UNIVERSITY OF NORTH CAROLINA
STUDIES IN THE ROMANCE LANGUAGES AND LITERATURES
Number 45

THE DEVELOPMENT OF THE *TRAGÉDIE NATIONALE* IN FRANCE FROM 1552-1800

THE DEVELOPMENT OF THE
TRAGÉDIE NATIONALE IN
FRANCE FROM 1552-1800

BY

GEORGE BERNARD DANIEL

CHAPEL HILL

THE UNIVERSITY OF NORTH CAROLINA PRESS

DEPÓSITO LEGAL: V. 166 — 1964

ARTES GRÁFICAS SOLER, S. A. — VALENCIA — 1964

CONTENTS

	Page
PREFACE ...	9
INTRODUCTION ...	11
CHAPTER I. The *Tragédie Nationale* in the Sixteenth Century ...	15
— II. The *Tragédie Nationale* in the Seventeenth Century.	36
— III. The *Tragédie Nationale* in the Eighteenth Century to 1789 ...	68
— IV. The *Tragédie Nationale* from 1789-1800 ...	124
— V. Factors Involved in the Presentation of Drama ...	183
— VI. Conclusion ...	200
APPENDIX. A List of *Tragédies Nationales* from 1800-1830 ...	205
BIBLIOGRAPHY ...	207

PREFACE

I wish to express my appreciation to the Faculty Reasearch Council of the University of North Carolina for a grant which made possible publication of this study. My sincere thanks are extended to W. L. Wiley, U. T. Holmes, Jr.; R. W. Linker, N. B. Adams, and J. E. Keller, for their active support and advice.

INTRODUCTION

The term *tragédie nationale* as applied to that branch of tragedy devoted to the dramatization of events taken from French history was not in general use until the time of the Revolution. Although French history as a source for tragedy had been referred to usually at infrequent intervals during the course of the sixteenth, seventeenth and eighteenth centuries, the most important manifesto espousing the cause of the *tragédie nationale* was the *Discours préliminaire* to *Charles IX*, written by Marie-Joseph Chénier, and presented at the Comédie-Française for the first time on November 4, 1789. Chénier not only sanctioned the use of French history as a source for tragedy but claimed also to be the first to write a work which could be properly termed *tragédie nationale,* an expression he defined as the faithful dramatization of an event from French history. [1] Chénier's contention was, of course, false. As will be demonstrated in this study, the national history had been tapped, although rarely, almost from the beginning of tragedy as a genre in French literature. [2]

The most recent study on the historical theater in France has been that of Lennart Breitholtz. [3] In his work, *Le théâtre historique en*

---

[1] Marie-Joseph Chénier, *Théâtre* (Paris: Foulon et Cie., Baudouin Freres, 1818), I, 92.

[2] Etienne Jodelle, an impulsive youth of twenty and steeped in the classical tradition, inaugurated French tragedy and comedy with *La Cléopâtre captive* and *Eugène*. Both plays were presented at the collège de Reims and the collège de Boncourt, probably near the end of 1552. For a description of the performances, see Etienne Pasquier, *Oeuvres* (Amsterdamm: La compagnie des libraires associés, 1723), I, 704.

[3] Lennart Breitholtz, *Le théâtre historique en France jusqu'à la Révolution* (Uppsala: A. B. Lundequistska, 1952).

France jusqu'à la Révolution, Dr. Breitholtz traces the growth of French historical drama, both serious and comic, from its beginnings in the medieval period to the eve of the French Revolution. The treatment of the comic theater during this period is particularly good. Clarence D. Brenner's dissertation, «L'histoire nationale dans la tragédie française du XVIII⁰ siecle», is the only other study that has been concerned solely with the development of the historical theater before the Revolution.[4] As with Breitholtz, Brenner concluded his study with the year 1789. Both works are extremely valuable for a listing of plays written before 1790 and dealing with French history. Both studies, although certainly worthwhile, show, however, little concern with the actual content of tragedies drawn from the national history.

For the period from 1789-1800 several invaluable works should be mentioned. That of Theodore Muret, *L'histoire de France par le théâtre, 1789-1851,* is of great aid in following the use of the theater as a vehicle of propaganda, and as a barometer to gage the social climate of the times.[5] The most scholarly and by far the most important book dealing with the theater during the Revolution is Henri Welschinger's *Le théâtre de la Révolution, 1789-1799.*[6] This work quotes from many priceless documents destroyed since by fire. Charles G. Etienne and A. Martainville, who lived during the time of the Revolution, left a vivid account of theatrical happenings in their voluminous work, *Histoire du théâtre français depuis le commencement de la Révolution jusqu'à la réunion générale.*[7] They presented a faithful picture of the many vicissitudes visited upon the troupes of the Comédie-Française during the fateful decade under consideration. *Le théâtre sous la terreur* is an exhaustive work by Paul d'Estrée in which he analyses the events relative to the theater during

---

[4] Clarence D. Brenner, «L'histoire nationale dans la tragédie française du XVIII⁰ siècle», *University of California Publications in Modern Philology,* XIV (1929-30), 195-329.

[5] Théodore Muret, *L'histoire de France par le théâtre,* 1789-1851 (Paris: Amyot, 1865).

[6] Henri Welschinger, *Le théâtre de la Révolution,* 1789-1799 (Paris: Charavay Freres, 1880).

[7] Charles G. Etienne and A. Martainville, *Histoire du théâtre français depuis le commencement de la Révolution jusqu'à la réunion générale* (Paris, Barba, 1802).

that shameful period.[8] The volumes of *A History of French Dramatic Literature in the Seventeenth Century*, by Henry C. Lancaster, and his subsequent works on French tragedy in the eighteenth century afford a storehouse of information on propagandistic writings.[9]

Since so very little has been done on the development of the *tragédie nationale* before 1789, the main body of the present study is aimed at filling the lacunae left by Breitholtz and Brenner. Likewise, an additional chapter is included to show both the vogue of the *tragédie nationale* during the years of the Revolution, and the use made of the theater as a public threshing floor for political beliefs. Much of this chapter will trace the peregrinations of the troupes of the Comédie-Française during the decade from 1789-1799. In the consideration of the propagation and growth of the *tragédie nationale* in France, and because they play such an important role, elements other than the tragedies themselves must be studied. Rather than overlook totally the physical factors such as buildings, seating arrangements, methods of lighting, *décors*, costumes, admissions, audiences and theatrical personnel, I have included a brief chapter treating these matters.

The purpose of the present study then is sixfold:

1. To trace the development of the *tragédie nationale* in France from 1552-1800, with critical analyses of fifty plays drawn from the national history. Of the total number of tragedies produced from 1552-1800 not more than seventy-five were drawn from French history.

2. To consider critical attitudes toward the use of French history as a source for tragedy.

3. To show the use of the *tragédie nationale* as a mouthpiece for propaganda.

---

[8] Paul d'Estrée, *Le théâtre sous la terreur* (Paris: Emile-Paul Frères, 1913).

[9] Henry C. Lancaster, *A History of French Dramatic Literature in the Seventeenth Century* (Baltimore: The Johns Hopkins Press, 1929). There are three separate volumes dealing with the eighteenth century: *Sunset, a History of Parisian Drama in the Last Years of Louis XIV, 1701-1715* (Baltimore: The Johns Hopkins Press, 1945); *French Tragedy in the Time of Louis XV and Voltaire, 1715-1774.* (Baltimore: The Johns Hopkins Press, 1950); and *French Tragedy in the Reign of Louis XVI and the Early Years of the French Revolution, 1774-1792* (Baltimore: The Johns Hopkins Press, 1953).

4. To follow the personnel of the Comédie-Française from 1789 through the Revolution.

5. To present a brief discussion in connection with the *tragédie nationale* of some of the physical factors involved in the staging of plays.

6. To include a list of tragedies inspired by the national history and written from 1800-1830 in order to establish the popularity of this field as a source for tragedy before the Romantic movement.

Because of their lack of literary appeal, copies of *tragédies nationales* are extremely rare. It was with great difficulty that I was able to obtain most of the tragedies discussed here. This study does not purport to be an exhaustive study on the *tragédie nationale*. It is hoped that by using materials already gathered, and seeking others, at present unavailable, I might one day be able to trace the *tragédie nationale* to the present day.

Chapter I

THE *TRAGÉDIE NATIONALE* IN THE SIXTEENTH CENTURY

According to literary historians of the Renaissance, there were about a hundred tragedies written in French from 1552 to 1600.[1] Only seven of these can be categorized as *tragédies nationales*. They generally contained five acts, were in verse, tended to obey loosely the three unities of time, place and action, depicted characters of noble station, had little or no mixing of the comic and tragic, permitted no violent action on the stage, and were highly rhetorical.

Jean Vauquelin de la Fresnaye (1536-1606) resumed most concisely in his *Art poétique* prevailing attitudes toward the use of history in tragedy, and more particularly national history, as expressed by most dramatic theorists before the time of Voltaire. Vauquelin advised those who wished to write in the tragic vein to seek their inspiration from ancient history:

> Au tragique argument pour te servir de guide
> Il faut prendre Sophocle et le chaste Euripide
> Et Seneque Romain: et si nostre Echafaut
> Tu veux remplir des tiens, chercher loin ne te faut
> Un monde d'argumens, car tous ces derniers ages

---

[1] The most valuable works consulted on tragedy during the Renaissance were: Emile Faguet, *La tragédie française au 16ᵉ siècle* (Paris: H. Welter, 1897); Gustave Lanson, «Etudes sur les origines de la tragédie classique en France», *Revue d'histoire littéraire de la France*, X (1903), 177-231 and 413-436; and Raymond Lebègue, *Tableau de la tragédie française de 1573 à 1610* (Paris: Société d'édition d'enseignement supérieur, 1951). The *Revue d'histoire littéraire de la France* will bear the abbreviation *RHLF* in subsequent references.

Tragiques ont produit mille cruelles rages.
Mais prendre il ne faut pas les nouveaux argumens;
Les vieux servent tous jours de seurs enseignemens.
Puis la Muse ne veut soubs le vray de contraindre;
Elle peut du vieil temps, tout ce qu'elle veut, feindre. [2]

Although not published until 1605, the work was begun in 1574. As was typical of treatises concerning drama, form was emphasized rather than content. Historical truth, as distorted from the Aristotelian dictum, was not malleable. [3] It was generally accepted without discussion that French history was not remote enough in time to allow the poet freedom to introduce fictional elements.

As far as I have been able to ascertain from a study of materials treating the French theater, the first tragedy in France that could be termed *tragédie nationale* was *La tragédie de feu Gaspard de Colligny*. Dated October 23, 1574, the approbation, issued by the Paris Faculty of Theology, and signed by Doctor F. Bérot, a learned Sorbonne professor, declared nothing unworthy in the tragedy. [4]

Colligny is obviously a treatment of the Protestant leader's murder which occurred on August 24, 1572. [5] The work, cast in the mold of a classical tragedy, was written by François de Chantelouve, a Catholic gentleman of Bordeaux, and *chevalier de l'ordre de Sainct Jehan de Jierusalem*. [6] Little more is known of him. In an analysis of this play, one notes to what extent hate can engender lies. Gaspard de Coligny, leader of the reformed cause during the devastating wars in the decade from 1560-1570, is represented as being a diabolical agent whose ambition is to seize the throne of France. History has, however, preserved the account of the unflagging loyalty of the admiral to

---

[2] Jean Vauquelin de la Fresnaye, *Art poétique*, Ed. G. Pelissier (París: Garnier, 1885), Book II, lines 1107 ff.

[3] See Preston H. Epps, *The Poetics of Aristotle* (Chapel Hill: The University Press, 1942), p. 19.

[4] Paul Lacroix (P. L. Jacob), *Bibliothèque dramatique de monsieur de Soleinne* (Paris: Administration de l'alliance des arts, 1843), I, 161.

[5] An interesting biography of Coligny is that of Walter Besant, *Gaspard de Coligny* (New York: G. P. Putnam's Sons, 1881).

[6] The edition consulted is that found in Pierre de l'Estoile, *Journal de Henri III ou mémoires pour servir à l'histoire de France* (La Haye: Pierre Gosse, 1744), I, 551-597. The first edition of Chantelouve's work was printed in Lyon in 1575. Since there were no divisions into scenes in the edition consulted, I have not inserted them in passages quoted.

his King and to France. Coligny was universally admired as a man of justice, moral uprightness, and honest diplomacy. A study of Chantelouve's drama is of interest only as an historical oddity and a link in the Catholic-Reformed controversy.

The work contains five acts, and is written in alexandrine verse. At the end of each act, a chorus of *peuple françois,* speaking in eight syllable rhymed couplets, reiterates the baseness of Coligny's character. There are no scenes and no tragic action. The word *tragedy* is only a convenient peg on which to hang what Chantelouve saw as a very noteworthy contribution.

The entire first act is in the form of a monologue. The admiral, frequently referring to mythology and fabricating new words, calls upon Hell to open its doors to him:

> O mort, ô rage, ô feu, ô Pluton, ô Furies!
> Courez, accablez-moi soubz vos fureurs aigries.
> O Satan, ô Calvin, ouvrez-moi les Enfers.

Continuing, Coligny curses God. He claims that Hell has power:

> Et non pas ce grand Dieu, qui fait peur aux enfans
> Et aux femmes, qui sont toutes courbees d'ans.

> Toute religion désormais je renonce.

The admiral presents his plan to seek the good graces of Charles IX and then dispatch him. For his accomplice Coligny would prefer Montgomery, the accidental murderer of Henry II. The act ends with a long lamentation by the chorus vilifying Coligny and Montgomery:

> Une femme ne t'a nourri,
> Mais une tigresse Hyrcanine,
> Non plus qu'à ton Montgoméri
> Fils d'une roche Marpesine
> Tous deux une Louve eshontée
> Avez en un antre tetée.

The chorus implores God to stop the admiral:

> Voy, Sauveur, voy ta pauvre Eglise
> En mille tronçons estre mise.

The strange allusions to pagan mythology mixed with elements of the christian religion form an incongruous concoction. The prolixity of Chantelouve's vocabulary is noted in the appearance of such unusual words as *hontoyer* (déshonorer), and *ensaffrané* (a word indicating the color of dawn).

In act two, Charles IX curses his fate. No matter which side he favors he will lose faithful subjects. The Privy Council advises there is only one choice: Decimate the Huguenots! The scene changes to present Cavagne and Briquemaut, fanatic Huguenots, who scheme to kill the King. The chorus agrees with the Privy Council. Catholicism is the only religion for France.

A return to paganism is the keynote of the third act. Mercury, often represented in Renaissance parlance as Christ, comes to reveal the secret plan of the gods for France. Mercury accuses Coligny of initiating the scheme to kill Charles.

> J'ai veu et fondé le courage
> De l'admiral, j'ai veu sa rage;
> Je sçais qu'il cherche, et je le voi,
> Couleur pour massacrer le Roi.

Mercury is charged with preventing the fruition of this diabolical plan. He will kill Coligny. This of course presages the massacre of Protestants on Saint Bartholomew's Day and exonerates Catholics from being guilty of carnage.[7] Montgomery then appears to curse the unlucky star which has made him so perfidious. The chorus closes the act with an accusation that Coligny was the root of all upheaval in France.

In the fourth act we meet the spirit of Andelot, Coligny's brother and cohort in crime, who testifies to the torments suffered by all Protestant companions in Hell.[8] Calvin is among the sufferers. In strange contrast:

> Ces prestres, Cardinaux, et toute la Prestaille,
> Que tant je mesprisois, que je tuai jadis,
> Sont morts, et sans douleur vivent en Paradis.

---

[7] Bartholomew, one of the twelve apostles, has his festival on August 24.
[8] François, Sieur d'Andelot (1521-1569), an active supporter of his brother in campaigns against the Catholics.

The admiral, surprised by the sight of his brother, is stunned when the furies remind him of his eventual doom also to the chasm of Hell. Nevertheless, Coligny is adamant in his murderous intentions to which has been added the Duke de Guise's name. In the closing scene the chorus implores God to stop the Huguenots.

The fifth act reflects the general rejoicing in the Catholic camp once the massacre of Huguenots is effected. As the act opens, Charles is again with his Privy Council which presses for the Huguenots' proscription. The King speaks the only line in the whole play not seeded with hate.

> Heureux le Roy qui n'est de cruauté vestu.

The meeting is interrupted by a report of a new conspiracy against the King:

> L'admiral, et les siens, d'une traitresse audace,
> A conspiré la mort de la Royale Race,
> Et devoit dans demain avec le traistre fer
> Tuer le Roy, la Royne, et messieurs à souper.

This spurs Charles to action. The very flighty and artificial language, typical of the entire play, is epitomized in the *récit* of the massacre as related by a messenger. After the news of the conspiracy had spread, Charles ordered the death of all Huguenots. The messenger describes the dawn:

> Avoir eu le conseil lorsque la blonde Aurore
> Chassoit les noirs chevaux de la Déesse More (night)
> Et que laissant le lict de son mari vieillard
> Ses couleurs pour le Ciel semoit de toute part.

The play ends with the hope that peace will now reign:

> Bref, et celui que desiroit la France,
> Seigneurie, en son désir felon
> Est possesseur, ô divine vengeance!
> Du plus haut lieu qui soit en Montfaulcon. [9]

---

[9] According to legend, the admiral was beheaded, the head taken to the King and Catherine, then embalmed and sent to Rome as a present to the

No observations would be strong enough to express the poor quality of this diatribe against one of France's noblest heroes. The extreme which Chantelouve allowed himself is repulsive not only because there is no truth, but also because the untruths were not said with naturalness. The grotesque manner of speech and the absence of action are sufficient reasons why such a work was never presented. Moreover, the dialogue was the form used for propagandistic writings. They were widely circulated and were a strong stimulus in fanning the flames of animosity between Protestant and Catholic.

Both groups used the theater to defend their ideas and to attack their adversaries. As early as 1533, students of the collège de Navarre in Paris had performed a play in which Marguerite de Valois, sister of François 1er, was attacked for her apparent sympathies in the Protestant reform. [10] In 1540 at Caen, Eloi du Mont, principal at the college bearing his name, composed and presented a play entitled *L'hérésie*. [11] The progress of new ideas offered the *écoliers,* inherently disposed toward satire, ample opportunities for manifesting their penchant. The clergy and religion were freely criticized. In 1556, the Parlement de Bordeaux followed example by forbidding dramatic presentations of «aucunes pièces concernant la religion ou foi chrétienne, la vénération des saints et des saintes institutions de l'église. [12]

One of the first and certainly one of the best plays in the repertory of the Company of Jesus was *L'histoire tragique de la Pucelle d'Orléans,* written by Fronton du Duc, professor of theology at the University of Pont-à-Mousson. The play was performed at Pont-à-Mousson in 1580, and published a year later. [13] Fronton had com-

---

Pope and the Cardinal de Lorraine. The remainder of the corpse was defamed and what remained eventually taken to hang by the feet at Montfaucon.

[10] L. V. Gofflot, *Le théâtre au college du moyen âge à nos jours* (Paris: Honoré Champion, 1907), p. 78.

[11] *Ibid.,* p. 79.

[12] *Ibid.,* p. 81.

[13] The work was published at Nancy by the Veufe Jean Janson. Dramatic performances at Pont-à-Mousson began around 1575 and continued up to the end of the eighteenth century. Until 1582, there was no *salle de représentations*. During that year, according to the historian of the university, Père Abram, a *grande salle* was built «dans le fond de la cour on construit une salle de la longueur de 90 pieds sur 40 de largeur, dans laquelle il y a un théâtre... et aussi des bancs en amphithéâtre qui servent aux académiciens lorsqu'il y a des actes publics». Le père Abram, *Historia universitatis et college Mussipontani,* 1650 (Traduction manuscrite à la Bibliothèque de Nancy). Cited by Gofflot, *op. cit.,* p. 134.

posed his work in honor of Henri III's anticipated visit to Plombières. Because of the plague, the King postponed his visit. The tragedy, originally planned for his entertainment in May, was given before Charles, Duc de Lorraine, on September 8.[14] Probably as early as 1439, an account of this peasant maiden's heroic and inspired struggle in raising the siege of Orléans on May 8, 1429, had been depicted in an anonymous work known as the *Mistère du siège d'Orléans*.[15] It is similar in form to the biblical and saint plays and is the only extant medieval dramatization in French of an almost contemporary event.[16] The author himself had probably fought in the battle which he wrote about.

From 1439 to the present day, in French alone, Jeanne d'Arc has been the inspiration of more than seventy dramatic works. Representing many who were still living at the time of its first presentation, there are one hundred speaking roles in the *Mistère du siège d'Orléans*. The action begins in England. At a council of war in which Salisbury is an important figure, it is decided Orléans must be reduced to complete the conquest of France.

---

[14] Les Frères Parfaict (Claude et François), *Histoire du théâtre françois depuis son origine jusqu'à présent* (Paris: LeMercier et Saillant, 1745-1749), III, 448.

[15] *Le mistère du siège d'Orléans*, 20,529 lines long, was published from the only manuscript, at the Vatican, number 1022, by MM. F. Guessard and E. de Certain in the *Collection de documents inédits sur l'histoire de France* (Paris: Imprimerie impériale, 1862).

[16] For forty-five listings of plays devoted to Jeanne d'Arc before 1875, see Théodore Joseph de Boudet de Puymaigre, *Jeanne d'Arc au théâtre, 1439-1875* (Paris: Duniol, 1875). Under the influence of the Hundred Years War there developed a patriotic type of drama of which *Le mistère du siège d'Orléans* is the most outstanding. The very day on which the siege was raised there was a procession in honor of the city's liberation. This procession became a regular occurrence. As a finale to the procession, a drama was always presented commemorating the deliverance of the city from the English. Processions similar to that in Orléans were staged throughout France. Among towns having such a demonstration of their patriotic fervor were Dieppe with the annual presentation of *Mitouries de la mi-août;* Guyenne (Compiègne) with *La déconfiture de Talbot advenue en Bordelais*, and Vienne (Dauphiné) with *Le léopard anglais jaloux et perfide dompté par des Français*. This work was presented in 1490 before Charles VIII during his visit to the city. Paris, Poitou, Abbeville and Troyes also had their processions and staged patriotic plays. Germain Bapst, *Essai sur l'histoire du théâtre* (Paris: Librairie Hachette, 1893), pp. 15-17.

Jeanne d'Arc does not appear until verse 7,060. While guarding her father's sheep, she is visited by Saint-Michael who enjoins her to go to the succor of Charles VII. Her first step is to see Baudricourt. Rejected, she returns to her flocks. The situation in France becomes more lamentable as the days pass. Jeanne is visited again by Saint Michael who encourages her to renew efforts to sway Baudricourt.

The next scenes take us to Chinon where Jeanne recognizes, in spite of the ruse concocted to test her sincerity, the King, Charles VII. With confidence in her, the King orders that she be questioned at Poitiers by his churchmen and councilors. After being highly recommended, Jeanne is handed over to the King's care. The next several scenes treat of Jeanne's white armor, her sword and standard. Jeanne sets out to raise the siege at Orléans. The drama does not end at the deliverance of Orléans, but only after the triumphal return from Patay.

The sequence of events as recorded by the anonymous author has proved to be historically true. Should one extract all of the passages in which Jeanne d'Arc figures in the *Mistère du siège d'Orléans*, it would be apparent that Fronton du Duc's play is very similar. *L'histoire tragique de la Pucelle d'Orléans* is dedicated to *Comte de Salm* (Jean), *maréchal de Lorraine, gouverneur de Nancy et seigneur, entre autres lieux, de Domremy.*[17] The play is divided into five acts, has twenty-seven characters, and is written in alexandrine verse. At the conclusion of each act, a chorus composed of children appears to resume the past action and to set the tone of the ensuing act. The lines spoken by the chorus are in seven or eight syllable rhymed couplets.

In the prologue Fronton du Duc explains why he chose a topic which had been neglected in drama since 1440:

>Messieurs, c'est à l'honneur du pays de Lorraine,
>Au fruict de la jeunesse, affin qu'elle s'aprenne
>Aux arts et aux vertus, que ce peuple joyeux
>Est venu pour ouyr, non de comiques jeux,
>Mais plus tost en poussant une voix plus hardie,
>On prétend vous montrer en une tragédie
>Un spectacle plus grave, affin que gravement

---

[17] The discussion included here is based primarily on material in Jean N. Beaupré, *Nouvelles recherches de bibliographie Lorraine, 1500-1700* (Nancy: Grimblot, 1856), pp. 20-60.

> L'esprit se norissant se forme sagement.
> Or, on n'a point choisy ung argument estrange
> Scachant que cil est fol, lequel ayant sa grange
> Pleine de grains cueillis, emprunte à son voisin,
> Laissant pourrir chez soi propre magasin;
> On a trouvé chez nous suffisante matière
> Pour d'un poème tel fournir la charge entiere
> On a doncques choisy les faits d'une Pucelle
> Qu'en France plus souvent d'Orléans on appelle:
> De Domremy, plus tost nous la dirons icy.

Act one, containing three scenes, reveals the present sad state of France, Jeanne d'Arc's holy mission to drive the English out of France, and the maid's acceptance by Charles VII. The first scene is in the form of a long monologue spoken by Louis de Bourbon, count of Clermont. He calls upon God to avenge France overrun and oppressed by the English. His vituperative yet colorful remarks against the English indicate a general tendency through the play. The verbal attacks carry a comic vein of which the author was obviously unaware. Louis angrily cries:

> ...ces sales baleines
> Ces veaux marins qui leurs humides plaines
> Delaissent pour venir s'enrichir de noz biens,
> Les fruicts de notre terre...

The scene switches to Domremy and Jeanne d'Arc. In a long monologue, she expresses her perplexity at having been visited by Catherine, Marguerite and Michael. Jeanne utters her disbelief at being chosen for the divine mission of saving France:

> Mais quoy! hé! quelle suis-je et quelle est mon pouvoir?
> Quelle addresse est en moy? quel conseil? quel scavoir?
> Pour aller à ung Roy qui commande à la France;
> Luy dire que de moy viendra la délivrance
> De ses pays saisies, et qu'il ne vaincra pas
> Les Anglois, que par l'heur de mes braves combats.

Her vacillation is soon dissipated. Saint Michael arrives, inspires her with renewed fervor, and in a vision the victory of Orléans is revealed to her.

Again the scene changes. This time we are taken to Bourges. The Count of Clermont announces Jeanne's arrival to Charles VII. Dressed as a man, Jeanne claims to have a secret only for the King's ears. The King attempts to hide among his courtiers, and, although the crown is worn by his cousin, Jeanne recognizes him. The act ends with the reiteration of her divine mission:

> En vain tascherait-on-faire broncher celuy
> A qui Dieu tient la bride.

In act two, Jeanne is accepted as leader of the French forces. As the first scene opens, Charles is with his Privy Councilors. There is a debate over whether Jeanne d'Arc is a charlatan or sincere in her mission. Charles ventures an opinion:

> Tout ce qui vient de Dieu ne peut estre inutile
> ... il semble que j'entends
> Une voix dans mon coeur, qui dit que trop j'attens
> Que contre l'esguillon je regimbe et rebelle,
> Repoussant le secours d'une main non mortelle.

Eighteen hundred men are recruited for Jeanne's army designated to raise the siege at Orléans. Before leaving from Chinon, she requests a sword, preferably from the King:

> Une épée qui est au moustier de Fierbois,
> En laquelle cinq fois est engravé le signe
> De la croix salutaire...

Jeanne meets with her soldiers. In a long sermon she exhorts them to remember the divine will of this expedition. There should be no hesitancy in following a woman since she is the agent of the divine will. She warns her troops not to swear, steal, or fraternize with camp followers.

At Orléans the English prepare for a very unorthodox battle. The Englishman Talbot expresses the consensus:

> Ils attendent, je crois, une folle sorciere
> Qu'on dit estre à Chinon: ceste habile guerriere
> Qui fait du capitaine.

The citizens of Orléans are encouraged and spurred on with new hope. Their confidence in Jeanne d'Arc is colorfully summarized by a soldier cursing the English, «Alors de sa venue, garde toy bien Anglois qu'on te coupe la queue».

Between the second and third acts Orléans, Troyes, Chalons and Rheims have been reconquered. Charles VII has also been crowned king. In the opening scene of the third act Charles VII thanks God for his omnipresent mercy. The King joins with René d'Anjou in anticipating the eventual expulsion of all English from France. All references to the English contain allusions to beasts. One of the most vehement is spoken by Charles, who entones his curses upon, «...ces viperes marines, ces madrés Léopards qui soufflent des narines». The widespread joy commonly expressed by the King and René is dampened by the news of Jeanne's capture at Compiègne. Dejected and horrified, Charles VII utters the premonitions of all valiant French, «On la verra bien tost des bourreaux poursuivie». The act ends with a chant by the chorus concerning Jeanne's betrayal and the inevitability of her death.

As the fourth act opens, Jeanne, tied to a heavy chain, is in prison at Rouen. The ransom offered for her release refused, she awaits death calmly. The pain which she foresees before her death is secondary. Instead, she has a very live fear that her honor is in jeopardy:

> Ce sont les durs efforts de ceux qui sont mes gardes
> Desquelz les sales mains et les langues paillardes
> Ne cessent mon honneur toujours solliciter,
> Et ma pudicité à forfaire inciter.

Her fears are somewhat allayed by Saint Michael who reassures her that she will die a virgin. He reveals the final plan of God for her, which is, of course, martyrdom.

The Duke of Sommerset and Talbot bemoan the slowness with which Jeanne's punishment is accomplished. Both vaunt the power of the English, and yet blush with shame to think a woman defeated them at Orléans. The shame inflicted upon their pride appears to be the only reason why Jeanne must die.

Jean Destivet, canon of Beauvais and Bayeux, will present the case against Jeanne d'Arc. She is charged with five cardinal crimes: necromancy, heresy, causing unrest, dishonoring her sex by wearing man's clothing, and permitting herself to be worshipped as a god. With these five counts Jean believes it virtually impossible for the court to declare the maid innocent, and promises she will never leave the prison walls alive.

In the trial, presided by Pierre Cauchon, Bishop of Beauvais, Jean Destivet describes Jeanne as a supreme sorceress. Medea, Urganda and Circe are innocent fledgelings in comparison. Jeanne d'Arc contends the present tribunal is not worthy of judging her:

> J'appelle le Pasteur de Rome pour refuge
> C'est lui seul que je veux estre mon juste juge.

Her opinions do not prevail. The sentence is life imprisonment. The chorus ends the act with a long diatribe against Pierre Cauchon in which he is compared to Judas Iscariot.

The last act begins with a long monologue pronounced by a citizen of Rouen in which he deplores the iniquitous sentence. A diametrically opposed attitude is expressed by Sommerset. Consumed with rage at the bland sentence, he storms:

> Qu'elle ne morra pas! que partout sera dit
> Qu'une femme a vaincu des Anglois le crédit!
> Qu'une infeste charongne, une vile sorcière
> Tellement a sillé des juges la paupière,
> Qu'ilz ne pourront pas voir sa grande iniquité
> Qui ja plus de cent fois la mort a mérité!
> Plustost sera Rouen du tout réduict en pouldre;
> Plustot accablera la pétillante fouldre
> De nos canons bruyants tous ces sots escrivains
> Devant que noz effortz soient rendus ainsi vains!

He threatens Fécamp who explains the ecclesiastical court issued the most stringent sentence in its power.

In the last scenes of the play, Fronton du Duc introduces spectators who saw Jeanne burned at the stake. A messenger relates the last moments before her death. One of the most striking elements of his account is the description of Jeanne d'Arc's dress which was nothing more than an imprinted sack:

> De serpentz venimeux et horribles crapaux
> Et des corps tres-hydeux des diables infernaux,
> Sur la teste elle avoit une mitre pointue
> De papier, où ung diable avec sa main crochue
> Estoit peint tirassant ung misérable corps;

> Et ung aultre sembloit donner mille morts
> Avec une tenaille; et en tel équipage
> Ils commencent sur elle à décharger leur rage.

Every part of her body, except the heart, was consumed by the fire. From the ashes there arose a white dove which winged its way straight to heaven. The English would not permit the martyr's remains to be gathered: «Mais ils les ont espars dans Seine par les flots». The chorus ends the play with a glowing tribute to the peasant heroine:

> Vierge très chaste et très forte,
> De la France le bonheur,
> Et de Lorraine l'honneur.

Although Fronton du Duc's *Jeanne d'Arc* was one of the first attempts at national historical tragedy, it is a very laudable effort. It differs from other plays of similar inspiration in several ways. There is a total absence of moralizing; no love element or secondary intrigue mars the main thread of the plot; the characters are very much alive, independent and individuals not walking automatons spitting forth moral axioms; the author selected primary events in Jeanne d'Arc's life and connected them logically without permitting contingent incidents to divert the spectator's attention; the language is not stilted and unnatural; Jeanne d'Arc is noble, simple and disinterested; and the thread of events adheres closely to historical truth.

Fronton du Duc, while obviously aware of the growing tendency in tragedy to follow set rules, very realistically ignores the unities of time and place. Nevertheless, the unity of action is masterfully handled. The very slight comic element, represented by invectives hurled at the English and reminiscent of the devils in mystery plays, exercises a salubrious effect in rendering the play more realistic. It is indeed lamentable such an excellent work is generally ignored in studies treating the development of French tragedy.

In addition to *La tragédie de feu Gaspard de Colligny*, several other Catholic propaganda plays were written. Around 1573 a certain De Gerland, of whom nothing is known, wrote a tragedy now lost which he called *Montgoméry*. In reality the work was a dialogued account of the troubles of France since the death of Henri II, in 1559, to 1573. Because most of them were destroyed or never circulated, I am unable to discuss any of the Protestant propaganda tragedies drawn from the national history.

La Guisiade, published in 1589, and written by Pierre Matthieu is a eulogy of Henri, Duc de Guise and his brother, the Cardinal de Lorraine, executed in 1588 at Blois.[18] There were three editions of this work in 1589. The name of the author, identified by the initials I. R. D. L. (Jacques Roussin de Lyon, the printer) in the first and second editions, did not appear until the third. Matthieu, in addition to identifying himself, presented arguments of a political, historical and moral nature before each scene. However, he refused to indicate the true names of his characters. This task was performed by Lenglet Dufresnoy in the *avertissement* and notes.[19]

Pierre Matthieu (1563-1621) was the son of a weaver. In spite of his low birth, Matthieu received a good education. He became a lawyer at Lyon and was an ardent admirer of the Duc de Guise. After the Duke's massacre on December 23, 1588, Matthieu wrote *La Guisiade* as a testimonial of his admiration. The principal theme of the drama is the flippancy and malevolence of Henri III as compared to the nobility and devotion to duty of Henri, Duc de Guise. In later years Matthieu changed his political sympathies to become an ardent adherent to the crown. He was rewarded with the post of royal historiographer, and remained in that position until his death at Toulouse in 1621. Among his more interesting works is the two volume *Histoire de France,* published posthumously in 1622 by his son.

Preceding the text of *La Guisiade,* an *épistre,* to Monseigneur le Duc de Mayenne, affords Matthieu occasion to complain of the dearth of good writing in sixteenth century France. He further observes that although his tragedy might not be a literary masterpiece, at least it will be historically correct. Matthieu's claim is false. The basic facts leading to the Duke's murder are recorded with some accuracy, but the most generally accepted historical truths are distorted. Matthieu shows Henri as being under the complete domination of *mignons* to whom is attributed the real cause of the Duke's death. As proven by history, this allegation is fallacious. Henri III, aware of the Guise family's ambitions for the crown of France, determined to reduce any

---

[18] The first edition was printed in Lyon by Jacques Roussin. The edition consulted was that appearing in Pierre de l'Estoile, *op. cit.,* III, 516-628.

[19] Lacroix, *op. cit.,* I, 161.

immediate threat as long as he was alive. He alone was responsible for the Duc de Guise's massacre on December 23, 1588. The manifest prejudice of the author is evidenced in a second historical falsehood. In his biased characterization of the Duke, Matthieu portrays him as devoted only to Catholicism and to France. The accusation, constantly reiterated by Henri III, claiming Guise was plotting to overthrow him, was true and not the result of groundless fear.

The Guise family played an important role in the religious struggles of the sixteenth century that all but destroyed France as an important power. The Guises are best known for their creation of the Ligue (1576), which was intended to perform in France the same functions as the Inquisition in Spain. In their aspirations to the throne of France, they ran afoul the petulant, proud and astute Henri III, who, although without issue, determined to rule France while he was alive. The crowning insult to Henri III was the barricading of Paris to his passage in May, 1588, by Guise sympathizers.

Following negotiations with the Duc de Guise and his followers, Henri convoked the Estates General for a meeting in Blois. The convocation was opened on October 2, 1588. It appeared, during the first weeks, as if Henri and the Guises might reach some happy solution. Nevertheless, Henri had long before intended the Duke's assassination and only waited for the propitious moment. Having readied the members of his Privy Council (forty-five members) to aid in the task, Henri summoned in the early morning hours of December 23 the Duc de Guise to his bedchamber. The Duke came in all haste. He was stabbed to death by those who waited to fulfill the King's command. His brother, Cardinal de Guise, was arrested the next day and condemned.[20]

In five acts and alexandrine verse *La Guisiade* contains a chorus which speaks after each scene. The play is devoid of action. The greater part of each act is in fact a long monologue. The entire first act, a monologue, serves to depict the intrepid Duc de Guise charged with the divine mission of extirpating every living Huguenot in France. The Duke deplores present conditions in which schism between Church and State increases daily in its proportions. The Duke is in the thick of the quarrel only to fight for his King and France:

---

[20] For a detailed analysis of events leading to the assassination of the Duc de Guise, see Jacques Vivent, *La tragédie de Blois, le roi de France et le duc de Guise, 1585-1588* (Paris: Hachette, 1946).

> Le Schisme et l'hérésie enflammant ses entrailles (France),
> Lui ont jà préparé ses tristes funérailles.
> Ses fils, ô creve-coeur! ses bastards, non ses fils,
> Lui donnent tous les jours un millier de deffits.

A very striking feature of the play is the caustic critiscim of Henri III, particularly in his relations with the *mignons*. The Duc de Guise attributes actual conditions in France to the *mignons*' destructive influence on the King. The chorus of the *Union de France* ends the act with a long lament upon recent tragic events of which France was the victim. Notable among these were the death of Henri II and the rise of the Huguenots. The speeches of the chorus are written in seven or eight syllable lines having alternate rhyme.

Act two pits Henri III against his mother, Catherine de Médicis. Matthieu strives to illustrate the stubbornness and inexperience of Henri, who believes the Guise family is seeking the crown. Catherine, on the other hand, is depicted as a gentle but firm mother. She tries to dissuade her son from harboring resentment. According to her, the Guises are fighting only for France and the Catholic church:

> Vous n'aviez plus de nom, de Sceptre, ni d'Eglise,
> Ni de Religion, sans la maison de Guise.

This strongly worded statement, instead of placating Henri, induces him further to punish the Guises. Catherine recalls her son's unholy life and admonishes him to be a King:

> Vous nagez dans les flots de vostre volupté,
> Aveques ces Mignons, ces gourmandes Harpies:
> Qui de meilleurs morceaux ont les griffes remplies,
> Dont le glout estomach du peuple prend le pain,
> Et tant plus ils sont saouls, tant plus meurent de faim;
> Esponger de la Cour, vos plaisantes délices,
> Polypes inconstans, gradués en tous vices.
> Comme un Ours qui permet se mener par le ne,
> Vous estes abusé par ce diable incarné,
> Ce traistre d'Espernon, qui perfide, practique
> Contre Dieu, contre vous, pour plaire a l'Hérétique.

Persisting in her condemnation of Henri's life, his policies and his ideas, the queen mother is finally successful in arranging an encounter between Henri and his cousin, the Duc de Guise. The chorus expresses the same opinion, as does Catherine, toward Henri III:

> Le Roy n'est de son coeur maistre.

Left alone, the King gives a long harangue of self-praise.

> Je suis l'oinct du Seigneur, je suis Roy grand.
> Je suis sur les François juge en dernier ressort,
> Ma poictrine et mon dos, comme d'une cuirasse,
> S'arme de mon bon droict, j'ai l'amour en la face,
> J'ai en main le pouvoir, et le courage au coeur.

When he sees the Duke, Henri III accuses him of continually inciting the people to riot. The Duke claims he is only fighting for God, Catholicism, Henri, and France. The Duke sees all of France crumbling under the invasion of heresy. The only recourse is for Henri III to become an ally of the holy Ligue. Henri agrees that heresy must be annihilated. The Duke, like Catherine, offers advice to the King. According to the Duc de Guise, Henri III will find his power greatly enhanced if: (1) he would expel Italian financiers; (2) punish the *mignons;* (3) break the trade treaty with the Ottoman Empire; (4) cease free interchange with England, which he spoke of as being, «Le puant cloaque de la France»; and (5) name a successor. To discuss these issues and other problems facing the kingdom, Henri consents to a meeting of the Estates General at Blois. The Duke swears his unswerving loyalty. The act ends with a choral plea to the stars:

> Ne trompez pas notre esperance
> D'une fausse opinion:
> Ne trompez pas la pauvre France,
> Qui se fie à l'Union.

Act three, in which all factions are sworn to fight heresy to the bitter end, opens with D'Espernon plotting the Duc de Guise's death. The chorus curses D'Espernon and praises the grandeur and strength of the Ligue. After an interminable scene in which all three estates vilify heresy and plead for the preservation of the *Saincte Ligue*, the King swears to fulfill the wishes of the Estates General.

An unrivalled example of Matthieu's ineptness as a poet is the King's closing harangue to the delegates: «Vous etes mes ruisseaux, je suis vostre ocean». The chorus is not duped by Henri's eloquence and false sincerity. The union has been cemented but:

> Plustost on verra l'impossible
> S'accorder avec le possible,
> Que l'Union soit sans pouvoir,
> Sans vertu, sans Foi, sans devoir.

In act four Henri brings to fruition his plot to kill the Duc de Guise and his brother, the Cardinal. Matthieu mitigates what to him seemed the heinousness of the crime by the inclusion of privy councilors who incited Henri to order the murder. The author hesitated to name the conspirators and in the play they are simply identified by the letters N. N.

In this act the Duke is presented as a messiah. He rejoices in the hope that with the King's solidarity France will again be happy:

> Nous tirerons des flots le basteau de l'Eglise
> Le Roy tient l'aviron, le Ciel nous favorise!

In spite of the rumor alleging that he is about to be murdered, the Duke prepares to leave for a meeting with the King. The chorus warns him:

> La perfide (Le Roy) ores conjure
> Ses quarante-cinq Bourreaux
> Sous le mot d'un Roy perjure
> D'estreindre deux grands flambeaux.

Having ordered the Guises' death, Henri III decries his heavy responsibility:

> J'aimerois beaucoup mieux que le Ciel m'eust fait naistre
> Un petit Laboureur: au moins je serois maistre
> Sous mon rustique toict que j'aurois pour Palais.

He oscillates in the final decision, but resolves that only he should rule. The chorus, in solemn tones, delivers an expression of its supreme contempt for Henri:

> La Foi mignonne de nos Rois,
> Leur pavois, leur rempart, leur guide,

Meurt par le dernier de Valois
Desloyal, cruel et perfide.

In act five a messenger relates, to the Duchesse de Nemours, the circumstances of her son's death. The play ends with a long lamentation by the mother and a prediction of the King's murder.

La Guisiade is noteworthy in that it reflects general attitudes toward such a sacrosanct person as the King, however, is its only interest. Matthieu's play, written before Henri III's assassination by Jacques Clément on August 1, 1589, contains many linguistic peculiarities. New words abound such as *sagette (flèche), brasiller (s'echauffer)*; he ignores aspiration; the word *le héros* is frequently written *l'héros*. The grotesqueness of his figures of speech is evident from the following line: «Depuis l'aube, ou l'on voit s'emperruquer le jour...» There is no characterization, no exposition, development or denouement of plot. The situations are independent episodes with total disregard of the unities. There is never any indication of time, and no mention of place until the fourth act. The total result is a diatribe written in very poor form. We can concur with the editor of the edition consulted for this study in that Matthieu was «an ignorant country bumpkin».

A second attack leveled against Henri III was *Le Guysien ou perfidie tyrannique commise par Henri de Valois*. Now lost, the work was written around 1592 and published by Jean Moreau, a royal printer.[21] Lacroix found the assassination scene of the Duc de Guise in this play particularly worthy of French tragedy. Yet in another scene, totally without reason, the *très-chrétienne* Catherine de Médicis, while deploring the crime of her son, suddenly invokes the wrath of Jupiter upon the murderer.[22]

Chilpéric, roi de France, second de nom was a very controversial *tragédie nationale*. Written and presented in 1594 at the collège des Capettes in Paris, the work was from the pen of Louis Léger, a regent of the college. Situated in the decade from 710 to 720, the play recounts the exploits of Chilperic as King of Neustria, a term used to indicate the old name of the western kingdom of the Franks, as opposed to the eastern kingdom, Austrasia. A protegé of Charles Martel, Chilpéric became King of Neustria in 715.

---

[21] The work was published in Troyes in 1592.
[22] Lacroix, *op. cit.*, I, 176.

Léger's work was quickly censored by the Parlement de Paris. The records of that body for August 23, 1594, reveal concern with the insolent boldness shown by Léger in depicting a French king on the stage. The entry states:

> Ce jour ce qui a été rapporté à la Cour, que par la ville a été mis des affiches, pour être demain au collège des Capettes, joué une tragédie intitulée *Chilpéric, roi de France, second de nom*. Le principal du collège mandé, qui a amené Louis Léger, un des premiers régents du collège, lequel a présenté à la cour le cahier de la dite tragédie en vieux français; lecture faite du prologue d'icelle, et en ces conclusions: la Cour ordonne que le dit Léger sera présentement mené et conduit à la conciergerie du palais pour être oui et interrogé sur le contenu du dit cachier; a fait et fait inhibitions et défenses au principal du collège de faire jouer ce qui a été affiché par la ville, et outre ordonne que présent arrêt sera signifié au recteur de l'Université.[23]

Although nothing is known of the contents of *Chilpéric*, the sudden concern over its presentation was probably due to the political unrest in Paris caused by difficulties between the Catholic League and Henri of Navarre.

In summary, French tragedy during the first fifty years of its development was sententious and oratorical. A passionate interest in antiquity was demonstrated and many doctrinists adhered to imitation as the most effective manner of creating a great national drama. In their enthusiasm, devotees of imitation were uncertain about the manner of imitating. Nevertheless, out of the uncertainty and the probing, a well-ordered formula was established for tragedy. Thus, the way was being opened for the efflorescence of the classical ideal as epitomized in the tragedies of Jean Racine.

In the field of dramatic theory Aristotle exercised an overwhelming influence. He was misinterpreted or distorted to sanction laws advanced by contemporary theorists. Dramatic theory in the century was carried on primarily by dramatists whose first concern was with style, not with general theory or doctrines.

The use of French national history as a possible source for tragedy was generally neglected because of primary concern with imitation of

---

[23] Cited by Gofflot, *op. cit.*, p. 61. No copy of *Chilpéric* is in existence.

the ancients. Only seven tragedies written between 1552 and 1600 can be classified as *tragédies nationales*. All of these except *Chilpéric, Clothilde* and *L'histoire tragique de la pucelle d'Orléans* were drawn from contemporary history.[24] The political and religious struggles nurtured the circulation of violent pamphlets against opposing parties. These pamphlets were called tragedies, since dialogue was the accepted medium of diatribe, and are contained in this study not only because they embrace some historical materials, but also because they serve to illustrate the tendency of national historical tragedy, from its inception, to be used as a vehicle of vituperation.

---

[24] *Clothilde*, of anonymous authorship, and written around 1580, was an account of the christian attributes of Clovis' wife. This work has also been lost.

CHAPTER II

THE *TRAGÉDIE NATIONALE* IN THE SEVENTEENTH CENTURY

A primary aim of tragedy in the seventeenth century was a study of psychology rather than emphasis on spectacle and action. Two essential ingredients of successful national historical drama, they divert the spectator from being too conscious of historical fact.

A listing of tragedies written in the classical period will reveal almost all drew their subjects from ancient history and mythology, especially from that of Greece and Rome. Modern and Biblical history were rarely used as sources. The prevailing attitude toward the use of sources drawn from modern history was poignantly summarized in the second *préface* (1676) to *Bajazet* (1672) of Jean Racine;

> ...On peut dire que le respect que l'on a pour les héros augmente a mesure qu'il s'éloignent de nous: *major e longinquo reverentia* (Tacitus: *Annals,* I, 47). L'éloignement des pays répare en quelque sorte la trop grande proximité du temps. Car le peuple ne met guère de différence entre ce qui est, si j'ose ainsi parler, à mille ans de lui, et ce qui en est à mille lieues. [1]

In the century from 1600 to 1700 there were written around two hundred dramatic works categorized as tragedies. Of these, less than thirty were based on French history. Except for an occasional mention of this field as a possible source for tragedy, references to it are indeed

---

[1] Jean Racine, *Bajazet,* Ed. Cuthbert Girdlestone (Oxford: Basil Blackwell, 1932), p. 4.

sparse. Jean Magnon, a very minor dramatist of the century, erroneously thought he would be the first to put French history on the stage, but seemed never to have carried out his plan. He stated such intentions in the dedication of *Josephat* (1647):

> ...moy mesme des premiers ie veux introduire sur le théâtre l'Histoire Françoise, bien loin que l'antiquité nous ait pu fournir abondance de matières, il nous a fallu beaucoup adjouster à ce qu'elle nous a dit de ces Héros, au lieu que dans notre siècle nous aurons un contraire travail, et nous serons en peine de retrancher du grand nombre de ces excellents sujets que notre Histoire nous donnera. [2]

The dearth of tragedies in the seventeenth century drawn from French national history was due, in large measure, to the ironclad interpretations applied to Aristotle and Horace and also to the blind obedience to rules governing the composition of tragedy.

Written by Virey des Graviers, with five acts and a prologue and published in 1600, the first historical drama of the century was the *Tragédie de Jeanne d'Arques, dite la Pucelle d'Orléans, native du village d'Emprenne près Vaucouleurs en Lorraine*. [3]

The names of the actors were noted in one copy that has been preserved. They were probably members of a guild in Rouen, and presented the tragedy which was written to commemorate Jeanne d'Arc's death in their city. A list of the actors is included below: [4]

ROLE	ACTOR
Charles VII	Maitre de l'Emprise
Le duc d'Alençon	M. Guillon
La Pucelle	Jehan Gohier
Le bâtard d'Orléans	Claude Gobier
Le comte de Suffolk (sic)	Duchon (?)
Glacidas	Langiboust
Talbot	Lapallissade

---

[2] Henry Carrington Lancaster, *A History of French Dramatic Literature in the Seventeenth Century* (Baltimore, The Johns Hopkins Press, 1929-1942), *The Period of Corneille, 1635-1651*, II, II, 652. The first numeral refers to Part, the second to Volume.

[3] Virey des Graviers, *Tragédie de Jeanne d'Arc* (Rouen: Raphael du Petit Val, 1603).

[4] Lacroix, *op. cit.*, I, 30.

Lucidam	Langiboust
Alide	V. Froneuphe (?)
Les filles de France	Marthon Plus (?)

In the first act Charles VII and the Duc d'Alençon, with long sepulchral phrases, discuss the misfortunes to which France has fallen lot. An example of the bombast will suffice to illustrate the style:

> Le François est semblable au saule verdissant
> Tant plus il est tordu et plus il va croissant,
> C'est un monstre à neuf corps, un hidre lerneen,
> Qui se rit ès combats du fait herculeen,
> Et pour son front coupe d'une main inutile
> Sept naissent à la fois sur sa teste fertile.

Act two is a pastoral scene. In the company of her admiring friend, Dunois, Jeanne explains how angelic visitations enlightened her for the divine mission of which a part is the trip to King Charles VII. Her language is sprinkled with pagan allusions:

> Et les songes ailez coulant dedans mom âme,
> Echauffèrent mon coeur d'une divine flamme;
> Puis comme messager du tout puissant Jupin,
> Me dirent en telz mots le but de mon destin:
>
> «Fille, le seul soucy de la chaste Lucine,
> Quitte, quitte les bois, arme, arme ta poitrine,
> Venge l'injure faite à ton propre pays,
> Et chasse par le fer, les douleurs, les ennuis,
> Qui comblent maintenant les sujets de ton prince».

Dunois listens attentively but doubts her ability as a warrior. He is more interested in her physical beauty.

> Peut-etre que vos yeux, flammesches immortelles,
> Que ce poil, que ce front, que ces lèvres junelles,
> Que ce teint peint de lis et que vostre beauté
> Pourroit (sic) vaincre et tuer autant de leur coste
> Que l'espee de l'autre.

Jeanne reminds him petulantly that her mission is divine and thereby its success is not dependent on her physical charms.

The third act, devoted partly to the English, and partly to Jeanne d'Arc, concerns the mutual animosity between France and England and the long awaited deliverance of Orléans.

Suffolk's interminable and bitter tirade against the French is abruptly ended by the arrival of Glacidas. He expresses the surprise of every English soldier at the sudden seemingly inspired onslaught of the usually sluggish French:

> Monseigneur, courez tost, hé! Voici l'ennemy
> Il n'est pas de besoin de retarder ici,
> Las! il tue, il prend tout; tout fuit devant sa face;
> Plusieurs que pris, que morts gisent dessus la place,
> Une femme enragée, une peste, un dégat,
> Un tonnerre, un malheur, sous les armes abat,
> Des soldats plus vaillants elle est presque maîtresse;
> Armez-vous vistement et courez à la presse.

Jeanne d'Arc soon arrives to celebrate her victory and the liberation of Orléans:

> Orléans qui est ceint d'un mur dardanien,
> Ouvrage merveilleux du blond lathonien
> Qui te laves les pieds dans le fleuve de Loire,
> Nourrisse de Bacchus, de Parnasse la gloire,
> Mere alme de Cérès et fille de Jupin,
> Ne crains doresnavant que le soldat mutin
> Esbranle ce tien front et que l'anglaise audace
> D'un canon essoufflé tonne devant ta face.

Act four is a long lamentation by Talbot bemoaning England's loss of Orléans. In act five Jeanne, now a prisoner of the English, reflects upon her imminent death. The *Filles de France* end the play with a panegyric of the simple maiden. They faithfully swear never to forget her sacrifice and to erect an altar to her memory. Likewise, they predict her renown will be as everlasting as France.

The frequent allusions in this play to pagan mythology create an anachronistic tinge bordering on travesty. Jacques Virey was unequal to the task of presenting a simple peasant girl inspired with a beatific vision. In the second act, which is the only time Jeanne is seen in her native milieu, Virey subjects her to the humiliating circumstance of a carnal love scene. The intent of the author was doubtlessly serious, but the effect is a parody.

Tradition has made Jeanne d'Arc an illiterate shepherdess. When she clothes her language, as appears here, in rhetoric and recondite allusions, naturalness and simplicity, her most admirable characteristics, are sullied. The literary result is displeasing and unworthy of serious consideration.

Much of the body of historical tragedy during the seventeenth century belongs to propagandistic literature. The first such work of the century appeared in 1607. This was *Le Triomphe de la Ligue*, a five-act tragedy in verse, written by R.-J. Nérée.[5] The author preferred to be known by a *nom de plume*. Sufficient reason is attested by the nature of his play, which is a bitter satire against the Catholic League that opposed Henri IV.

The characters are indicated by anagrammatic names. The main theme of the plot is woven about the campaigns of Henri against the *Ligue*. The events are reported with amazing accuracy, and the author shows great poetic genius in his expression. For example, in discussing details of the battle of Coutras, he depicts Henri's unassailable courage as follows:

> Tant qu'il semble, à le voir nous brêcher, fendre, occire
> Que sa lance est de feu et nos armes de cire.[6]

Lacroix believed Nérée was none other than N. Rapin (1540-1608), one of the principal authors of the *Satire Ménipée*.[7] Lacroix also believed Henri commissioned Rapin to write this work to relate his great prowess as a warrior. The main opinion of Lacroix' argument was based on an analogy between the style of *La Satire Ménippée* and *Le triomphe de la Ligue*. Likewise, Rapin was ordered to court in 1607, the year in which *Le triomphe* was published. Another convincing argument advanced by Lacroix in favor of Rapin was that the manuscript of the play bore Rapin's initials along with Nérée's name.[8]

---

[5] R.-J. Nérée, *Le triomphe de la Ligue* (Leyde: Thomas Basson, 1607).

[6] The battle of Coutras was fought against the Duc de Joyeuse, on October 20, 1587. This battle ended the War of the Three Henrys waged between Henri IV, Henri, Duc de Guise, and Henri III, King of France.

[7] Celebrated political pamphlet directed against the *Ligue* (1594).

[8] My discussion is based entirely on materials found in Lacroix, *op. cit.*, I, 192-193.

Claude Billard, Sieur de Courgenay (1540-1618?) was the most prolific writer of national historical tragedy in the seventeenth century. Of his eight tragedies, three are drawn from French history. They are *Gaston de Foix* (1607), *Mérovée* (1607) and *Henri le Grand* (1610). Each is in five acts and in verse. Frequent use is made of the chorus.

Gaston de Foix recounts the tragic death of this fearless soldier on April 11, 1512, in the battle of Ravenna, which he won from the Spaniards. Gaston was the son of Jean de Foix, Vicomte de Narbonne, and of Marie d'Orléans, the sister of Louis XII. In 1512 he replaced the Duc de Longueville as commander of the French army in Italy. Louis XII was actively engaged there in a campaign against the Sainte-Ligue, a coalition formed by Pope Julius II with Spain and Venice. Only twenty-two years old, Gaston proved himself a general of uncanny ability.

As it develops, the play is a monologue honoring Gaston.[9] In act one he appears to praise his abilities as a warrior. While sprinkling his monologue with frequent classical allusions, the young general elevates himself to the ranks of the world's greatest men. He is particularly fond of comparing his genius to that of Alexander the Great.

As if Gaston's monologue in praise of himself were not enough to establish his greatness, a chorus of French soldiers punctuates their leader's opinions with further praise. The chorus also predicts Gaston's imminent death:

> Au premier Apvril de ses ans,
> Il peut s'esgaler aus plus géans,
> Desja chenu d'experience:
> Je crains que ce fruit avant-neur
> Soit en l'hyver dès son enfance,
> Et qu'il se perde en sa valeur.

In act two leaders of Julius' coalition, gathered for a meeting to plan strategy, take their turn at praising Gaston. The general concensus is that «on n'a rien veu de tel». Nevertheless, it is imperative to engage the French forces in battle as quickly as possible. If Gaston is surprised perhaps there will be some chance of befuddling his plans.

---

[9] *Claude Billard, Gaston de Foix,* Ed. Eliot H. Polinger (New York: Publications of the Institute of French Studies, Inc., 1931).

In an endless monologue Cardinal de Médicis deplores the present state of the world in which there seems to be no peace or desire for it. In anticipation of victory in battle, a chorus of Italians ends the act.

In act three Louis XII avails himself of the occasion to laud his nephew who, although opposed by powerful forces, will surely win through his ability to out-manoeuvre the enemy.

The King's monologue is followed by a charming interlude in which a chorus composed of the Dames de la Cour advances the claim that their beauty has been responsible for the victories of the French army and not the leadership of Gaston:

> On n'a vaincu par les armes,
> Ce sont nos yeus, et nos charmes,
> Les seuls coups de nos beautez
> Ont les ennemis domtez;
> Les eclairs de nos oeillades
> Les ont rendus si malades.

The concluding scene of the act presents the dilemma of the queen of Spain who, by duty, is bound to pray for the victory of her husband's forces, but since she is Gaston's sister, her emotions favor him. After all she does not love the old king of Spain and if it were not her duty to be faithful to him, she would incite a revolt. This confidence evinces the liveliest protestations from her companion, *la nourrice*.

The Queen has a strange sensation that warns of her brother's death. A striking example of Billard's propensity for periphrase is evidenced as she gives voice to her fears:

> Une pale tremeur ondoyante dans moy,
> Fait dresser mes cheveus, me met en tel esmoy
> Ceste ame toute esmeue, et ces veines poussées
> Sous un pous tressaillant des terreurs plus glacées
> Que je vogue chetive, ainsi qu'on voit les flos
> Vaguer encore esmeus, couvers d'un vain repos
> Des assauts de l'Autan dont les ailes humides
> Ont bouleversé l'air, et le sein de Nereydes.

Alarmed at the Queen's audacious expression of will, the chorus, obviously voicing the author's opinion, reproves her with a long discourse treating the two kinds of Love: that of blood ties and that of marriage. The latter is far more important since it presupposes an inseparable unity of soul which the chorus Platonistically calls Androgine:

>Deux moitez jointes en un
>Ne tiennent rien du commun.
>Cest amour inseparable
>N'a le mouvant, ny le sable,
>Ny de l'Ocean venteus,
>Ny de l'Autan impiteus.

Final preparations are made for battle in act four. In the first scene the Marquis de Pesquaire, a young Spanish officer, flaunts his courage as being equal any day to that of Gaston. We now see the vast battlefield, and Gaston's genius is revealed through his easy command of every detail of the battle which will soon ensue. The chauvinism of the French soldiers is revealed through their lavish praise of Gaston:

>Sous un Guaston genereus,
>Les cerfs seroient valeureus;
>Que pouvons nous moins attendre
>Que le voir un Alexandre?

Although victorious, while routing a detachment of Spanish soldiers, Gaston was set upon and mortally wounded. The final preparation for the acceptance of his death is the main concern in act five. As the scene opens a third premonition of Gaston's death is expressed. In a conversation with his cousin, the Cardinal d'Amboyse (died 1509), Louis XII tells of a dream in which he saw Gaston pierced with wounds inflicted by lions. This is evidently symbolic of the lions of Aragon:

>Je songeoy qu'en un champ, ce genereux vainqueur
>Assailli des lions rovoit sa large espée
>Au pourpre de leur sang, d'heur en heure trempée
>Qu'il estoit fort pressé, qu'en fin je le voyois
>Atterré dessous eus, et rendant les abois:
>Que deschiré de coups, sa face blemissante,
>Mi-morte ressembloit une ombre palissante,
>Qui des ondes de Stix vient de nuit apres nous,
>Pour nous espouventer, compagne des hybous.

The cardinal reassures Louis that he should not be disturbed. Gaston is destined to be victorious. Their conversation is cut short by news that Gaston died in close battle with Spanish forces. This shocking news almost overwhelms the King and all Frenchmen. Gaston is cited as having been an invincible warrior and a great boon to France. All resolve to avenge his death by putting every enemy soldier to the sword. The chorus ends the play with a lament in honor of Gaston. Although his death was untimely; he is now in Paradise and infinitely happier than on earth:

> Mais las! essuyons nos yeux:
> Plorer ceux qui sont ez cieux
> C'est leur porter de l'envie;
> Ce sont eus qui sont en vie;
> Celle qu'on vit icy-bas
> Est la vie du trespas.

Billard dedicated his tragedy to the Duc de Nevers, a descendant of the family of Foix. From the lavish praise with which he honored that family's name, Billard obviously hoped for a generous pecuniary remuneration. The play resembles more a declamation than a tragedy. It is characterized by long monologues, no action or development and introduces characters unnecessary to the dénouement. There is no consideration of the unities. The scene switches at will from Ravenna, to Paris, then to Aragon and back to Ravenna. Although the action could have very easily been encompassed within the twenty-four hour rule, there is no indication that this was the author's intention. Except for the unifying element of praise for Gaston, there is no *liaison de scènes*. The queen of Spain's tirade against her husband and the ensuing comments of the chorus form an entirely independent episode. In spite of the liberal references to mythology and history, the language is colorless. The endless string of superlatives offered in honor of Gaston leads to a parody rather than sincere expression. As a consequence, Gaston appears as an over-confident and jaunty youth about to launch upon some innocent distraction rather than an intrepid general as Billard hoped to picture. None of the other characters receive any development. The total result of the work is soporific. Luckily, there is no evidence it was ever presented.

From the consideration of an almost contemporary event in *Gaston*, Billard turned to the earliest chronicles of French history for the source of his second tragedy, *Mérovée,* written also in 1607.[10] Although the work bears his name, Mérovée appears only once; emphasis is placed on the diabolical Frédégonde, second wife of Chilpéric I (564-584). Frédégonde was a daughter of a peasant, and equally distinguished for her beauty, her talents and her crimes. Inspired by a violent passion, Chilpéric sought her love. In order to name her his queen, he repudiated his first wife Audovera, and strangled his second, Galsonde. Once married to Chilpéric, Frédégonde exercised even a more pernicious influence over him. In her campaign to eradicate every possible candidate to the throne that stood in the way of her own sons, she carried on devastating intrigue and war. She forced Chilpéric into war with Austrasia, and pressed for the assassination of Sigibert, one of Chilpéric's four brothers; she tortured many people who were accused of trying to thwart her ambitions, and was involved in a scandal which claimed she instigated the murder of Chilpéric.

In five acts, in verse, and with choruses, *Mérovée* has long monologues, the distinguishing characteristic of Billard's dramatic works.

The play opens on the eve of Mérovée's death at the hands of assassins engaged by Frédégonde. The first act is a long monologue by the fury, Tysiphone, who has come to effect ruin upon the Franks. She predicts Mérovée's death, and gloats over Sigibert's assassination. Disheartened by the sad state of affairs, the chorus regrets that violence has free rein.

In act two Mérovée, separated from his beloved Brunehaut, deplores the situation in which fate has placed him. Brunehaut had married Sigibert in 567. Jealous of the renown which this marriage brought to his elder brother, Chilpéric married Galsonde, Brunehaut's sister. Outraged by this action, Frédégonde prevailed upon her lover to strangle his wife. This murder initiated a long series of costly wars between Chilpéric and his brother. The wars ended in 575 with Sigibert's assassination. Made captive, Brunehaut was successful in escaping death by marrying Mérovée, the son of her conqueror.

Sensing his life is in grave danger, Mérovée wonders why his father is so outraged. The answer is simple. He had married Brunehaut in spite of his father's opposition. In trying to dissuade his son from persisting in this marriage, Chilpéric had presented the argument of

---

[10] Claude Billard, *Mérovée* (Paris: Denys Langlois, 1610).

illegality. Since Brunehaut was the widow of Mérovée's uncle, only a dispensation from the Pope could correct matters. Chilpéric intended, of course, to block the dispensation. Bosson arrives to console Mérovée, who, instead of being freed from his unhappiness, threatens suicide. The chorus closes the act with a dialectic on the evils of love. The general conclusion is that all characters in the play face eternal damnation because they are victims of the guiles of love.

Although Frédégonde's fiendish ambition has been the mainspring of the previous action, she does not appear until the third act. She is presented as a horrible monster artfully dressed to appear stunningly beautiful. In her drive for absolute power, she deems Mérovée's death the next move. As she spins her web of intrigue, Frédégonde avows her love for Landry and assures him that her crimes have been committed only for the future benefit of his children and her own. Mérovée must be eliminated. Interspersed with praises of her beauty, Landry suggests that an effective means to assure certain death to Mérovée would be to direct Chilpéric's anger against him. Overjoyed by the ingenuity of her lover, Frédégonde admits her desire to build an empire of her own.

The chorus woefully regrets the existence of such people as Frédégonde, but agents of the devil are always in our midst. The act concludes with a long diatribe against unfaithfulness, creator of major crimes.

The hopeless contortions of a man trapped in the clutches of Frédégonde are the main reflection of act four. Demoniacally inspired by Frédégonde, Chilpéric is consumed with hate for his son. Although he is driven to do as Frédégonde bids, Chilpéric sees Brunehaut as the real cause of his troubles. Mérovée's youth and the workings of fate would excuse him. In a moment of remorse Chilpéric admits that he committed an odious crime in the murder of his wife, Galsonde:

> Sans m'avoir offensé, sans auvoir onc meffait
> Que pour aymer par trop celuy qui l'a deffait
> ...i'ay honte: helas ie tremble
> Lors qu'il me ressouuient de l'heure et du moment.

However, he is slavishly subservient to Frédégonde's wishes. Nevertheless, he resolves to pardon his son, and although Frédégonde threatens him with dire results, he remains steadfast in his previous decision.

The scene now switches to Brunehaut. In her longing to be with Mérovée, she reviews the unhappy life that has been a constant companion since departing from Spain.[11] She has a foreboding of Mérovée's eventual death at the hands of his close companion Bosson, really an agent of Frédégonde. In spite of her foreboding of evil, Brunehaut hoped to start anew with Mérovée:

> Nous en fussions allez aimants avantureus
> Chercher autre fortune, autre part plus heureuse.

The treason is completed in act five. Happy that Bosson fulfilled his duty, Frédégonde is afraid that her assassin will reveal the truth and orders his murder. Landry, who reluctantly agreed to murder Bosson, can rejoice that his son will soon be king. Filled with remorse, Chilpéric weepingly claims his vacillation is inspired by some infernal demon. The chorus warns of the consequences of unchaste love, especially among the great. Chastity is love's greatest safeguard. In the last scene Brunehaut, dejected and overwhelmed with grief, clamors for death to overtake her. The chorus reiterates the main theme of the play, and reminds all once again of the great bloodshed that ensues from the bonds of unholy love.

Although Frédégonde is one of history's most forceful sorceresses, Billard was incapable of creating a dramatic situation. He needlessly introduced Tysiphone whose presence obfuscated the entire first act. Brunehaut, who had probably married Mérovée to seek revenge for Sigibert's death, was as full of wiles as her enemy, Frédégonde. Although presented here as a hapless victim of circumstance to offset the ferocious domination of Frédégonde, Brunehaut's plaintive cries do not ring true. Mérovée is scarcely considered, and when he appears, his role is only to lament the separation from Brunehaut. Chilpéric, who is plagued by the only real struggle, is allowed to disintegrate into a senile maniac. The language is highly rhetorical, periphrastic and abounds in antitheses. The unities are scarcely in evidence, and the tragedy evolving from Frédégonde's ambition is clouded by useless bombast.

As the title indicates, *La tragédie du Roy Henry le Grand* concerns the assassination of Henri IV on May 14, 1610. Published in

---

[11] She was the daughter of the king of Spain.

1612, the work was probably composed shortly after the King's murder.[12] No figure in France has been more popular than that of «Henri le Grand». The materials set down in Billard's play followed historical account very closely. In 1609, the opening of the question of the succession of John William the Good, Duke of Clèves, of Julich and of Berg, led Henry, in spite of his own hesitations and those of his German allies, to declare war on the emperor Rudolph II. This enterprise, referred to throughout the play, was severed by François Ravaillac. Henri's marriage to Marguerite de Valois was fruitless. He renounced this union formed in 1572, and, in 1600, married Marie de Médicis, niece of the grand duke of Tuscany. There were five children from this union: Louis XIII; Gaston, Duc d'Orléans; Elizabeth, who married Philip IV of Spain; Christine, Duchesse de Savoie; and Henriette, wife of Charles I of England.[13]

In five acts and in verse Billard's work is a phrenetic harangue against Catholics. With the appearance of Satan in act one, the stage is set for Henri's murder. As is typical of Billard, a long monologue introduces the theme. For nine pages Satan, about to bathe his hands in the blood of the invincible Henri, deplores the manner in which he has been served since his fall from God's grace. He alone will mastermind the plot to take Henri's life. The act is concluded with the chorus rejoicing in the good fortune of France. The good king Henri, about to go off to war, has just arranged for his queen, Marie de Médicis to rule in his absence.

Frequently used by Billard to prepare the setting of his tragedies, a dream, foretelling Henri's death, is the principal concern of act two. When the act opens, Henri, in good spirits, spends five pages rejoicing in anticipation of his imminent departure for war:

> I'ay vieilly souz la paix, ceste sombre saison,
> Ce seiour de Paris m'a rendu si grison.

He will not wage unnecessary wars, but a part of his design is to try to eventually bring the Empire of the Crescent under the sway of

---

[12] Claude Billard, *La tragédie du Roy Henry le Grand* (Paris: Léopold Collin, 1806). Lacroix claims the tragedy was presented at the request of Marie de Médicis in 1610. Lacroix, *op. cit.*, I, 192.

[13] A recent and well-written biography of Henri IV is that of Maurice Andrieux, *Henri IV* (Paris: Artheme Fayard, 1955).

Christianity. Sully admonishes Henri to depart forthwith for his war in Germany, and suggests he use ruse in preference to force. Henri declares he will resort to both. Harassed by bad omens and dreams, in which she saw Henri covered in his own blood, the Queen, in the rôle of Caesar's wife, voices her fears to the Princesse de Couty and is somewhat reassured by her friend's frivolous banter. The chorus hopes to see Henri conquer the Moslem lands, but fears some treachery from the enemy, hopeless of victory.

The introduction of the Dauphin, Louis, gives rise to a humorous situation. Apprehensive that his father will leave nothing to be done, Louis hopes to see him fall victim to a mild siege of the gout. Louis does not like books and, instead of being constantly besieged by headaches that come from study, he would prefer to play soldier with his father. Although already refused permission to accompany Henri, the Dauphin thinks he will be able to convince his tutor that the wars will be more beneficial to his maturity than the contents of ill-phrased books. A chorus, composed of Louis' companions, concur in their disgust with study and especially:

> Je ne puis mettre dans ma teste,
> Ce meschant Latin estranger
> Qui met mes fesses en danger;
> Ces livres me rendent peureux.

In act three a series of warnings, mostly announced through dreams, and astrological predictions, aid in convincing Henri to take every precaution. First, he dismisses the warning of the Duc de Vendôme. Perturbed by dreams, Marie had sought the advice of an astrologer. She tells Henri of her experience in which it was predicted the King would die that very day. However, if through the persuasion of the Queen, Henri escaped death on the day noted, he would live another thirty years. Although he has no faith in the nonsense peddled by astrologers, Henri consents to cooperate if only to please his wife. A chorus of Parisians honors the good fortune of their city, the brightest jewel in France. The country is singularly blessed by having Henri as its king, and he in turn is to be congratulated for the happy choice of Marie as his queen.

Having had frequent unnerving dreams himself, Henri decides to seek the advice of a famous patriarch, the Hermite de Surayne. The hermit denigrates astrologers and oracles claiming them instruments of the devil, but he feels no harm could come from taking safety measures. After a little coaxing, Henri agrees to remain within the palace. Alone, Henri offers a prayer begging God to deflect the evil which seems to be inevitable. Feeling the nation is too prosperous, the chorus lends its voice to the suspicion that Henri's life is in danger.

Act four depicts events leading to the King's death. As the scene opens, the Parricide appears, his soul torn in a conflict in which he seems to be a helpless bystander. Although goaded by demons to stab the King, the Parricide hopes to overcome their bewitchment by looking into the King's eyes whose dazzling radiance commands only respect. Detesting himself and yet driven to commit the odious crime, the Parricide writhes in the grips of Satan who possesses him. Satan gloats in his power:

> C'est moy, c'est ma fureur,
> Qui t'anime, te pousse, et t'enflamme d'horreur.

Very pleased with the quiet atmosphere of peace that has settled over Paris, Henri conveys his thoughts to three staunch Catholics: de Lavardin, d'Espernon and de Monbazan. The King is reminded that peace reigns only because he changed his religion. There has been no change of attitude in Parisians. Marie complains of Henri's indifference to her and her sons. While with the Mareschale d'Ancre, she hears of the King's death and reiterates how her fears were well founded. Commenting on Henri's death, the chorus asserts that the great are often murdered because their excessive courage, pride and fear of being called cowards require them to take minimum precautions. The great are subject to fate; the valorous grieve often; the best life is a secure, mediocre one.

Details of Henri's death and the reaction of several people to his passing occupy act five. In the solitude of his abode, the Hermite de Surayne is glad to be far from the busy life of Paris. He does not sanction the frivolity of city life whose iniquity causes unhappiness. While meditating on his interview with Henri, the hermit recalls the deaths of Henri II and Henri III and fears for the present king's life. Paris is in an uproar. In the wake of Henri's death, the Duc de Guise assumes the initiative in establishing some plan of government. He urges that Louis XIII be placed on the throne under the regency of his mother, Marie de Médicis.

THE SEVENTEENTH CENTURY 51

Broken with grief, the Queen requests the chorus to relate the details of Henri's death. Resolved, in spite of warnings, to leave the palace, Henri had thought to spare the Queen's nerves by setting out in haste. With this intention, he had dismissed his personal guards. Since his departure was secretive, and the streets of Paris were always crowded, the King's coach had been forced to stop. One valet had gone ahead to clear the way and another had stopped to fasten his garter. Thus unattended, the assassin's way was made easy. He leaped upon the coach and fatally wounded the King in the breast. The body was returned to the palace by courtiers. The assassin has been captured and will be duly tortured in order to discover the reasons for his crime.

Although the characters in this play are as wooden as those in Billard's other dramatic works, his treatment of Henri deserves comment. As would be expected, Billard paints a flattering portrait. Bored with the peaceful life at court, Henri is proud to be a warrior again, a suitable job for his tastes. Nevertheless, he is not interested in war just for the pleasure of it. Indeed, he has made every effort to avoid calling his subjects from their peaceful pursuits, but the enemy has flaunted his power by breaking treaties and creating tensions that were destined to eventually erupt in war. Presented first as essentially a soldier, Henri is then shown in the rôle of benevolent king. Almost fanatically loved by his subjects for the demostrations of his interest in their common good, Henri's prime concern continues to be in the welfare of his nation and its people. Henri is constantly shown as a dutiful and lovable husband. It was out of consideration for the queen that he left the palace secretly and thus facilitated the assassin's way. The King is depicted as a good and staunch Catholic. His religious leanings are brought into relief by the reminder that it is he who has changed and not Parisians. His humility is shown in the prayer in which he beseeches God to prevent the impending doom that seems to hover over him. That Henri is a man of decided opinions, Billard leaves no doubt. While surrounded by relatives, friends and advisers who have implicit trust in astrology and are eternally filled with dread by superstitions, Henri spurns contact with them. Energetic warrior, benevolent king, lovable husband, dutiful Catholic, humble Christian and champion of common sense, all noteworthy traits, are submerged in the stultified language of Billard.

Of the lesser characters, little can be said. To emphasize the grief which she is said to have had on the death of the King, Marie is seen as a tearful wife surfeited with superstitions and forebodings. Sully is seen only briefly to show his great esteem for the King. With his childish antics against study and desire to go to war, Louis XIII lends a humorous atmosphere to the development. Satan is an interesting but unnecessary character. He appears as a hideous figure created specifically to plot the death of Henri for preventing the triumph of evil by turning Catholic. Satan's agent is far more important as a dramatic creation. He has the only psychological struggle in the entire play. He actually praises his intended victim and hopes to avert disaster by looking into Henri's eyes. He can do nothing and writhes helplessly in the magnetized grip of a consuming fury.

Although the author was obviously unconcerned with making his play conform to the unities, they are followed. The action comes well within the twenty-four hour rule; all events occur in Paris; and the scenes are closely connected. Their unity is somewhat impaired by the choruses which only serve to echo action already introduced.

Jean Prévost (1580-1622), highly regarded as an alchemist, devoted one of his tragedies to Clotilde, the wife of Clovis.[14] Published in 1614 with some of Prévost's other works, *Clotilde* is in five acts and in verse. The only fact drawn from French history is that Clotilde is the wife of Clovis. In the *épître dédicatoire* the author explained why he distorted history so freely:

> J'ay taché par mon artifice d'embellir ce sujet,
> Qui representé nuement, ne contenteroit pas ces curieux...[15]

The theme of the play was inspired by the legend in which Saint Léonard of Limousin saved Clotilde's life in childbirth. The play begins shortly after the conversion of Clovis. In a discussion with his adviser Sigibert, it is decided not to assume control of the land of the Visigoths. Clotilde is introduced near the end of the first act. Her high esteem for Léonard prompts the suggestion that he be made a bishop.

---

[14] H. Carrington Lancaster, *The Pre-classical Period 1610-1634*, I, 111. Lancaster calls *Clotilde* a tragi-comedy. *Clotilde* was published in Poitiers by Julian Thoreau, 1614.

[15] Frères Parfaict, *op. cit.*, XIV, 202. Prevost's work is based on the story in *The Golden Legend* by Jacobus de Voragine (London: J. M. Dent, 1900), III, 193-195.

In the second act Clotilde, eight months pregnant, is allowed to accompany her husband on a hunting expedition. While trailing her husband, Clotilde falls ill in the third act. A messenger, on his way to warn Clovis, meets Léonard and blurts out the news of Clotilde's illness. In the fourth act a physician's quick appraisal establishes the seriousness of Clotilde's condition. She cannot live, but perhaps an operation would save the child. Overwhelmed with the sudden turn of fortune, Clovis thinks of suicide. In the meanwhile, Clotilde, ready for death, fills the air with lamentations abounding in pagan allusions. Such behavior on the part of a Christian is sorely criticized by Léonard, a surprise visitor. At his beckoning, both Clovis and Clotilde pray to God.

In the last act the physician reports Clotilde's complete recovery due entirely to the attentions of Léonard. Filled with gratitude, Clovis wishes to reward the hermit, but is rebuffed in his advances. A group of his neighbors calls on Clovis and informs him that he and Léonard are related. Léonard accepts his pay in land which he offers to his friends. In the closing scene Léonard predicts good fortune for France, making special mention of the crusades and of Jeanne d'Arc.

The entire first act is unrelated to the details of the play. There is no tragic action. Clovis and Clotilde are inconsistent. This is particularly noticeable in the fourth act, when, faced with death, both call upon pagan gods rather than the Christian for whose glory they struggled so ardently. Clotilde, who is evidently the main character, fades into a secondary position with the appearance of Léonard. His rôle is much more natural than any other. Depicted as an humble, but good man, Léonard consistently upholds that opinion. His language is natural, and his actions well motivated. Although *Clotilde* is by no measure a work of art, the language is far less diffuse than was evidenced in Billard's tragedies.

One of the most popular political satires of the seventeenth century was *La magicienne estrangere* (1617), a seething attack against Léonor Galigay, the wife of Concini, and close friend to Marie de Médicis.[16]

In four acts and in verse, the work, written perhaps by Pierre Matthieu, was tremendously popular. There were eight editions issued in

---

[16] Rouen: David Geuffroy et Jacques Besongne, 1617.

the seventeenth century. The purpose of the play as stated in the preface is to:

> montrer les tirannicques comportemens, origine, entreprises, desseins, sortilèges, arrest, mort et supplice, tant du Marquis d'Ancre que de Léonor Gallygay sa femme, avec l'advantureuse rencontre de leurs funestes ombres. [17]

Dedicated to Louis XIII who ordered the execution of Concini and his wife, the work reflects violent hate for Italians. Due to its violence the author refused to identify his characters who are simply indicated by anagrams. The leading character is Louis XIII appearing under the name of «Le grand Pan françois». Others are the Duc de Luynes (Léontide de V.), the Duc de Nemours (Almidor de N.), the Duc du Maine (Argente du M.), Duc de Longueville (Lucidor de L.), le Président Deslandes or de Verdun (Le Solon françois), Galigay, Concini, three furies, a guardian angel, two councilors, an executioner, the ghosts of Concini and Léonor, Tenebrion, and two savants. [18]

The first act begins with Louis XIII and his advisers in a meeting of which the discussion concerns Léonor's projected execution. Upon hearing the fretful news, the furies prepare to come to Léonor's aid, but are restrained by the guardian angel of France.

The trial ensues in act two. Interrogated by Solon and the councilors, Léonor is accused of sowing discord, plotting against the government, and practicing sorcery. She gives the recipe of her potions:

> Tantost des loups garoux j'amassois les entrailles,
> De la graine de chus, des testes de cornailles,
> Du duvet de lanier, du myrthe papien,
> Du pavot endormant, du sable oegyptien,
> De l'encens masculin, des pepins de citrouilles
> Du suaire de mort et des os de grenouilles.

Having been decapitated and burned, Léonor wanders to Hades. In the third act she meets the ghost of her departed husband. The justification of the death of Concini and his wife is shown in the fourth

---

[17] Lacroix, *op. cit.*, III, 296. My discussion is based on materials found in the reference cited and also in Lancaster, *op. cit.*, I, (1610-1634), 155.
[18] Lacroix, *op. cit.*, III, 296.

act. A long enumeration of their evil deeds would indicate the need of extermination. The play closes with praise of Louis XIII and Henri IV. The work is of interest only as a reflection of public opinion during the time.[19]

A more interesting pamphlet was *La Rocheloise* (1629). In four acts and verse, the play was probably never acted. As the title indicates, the work is concerned with the defeat of the Protestant stronghold at La Rochelle in 1628.[20] Alleged by Lacroix to have been written by Pierre Matthieu, the manuscript simply bears the initials P. M. Lacroix' calculation is highly doubtful. Since the central theme of the plot is the defeat of La Rochelle in 1628, it should be noted that Matthieu died in 1621.

In the first scene the guardian angel of France compares La Rochelle to Troy, Babel and Sodom. The second act is devoted to an argument between the inhabitants of La Rochelle and their English allies as to whether the city should be surrendered. A notable passage in this act is the glowing tribute paid by the English to Jeanne d'Arc. In the third act the town asks for terms. In the fourth the English depart. The population of La Rochelle recants its evil ways and promises to be faithful.[21]

François Hédelin, abbé d'Aubignac (1604-1676), known primarily for the *Pratique du théâtre* (1657), wrote three prose tragedies. All were turned into verse by other dramatists. Neither *Zénobie* (1645) nor *Cyminde* (1642) concern us here. *La Pucelle d'Orléans*, acted in 1641 and published in 1642, was exceptional in its choice of subject and development of plot.[22]

---

[19] A companion diatribe against the Concini was *La victoire du Phébus françois contre le python de ce temps*. It is a dialogued account of the Maréchal d'Ancre's death, and is termed a tragedy, Rouen: Thomas Maillart, 1617. There are four acts in verse. The author is unknown. See Lacroix, *op. cit.*, III, 297.

[20] Troyes: Jean Jacquard, 1629. My discussion is based on the analysis contained in Lancaster, *The Pre-classical Period 1610-1634*, I, 367-368.

[21] Other examples of propagandistic writings during the seventeenth century classified under tragedy were: *Le Marquis de Louvois sur la sellette, criminel examiné, jugement par l'Europe*, five acts, prose, 1695; and *La balance d'Etat* by H. M. D. M. A., with no date, a penetrating satire of Mazarin.

[22] François Hedélin, *La Pucelle d'Orléans* (Paris: François Targa, 1642).

D'Aubignac's saccharine treatment of Jeanne d'Arc was an indication why, during the century, national historical tragedy never became important. The dramatists who endeavored to tap the rich sources of French history were inferior and unsure. They twisted history to such a degree that little or no element of historical fact remained. The result unfortunately was a melodramatic slush that revolted even the least sensitive spectator.

When d'Aubignac wrote *La Pucelle*, he did not sign his name. François Targa, who published the first edition from a manuscript surrendered to him by some actor, told how he would have run into difficulties with the authorities if d'Aubignac had not identified himself as the author and in turn authorized publication of the play, already completely printed.[23] Targa also had much to say about the subject of the play, the actors who interpreted it, and the scenery which was used:

> L'histoire de la Pucelle d'Orléans est un grand et magnifique sujet pour un poème héroique,... mais pour un poème dramatique, c'est, à mon avis, un sujet bien difficile et peu capable du théâtre; car ce poème ne pouvant représenter aux yeux des spectateurs que ce qui c'est faict en huit heures ou pour le plus en un demy jour, ou n'en peut fonder le dessein, que sur un des plus signalez accidents.[24]

Continuing, he complained of the ignorance among the actors who presented his play. According to him they were even too stupid to read the rôles even with a copy in their hands.

Targa described the scenery as deplorable:

> Au lieu de faire paroistre un ange dans un grand ciel, dont l'ouverture eust faict celle du théâtre ils l'ont fait venir quelques fois à pied et quelques fois dans une machine impertinemment faite et impertinemment conduite; au lieu de faire voir dans le refondrement et en perspective l'image de la Pucelle au milieu d'un feu allumé et environné d'un grand peuple, ils firent peindre un méchant tableau sans art, sans raison et tout contraire au sujet... Et au lieu d'avoir une douzaine d'acteurs sur le théâtre pour représenter l'émotion des soldats contre le conseil au jugement de son procès, ils y mi-

---

[23] Lacroix, *op. cit.*, I, 207.
[24] Lacroix, *op. cit.*, I, 267.

rent deux simples gardes qui semblaient plus tost y estre pour empescher les pages et les laquais d'y monter que pour servir à la représentation d'une si notable circonstance de l'histoire. [25]

D'Aubignac allowed himself complete freedom in the treatment of his subject. The most striking derivation from history is in the circumstance of having Jeanne d'Arc in love with the Count of Warwick. The Countess, his wife, is indeed jealous of this peasant maiden who seeks to steal her husband.

The extreme which the author allowed himself was explained away in the *Pratique du théâtre*:

> Ils (les poètes) prennent de l'histoire ce que leur est propre, et y changent le reste pour en faire leurs poems, et c'est une pensée bien ridicule d'aller au théâtre pour apprendre l'Histoire. [26]

Appearing in 1642, the verse translation of d'Aubignac's tragedy was attributed to both Benserade and La Mesnardière. Nevertheless, it was first included in the dramatic works of Benserade. [27] The Benserade-La Mesnardière version is almost a phrase by phrase translation of the original.

Claude Boyer (1618-1698), one of the contemporaries of Corneille and Racine, wrote one historical tragedy, *Clotilde* (1659). [28] The tragedy, containing five acts and in verse, was performed on May 18, 1659, at Bernay and destined to «augmenter la munificence d'une fête que M. le comte de Lyonne donna au Roy (Louis XIV)». [29] The action of the play takes place in the royal palace one month after the arrival of Deuthère and her daughter Clotilde at the court of Théodebert, King of Metz. [30] Elements of a romanesque love triangle are in-

---

[25] Puymaigre, *op. cit.*, p. 37.
[26] François Hédelin Aubignac, *La pratique du théâtre*, Ed. P. Martino (Alger: Carbonel, 1927), II, 68.
[27] Paris: Anthoine de Sommaville, 1642. Lacroix, *op. cit.*, I, 207.
[28] A recent study on Boyer was made by Clara Carnelson Brody, *The Works of Claude Boyer* (New York: King's Crown Press, 1947).
[29] Frères Parfaict, *op. cit.*, VIII, 268.
[30] The edition consulted was that of Paris: Gabriel Quinet, 1669. The work was first published in Paris: Charles de Sercy, 1659. The Clothilde referred to in this drama was a daughter of Deuterie, mistress of Théodebert, King of the Goths from 534 to 547.

troduced in act one. Clotilde is in love with Clidamant, a favorite of Théodebert and benefactor of Deuthère; Clidamant loves Deuthère, who is ambitious to be crowned queen; Théodebert grows fonder of Clotilde with the passing of time; Deuthère is very jealous of the attentions to her daughter; Clodomire, Théodebert's son, is also in love with Clotilde but has not revealed his feelings.

As the play opens Clotilde admits her affection for Clidamant:

> Clidamant seul peut estre avouë de mon coeur
>   Ses yeux ont pour les miens ie ne sçay quoy d'aimables
>   (Act I, Scene I)

She is even jealous of her mother, and although Clidamant has said nothing about it, Clotilde believes he loves her. Deuthère also reveals her love for Clidamant and is reminded her duty should lie in being faithful to Théodebert. Angered to learn of Deuthère's intention of marrying the King, Clidamant accuses his friend of treason. Deuthère haughtily replies that she desires the crown upon her head. Clidamant warns of his power with the King. This outburst warrants a word of precaution from Lucinde. Deuthère retorts that she is capable of handling any enemy. Trying the scheme of diplomacy, Théodebert suggests to Deuthère that she marry Clidamant, and relinquish her daughter to him. Filled with rage that Théodebert, a man her own age, would advance such a weird proposal, Deuthère storms at her suitor who meekly replies: «J'adore en vostre sang vostre vivant portrait». (Act I, Scene V). Moved to the need of confession by Deuthère's fit of anger, Théodebert confides in Sigile. The latter cautions the King of the extravagance of his thoughts. To this, the King answers cavalierly:

> Qu'importe à mon repos celuy de mon Empire?
> Mon amour n'est plus cher que l'Empire et le jour.
>   (Act I, Scene VI)

Having met with little sympathy, Théodebert tells Clodomire of his love for Clotilde, and commissions his son to bear the message of his love to her.

In act two Deuthère, whose increasing jealousy has left her dazed, promises her daughter first to Clidamant and then to the King. Deuthère believes Clotilde's aspirations for the throne have usurped the power of her own charms over Théodebert. Seeing the scepter rapidly disappearing from her grasp, Deuthère exclaims:

> Qu'un peu plus de beauté que ma Fille à sur moy
> Qu'un peu plus de jeunesse a fait manquer de foy.
>
> Je meurs de jalousie et de haine et d'amour.
> (Act II, Scene II)

When confronted by her mother, Clotilde declares nothing could persuade her to become Théodebert's wife. Deuthère accuses her daughter of lying. Clotilde then confesses her love for Clidamant. Deuthère immediately promises to support her daughter in this affair. Clidamant arrives at a propitious moment, and when informed that Clotilde is his for the taking, he accuses Deuthère of using her daughter as a pawn. He says to Deuthère:

> Non, je vous aime encore; ny son coeur, ny tout autre,
> Ne scaureit me venger de la perte du vostre;
> Rendez le moy ce coeur... (Act II, Scene V)

In her confusion Deuthère offers Clotilde to Théodebert. Clidamant realizes Deuthère's sudden change of heart is not sincere. Nevertheless, the King, having heard the news he has been longing for, dispatches Clodomire on the happy mission to tell Clotilde she will soon be queen. With no quarter Clodomire blurts out his passion for Clotilde. Finding himself suddenly the rival of his own son, Théodebert pleads for understanding! «Si tu pourrois, mon Fils, te vaincre en ma faveur». (Act II, Scene IX).

In act three Théodebert almost concedes defeat in the struggle between himself and Clodomire for Clotilde's love. In order to seek vengeance upon Clidamant Deuthère decides to permit the marriage between Clodomire and Clotilde. On the point of recanting his love for Clotilde, Théodebert's passion boils anew upon seeing her. Clotilde primly accuses her suitor of infidelity. This increases the King's esteem for her all the more. Clidamant claims Clotilde is acting so coyly only out of obedience to her mother. He admonishes Théodebert to ignore Clodomire with the assurance Clotilde will be the new queen.

Clidamant's determination to have Deuthère or murder someone in the process is the main theme of act four. Deuthère reassures a hopeless Clodomire. Clotilde calmly notifies her mother she will obey as a dutiful daughter, but after all Deuthère has freed her to pursue Clidamant. In her blind fury Deuthère presumes Clidamant must be exterminated. Clodomire threatens Clidamant who scarcely pays any attention. The act ends with Clidamant's appraisal of his fate:

> J'estois né pour aimer, et le ciel à mon âme
> Avoit fait en naissant un destin tout de flâme.
> (Act IV, Scene VI)

Having found his destiny impeded, Clidamant's attitude has changed to hate: «Je me perdray moy-même afin de me venger». (Act IV, Scene VI).

The puzzle is resolved in act five with the suicide of Deuthère and Clidamant. Clodomire will marry Clotilde and Théodebert will bury his chagrin in busying himself with affairs of state. Clotilde expresses her independence in refusing to marry Clodomire. In the only interview with Clidamant, she discovers his obstinacy. Although she denies any desire to be queen, Clidamant claims she is at the mercy of her mother's diabolical schemes. She defends her position eloquently while telling Clidamant openly that he is more important to her than her mother and the throne. Clidamant answers: «Si vous m'aimez, scachez que je n'en veux rien croire». (Act V, Scene II). Clotilde is naturally offended by Clidamant's manner. In the meanwhile, Deuthère has decided her daughter can love whom she pleases. Disgusted with the intrigue surrounding her, Clotilde chooses to love no one. Deuthère misunderstands her daughter's sincerity and interprets it as another of her ruses to deceive Théodebert. The King wants fo force Clotilde to marry him. He meets his son, sword in hand mistakingly thinks Clodomire has come to kill him. The sword is for Clidamant whom Clodomire intends to murder. Théodebert has a change of heart which involves punishing Clidamant and marrying Deuthère.

Clidamant recounts a fantastic adventure he has just experienced with Deuthère and Clotilde. He surprised Deuthère on the point of killing her daughter with a sword, and, to prevent the catastrophe, he jumped between the two. Clotilde fainted, and Deuthère, full of remorse and thinking her daughter dead, committed suicide by thrusting the blade of the sword in her heart. Before dying, she pronounced a curse upon Clidamant. Immeasurably happy, Clidamant wants to die because Deuthère is dead. Théodebert summons him to choose the manner in which he wishes to die. Full of self-reproach because of the unhappy turn of events, Théodebert is assured by Clotilde that she is responsible; Clodomire blames everything on Clidamant. Presently Sigile reports Clidamant's suicide. The king benevolently offers Clotilde to Clodomire.

This is a tragedy written according to the classical rules. The plot, involving four separate intrigues, is somewhat diffuse, but the development is so well handled the reader is unaware of this shortcoming. Although there is no mention of the unity of time, the events could have taken place within the twenty-four hour period. The unities of place and action are closely followed.

Although the name of the play is *Clotilde,* the leading character is Deuthère. Major emphasis is placed on the outcome of her ambition to become queen. Placed by the author as the scheming competitor of her daughter, Deuthère's blinding ambition evolves into a jealous passion that drives her to attempt murder and then suicide. The analysis of Deuthère's emotions anticipates the tragedies of Jean Racine. Clotilde's gentle and predisposing character is in striking contrast to that of her impetuous and frenzied mother. Clotilde would emerge as a meek and nondescript daughter if it had not been for a surprising development in the fifth act. In her refusal to follow the wishes of Deuthère and marry Clodomire, Clotilde expresses an independence of spirit that makes her a real personality. However, her usual equilibrium is cast awry by the unprovoked charge, in the third act, against Théodebert for infidelity. Although Boyer was evidently attempting to project woman's coquettish nature, it is incongruous to believe Clotilde ever had the faintest romantic inclination toward Théodebert.

Cast in the roles of anguished competitors for the same woman's love, Théodebert and his son Clodomire are ludicrous. Instead of being concerned with affairs of state as is natural to a man of Théodebert's age, the King subjects himself to the romantic sufferings of a stripling. His occasional flashes of reality only serve to heighten the burlesque character of the situation.

Clodomire's timid nature is accentuated by his hesitation in admitting his love to Clotilde, and, instead of creating interest, his state is made all the more ridiculous. The prince's harried maneuvers enter the realm of the burlesque when, in the fifth act, he brandishes his sword, intended for the murder of Clidamant, and it is mistaken by Théodebert as his own death weapon.

Although the past relationship between Deuthère and Clidamant is referred to only vaguely, it plays an important part in their present status. Depicted as a fatal man born only to love, Clidamant has had time to fall deeply in love with Deuthère and become insanely jealous of her. When she dies by her own hand, he can triumph only by committing the same act. Although Boyer inadvertently created a comic character in Théodebert and introduced a needless complication of plot with intrigues of love, his mastery of the alexandrine and the analysis of Deuthère's overpowering obsession to be queen are indeed noteworthy.

According to Loret, reporting in *La Muze historique* of May 24, 1659, Clotilde was favorably received at the Comte de Lyonne's festival:

> Ensuite la Troupe Royale...
> *La Clotilde* représentèrent,
> Que les Auditeurs admirèrent,
> Pièce digne d'un grand loyer,
> Dont est Auteur le Sieur Boyer,
> Qui, dit-on, d'une force extrême,
> A réussi dans ce Poëme,
> Bref, qui fut lors en vérité,
> A merveille représenté. [31]

Louis Ferrier wrote one historical tragedy, *Anne de Bretagne*. In five acts and in verse, the play was presented in 1678 and published a year later.[32] The work contains an important preface in which the author defends his choice of subject and discusses the unfavorable attitude of the enlightened public toward the use of French history as a source for tragedy:

> La nouveauté de son sujet lui a attiré bien des censeurs, et j'ai été surpris de voir qu'elle n'ait pas plu à de certaines gens, par l'endroit même ou je croyais qu'elle devait plaire le plus. Ils ont dit que notre histoire était mal propre à nous fournir des sujets de tragédie, qu'il fallait mener le spectateur dans un pays éloigné, remplir son oreille par des noms

---

[31] Cited by Brody, *op. cit.*, p. 33.
[32] Louis Ferrier, *Anne de Bretagne* (Paris: Jean Ribou, 1679).

plus pompeux, lui imposer et l'éblouir en quelque façon... Je ne me repens point d'avoir fait paroitre *Anne de Bretagne* sur notre théâtre: il est vrai que si j'étais à le faire, je pourrois réfléchir plus murement avant que de l'entreprendre. Je vois trop combien il est dangereux d'entrer le premier en lice, et qu'on y trouve des difficultés que l'on n'a souvent point prevues. Car enfin... peut-être Apollon aidant, je ferai à l'avenir de meilleures pieces qui me donneront sans doute, moins de peine que celle-ci. Je n'ai pas osé m'élever trop haut, de peur d'entrer dans le grand cothurne; et j'ai craint de descendre trop bas, en évitant cette élévation, que la simplicité de mon sujet ne me permettoit pas... J'ai altéré l'histoire en quelques endroicts...[33]

Anne de Bretagne (1477-1514) had a very interesting career. She was the daughter of François II, Duc de Bretagne, and Marguerite de Foix. She succeeded her father as Duchesse de Bretagne in 1488. Charles VIII, King of France, wished to establish his authority over her; Alain d'Albret wished to marry her; Jean de Rohan claimed the duchy; and her guardian, the Maréchal de Rieux, was soon in open revolt against Charles VIII. In 1489 the French army invaded Brittany.

Anne formed an alliance with Maximilien of Austria and married him by proxy in 1490. Affairs in Austria kept Maximilien too busy to consider helping his bride. With no help from her husband, Anne, besieged at Rennes, was compelled to seek negotiations with Charles. The terms of the treaty stipulated that Anne should marry the French king. This, of course, meant that France would have jurisdiction over Brittany. Anne concurred in the terms of the treaty, broke her marriage with Maximilien, and became queen of France.

After the death of Charles VIII in 1498 Anne returned to Brittany, and in 1499 she married Louis XII, thus again becoming queen of France. In 1504 she made an agreement for the marriage of her daughter, Claude de France to Charles of Austria, the future Emperor Charles V. This agreement was broken and Anne arranged for her daughter to marry François d'Angoulême, who became, in 1515, François Premier, King of France.

The theme of Ferrier's play is concentrated on the efforts of Anne to select a husband. As the play opens it is revealed that Anne is sought by three men: the Maréchal d'Albret, Maximilien of Austria and Char-

---

[33] Frères Parfaict, *op. cit.*, XII, 124-125.

les VIII of France. None of these intrepid warriors is to her liking. She loves the Duc d'Orléans (Louis XII), and would marry the latter except for a fit of ill-conceived jealousy which makes her choose Charles VIII. [34]

The so-called tragedy was praised by the *Mercure galant* of November, 1678:

> Anne de Bretagne, dont l'Hôtel de Bourgogne nous a deja donne quelques représentations, est la première piece nouvelle qui ait paru au théâtre cet hyver. Elle est de M. Ferrier. Les vers en sont fort aises, et les pensées naturellement exprimées. [35]

The *Mercure* mentioned the pleasure of the King and Queen with a performance they attended. Even though characterization in the work is acceptable to us today, there is little unity of action and practically no interest. Ferrier distorts history to such a degree that the queenly Anne becomes a soap opera heroine. Fortunately Ferrier had no influence on his contemporaries. It is lamentable, however, that no great tragedy writer in France opened successfully the rich field of French history.

Another national historical tragedy presented in 1678 was the unpublished *Princesse de Clèves* based on the novel by the same name of Madame de La Fayette. The only two performances took place at the *théâtre de Guénégaud* in December, 1678. This play, by Edne Boursault (1638-1701), was allegedly later known under the title of *Germanicus*.

In a letter written to a lady friend, Boursault explained the miserable failure of the *Princesse de Clèves*:

> ...Toutes les fois que vous allez à la première représentation d'une pièce sérieuse, vous croyez, dites-vous, aller à Athènes, ou à Rome: vous ne trouvez en votre chemin que des Grecs et des Romains; encore font-ils tous défigurés depuis que Corneille ne les a fait plus parler. Il vous semble que

---

[34] The *Mémoire de Mahelot*, Ed. H. C. Lancaster (Paris: Champion, 1920), p. 121, has an interesting statement regarding the scenery needed for *Anne de Bretagne*. «Théâtre est une salle de palais. Au second acte, il faut deux fauteuille et deux tabourest».

[35] Frères Parfaict, *op. cit.*, XII, 123.

> les Auteurs, qui ne peuvent faire tenir le même langage à leurs Héros, feroient mieux de les choisir dans un pays où l'on ne les ait pas tant mis en oeuvre; et vous dites qu'un grand homme de notre France, dont la vie seroit pleine de belles actions, et qu'on feroit parler comme naturellement les honnetes gens y parlent, feroit pour le moins autant de plaisir à voir, que des Heros, dont les noms paroissent uses, à force de les entendre repeter...
>
> Je ne vois rien dans notre langue de plus agreable, que le petit Roman de *La Princesse de Clèves*... J'en fis une Piece de Théâtre dont j'esperois un... grand succes. [36]

Because of the comparatively recent date (sixteenth century) of its events, Boursault knew that an audience would not appreciate his work. With this in mind he had written a prologue in defense of subject matter for tragedy being drawn from French national history. The prologue was in the form of an allegory with Fame and Melopene discussing the problem under consideration. Melopene, surfeited with subjects taken from ancient history, seeks new outlets for tragedy. Fame suggests: «Et depuis si longtemps que la France a des Rois, ne s'en trouve-t-il point que meritent ton choix? Choisis quelque grand nom sur les bords de la Seine». [37]

One other *tragédie nationale* written in the century was *Le jugement équitable de Charles le Hardy, dernier duc de Bourgogne*. The Frères Parfaict have a long analysis. [38] The essential action centers around Rodolfe, governor of Mastric, and admirer of Mathilde, the wife of Albert. In order to fulfill his desire to have Mathilde, Rodolfe accuses Albert of treason and has him executed forthwith. Once Albert is dispatched, Rodolfe's passion becomes a frenzied desire, and he attempts to violate Mathilde. She faints at the propitious moment. After the spell has passed, Mathilde seeks out Charles, Duc de Bourgogne, who has been spending a few days in Mastric. The Duc orders that Rodolfe marry Mathilde. The marriage is performed, and Rodolfe is hastily imprisoned to await death. A lady, Frédégonde, appears to plead Rodolfe's case. He is really the son of Charles and a dead sister

---

[36] *Ibid., pp.* 131-132.

[37] Ibid., p. 135. There remain no commentaries on the contents of *La Princess de Clèves*.

[38] Frères Parfaict, *op. cit.*, VI, 280-283. The materials in the play were inspired by an account in Pierre Matthieu's *Histoire de Louis XI*.

of Frédégonde. It is too late to retract the sentence, since, at the very moment Charles commanded a messenger to relay his order sparing Rodolfe, another messenger brings the unhappy news that he is dead.

The play is extremely melodramatic and rhetorical. Too much of the plot is left up to chance. The Frères Parfaict commenting on the work admired the author's mastery at development, but considered the theme unsuitable for French tragedy. [39]

As has been noted, the main source of tragedy throughout the seventeenth century was ancient history and mythology. Histories of other nations were of much less importance. Although there was some criticism in favor of using French national history, novelty in the choice of subject matter was not sanctioned by the public. The only successful play derived from modern history was *Le Comte d'Essex* (1678) of Thomas Corneille. [40] Modern subjects, however, were frequently disguised in order to give them an ancient or Byzantine setting. Notable among these was *Andronic* (1685) of Campistron in which is recounted the tragic story of Prince Don Carlos, son of Philip II of Spain.

As in the sixteenth century much of the political satire of the seventeenth was written in dramatic form and belongs to political rather than dramatic history. Brief mention is made of such plays in this study only because they were classified as tragedy. They were actually nothing more than pamphlets in dialogue form. Many were published outside of France and circulated surreptitiously in the country. Among famous people, the Maréchal d'Ancre and his wife, Richelieu, Mazarin, Louvois, and Mme. de Maintenon were the object of bitter satire. Of course, the old animosities between Protestants and Catholics were kept alive.

Due to a predilection for the classical ideal of *imitation, règle* and *goût* innovation in tragedy was discouraged. Infrequent references to the use of French history as a source for tragedy drew little attention or passed completely ignored. Of the more than two hundred tragedies that appeared during the century, less than thirty were drawn from French history. Only four of these works were inspired by events from

---

[39] *Ibid.*, p. 238.
[40] For a study on the vogue of English history as a source for French dramatic writings, see: L. Alfreda Hill, «The Tudors in French Drama», *The Johns Hopkins Studies in Romance Literatures and Languages*, XX (1932), 1-171.

the national history occurring before the fifteenth century. The entire production of national historical tragedy was highly propagandistic, prolix, periphrastic and stripped of interest.[41]

---

[41] Among the tragedies lost during the seventeenth century, three titles belonging to the *tragédie nationale* are noted. They are *Godefroy de Bouillon* (1614), *Philippe-Auguste donteur des rebelles en la journée de Bouvines* (1622), and *Guillaume d'Aquitaine* (1632). See Lancaster, *The Pre-classical Period 1610-1634*, I, 155 and footnote 5, 103.

Many references to tragedies performed at the colleges indicate the surprising popularity of the *tragédie nationale*. For example, among patriotic plays presented at the Collège Louis-Le-Grand in Paris were: *Carolus Magnus* (1684) and *Clovis* (1686).

Chapter III

THE *TRAGÉDIE NATIONALE* IN THE EIGHTEENTH
CENTURY TO 1789

Before the Revolution tragedy could be played publicly in Paris only at the Comédie-Française. About two hundred new tragedies were performed there from January 7, 1700, the date of *Vononez* by Belin, to November 4, 1789, the date of Marie-Joseph Chénier's *Charles IX,* which for all practical purposes marked the initiation of the French Revolution in the theater.

Tragedy in the eighteenth century underwent an agonizing struggle for survival. Corneille and Racine, themselves imitators of the ancients, were the models for writers of tragedy in the century. The imitation of an imitation would have led inexorably to a complete, if slow, disintegration; yet authors, by their servile attempts to introduce *nouveautés* such as complexity of action, *coups de théâtre*, bombast, recondite declamation, hyperbole, periphrase, disguises, horrific scenes and spectacle, imitated obviously the faults of their models, thus hastening the demise of French classical tragedy. The willing subservience to rule and form as created and practiced in the writing of classical tragedy became the most salient weakness of that genre in the eighteenth century. Although the unities were not strictly observed, tragedy continued to have five acts, be in verse, have characters of a noble station, prevented mixing of the genres, and used ancient history and mythology as primary sources. Many of the *nouveautés* introduced by Crébillon père and Voltaire were deprecated by those wishing to continue the strict limitations required in classical tragedy.

Rule and form demand *goût*; nevertheless, the tenor of audiences, particularly after 1760, had changed so remarkably from the days of

Corneille and Racine, it was imperative for tragedy to embody elements unnatural to classical tragedy. No man came with the genius of a Racine to meet the challenge which demanded reconciliation of taste with form. The changing tastes of the audiences of the century were reflected, for example, in the acceptance of murder on the stage. Strenuously forbidden in classical tragedy, the first murder transpiring on the French stage in the eighteenth century was in *Edouard III* by Jean Gresset (1709-1777). Performed on January 22, 1740, at the Comédie-Française, the play was warmly applauded. [1]

Many critics, among whom were Des Fontaines, Clément, Charisson, Collé, Fréron, La Harpe and Raynal, viewed any innovation with alarm. The volatile state in which tragedy found itself led to the creation of new dramatic forms of a serious nature. The *comédie larmoyante*, championed by Nivelle de la Chaussée, was a prelude to the *drame sérieux*, a middle ground between comedy and tragedy. [2] The major emphasis in plot development of the *drame sérieux*, as conceived by Denis Diderot, was the portrayal of conditions, not character. [3] Effect was achieved through tableaux, not through psychological analysis.

The essential characteristic of the classical tragedy was to please. Moral instruction was a natural result rather than a *parti pris* of the author. In the eighteenth century the theater became a platform from which authors could harangue the public into accepting biased political or moral theses as principal tenets of drama. An increasing interest among people in the theater provided a very appropriate occasion for preaching. [4] The Horatian *utile*, no longer a companion of the *dulce*, assumed total ascendancy. The end result, therefore, was far from being artistic. The growing demand for variety in plot and execution encouraged writers to seek inspiration in the vastly different field of English tragedy. Through the endorsement of Voltaire, Shakespeare

---

[1] According to A. Johannidès, *La Comédie-Française de 1680 à 1900* (Paris: Plon, 1901), p. 49, *Edouard III* was presented nine times. Jean-Louis Baptiste Gresset, *Edouard III* (Paris: Prault père, 1740).

[2] See: Denis Diderot, «Discours sur la poésie dramatique», (1759). Cited by Francisque Vial et Louis Denise, *Idées et doctrines Littéraires du 18ᵉ siècle* (Paris: Delagrave, 1920), p. 246.

[3] *Ibid.*

[4] See: John Lough, *Paris Theatre Audiences in the 17th and 18th Centuries* (London: Oxford University Press, 1957).

was the English writer who exerted more influence than any other on the course of French tragedy during the eigteenth century.[5]

Dramatic criticism in the eighteenth century was carried on through the pages of periodicals, in correspondence, secret memoirs, treatises and prefaces. Periodical criticism did not exert such an important influence upon drama as it does today. Félix Gaiffe summarized its inadequacies as follows:

> D'abord les feuilles quotidiennes se bornent à un compte rendu rapide et sommaire au lendemain de la représentation, quitte à revenir sur l'ouvrage avec plus de détails au moment ou il est imprimé. Quand les autres font paraître leur article, plusieurs jours, plusieurs semaines parfois se sont déjà écouléees et les spectateurs ont eu le temps de se former une opinion indépendante. De plus la critique dramatique, telle qu'elle est comprise alors, n'est guère de nature à orienter nettement dans un sens ou dans l'autre le goût du public; les articles consistent surtout en une analyse extrêmement détaillée de la pièce, avec quelques observations menues et mesquines sur la marche de l'action et le développement des caractères, encadrées quelquefois de considérations générales d'une désolante banalité; aucune idée directrice n'apparaît, si ce n'est le désir de flatter un auteur très protégé, ou de mordre à belles dents un confrère trop applaudi; il faut feuilleter des volumes et des volumes du *Mercure* ou de *L'année litteraire*, pour découvrir une discussion un peu approfondie sur un point d'esthétique théâtrale.[6]

---

[5] Saint-Evremond was perhaps the first Frenchman of letters to make mention of Shakespeare's name, alluding in the *Essai sur la comédie* (1677) to *The Merchant of Venice*. Other references to Shakespeare during the seventeenth century were made by Adrien Baillet in the conclusion of his *Jugement des Scavans sur les principaux ouvrages des auteurs* (1686), and by Pierre-Antoine Le Motteux, the founder of *The Gentleman's Magazine* (1693). For an interesting account of translations of Shakespeare's works into French, consult Albert Dubeux, *Les traductions françaises de Shakespeare* (Paris: Les Belles Lettres, 1928). For a list of thirty-nine English dramatists translated into French during the eighteenth century, see Charles A. Rochedieu, *Bibliography of French Translations of English Works 1700-1800* (Chicago: The University of Chicago Press, 1948).

[6] Félix Gaiffe, *Le drame en France au XVIIIe siècle* (Paris: Armand Colin, 1910), p. 127. Important periodicals and private correspondence in the century are listed below: Des Fontaines: *Le nouvelliste du Parnasse* (Paris, 1731); *Observations sur les ècrits* (Paris, 1735); *Jugements sur quelques ouvrages* (Avignon, 1744). Clement, *Les cinq années littéraires* (La Haye, 1754). Chassiron, *Réflexions sur la comédie larmoyante* (Paris, 1749). Collé,

The most enlightened literary criticism in the century came from the pen of Frederick Melchior Grimm (1723-1807). Grimm's *Correspondance littéraire* was begun in 1753 and lasted for more than forty years. During that period it was a decisive instrument in spreading news throughout Europe of events in the French literary world.[7]

The *Mémoires secrets pour servir à l'histoire de la république des lettres en France depuis 1762 jusqu'au 1787* was another work devoted to dramatic criticism in the eighteenth century.[8] Comprising thirty-six volumes, it was begun by Petit de Bachaumont. Whereas Grimm had detailed analyses and expressed critical opinions of the plays under consideration, Bachaumont and his associates were principally concerned with sensational events that occurred in connection with the theater.

The use of French national history as a source for tragedy was reiterated for the first time in the eighteenth century by Voltaire. He wrote in the preface to *Zaïre* (1732):

> C'est au théâtre anglais que je dois la hardiesse que j'ai eue de mettre sur la scène les noms des rois et des anciennes familles du royaume. Il me paraît que cette nouveauté pourrait être la source d'une genre de tragédie qui nous est inconnu jusqu'ici et dont nous avons besoin. Il se trouvera sans doute des génies heureux qui perfectionneront cette idée, dont *Zaïre* n'est qu'une faible ébauche.[9]

The only elements in *Zaïre* inspired by French national history were the names of Nérestan and Châtillon, French knights, and Lusignan, prince of the blood of the kings of Jerusalem.[10] Of his other tragedies

---

Journal historique (1748-51) (Paris, 1895). Fréron, *Année littéraire* (Amsterdam, 1754). La Harpe, *Lycée, ou cours de la littérature* (Paris, 1734). Palissot, *Petites lettres aux grands philosophes* (Paris, 1779). Raynal, *Les nouvelles littéraires*. Marmontel, *Eléments de la littérature* (Paris, 1781). Voltaire, *Oeuvres*.

[7] Frederick M. Grimm et Denis Diderot, *Correspondence littéraire philosophique et critique, 1770-1782* (Paris: F. Buisson, 1812).

[8] Louis Petit de Bachaumont, *Les mémoires secrets pour servir à l'histoire de la république des lettres en France...* (London: John Adamson, 1780-1789).

[9] Voltaire, *Oeuvres complètes*, Ed. Louis Moland (Paris: Garnier frères, 1877-85) II, 542.

[10] Lusignan is the name of a family which sprang from Poitou and long held the kingdom of Cyprus (1192-1475). In the last quarter of the twelfth

connected with French national history, none was too well received. *Adélaide du Guesclin*, performed at the Comédie-Française on January 17, 1734, was a miserable failure. The author revised it and had it presented under the title of *Amélie ou Le Duc de Foix* (August 17, 1752). This time the success was moderate even though Le Kain played the role of Vendôme. Rejected by the audience in 1734, the play abounds in elements of *effets théâtraux* such as the appearance on the stage of the wounded Nemours, his fainting there, and the cannon shot in the fifth act. [11]

In 1765, following a revival of the play, Voltaire wrote of its acceptance thirty-one years before:

> Elle fut sifflé dès le premier acte, les sifflets redoublèrent au second, quand on vit arrivé le duc de Nemours blessé et le bras en écharpe; ce fut bien pis lorsqu'on entendit, au cinquième, le signal que le duc de Vendôme disait: Es-tu content, Coucy? Plusieurs bons plaisants crièrent: Couci-Couci. [12]

Tancrède, performed on September 3, 1760, evinced Voltaire's most ardent support of French national history as a source for tragedy.

> Je ne saurais trop recommander qu'on cherche à mettre sur notre scène quelques parties de notre histoire de France. On m'a dit que les noms des anciennes maisons qu'on retrouve dans *Zaïre*, dans *Le Duc de Foix*, dans *Tancrède*,

---

century the two brothers Amaric and Guy, sons of Hugh de Lusignan (le Brun), played a part in the history of the Latin East. Around 1180 Amalric was constable of the kingdom of Jerusalem. His brother Guy married in 1180 Sibylla, the widowed heiress of the kingdom. On the death of Baldwin V in 1186, Guy became King of Jerusalem. He ruled in Jerusalem until 1192. His brother Amalric became king in 1197. Amalric was the founder of a dynasty of kings of Cyprus, which lasted until 1475, while after 1269 his descendants also bore the title of kings of Jerusalem.

[11] Voltaire wrote in the preface: «Le fond de cette tragédie n'est point une fiction. Un duc de Bretagne, in 1387, commanda au seigneur de Bavalan d'assassiner le connétable de Clisson. Bavalan, le lendemain, dit au duc qu'il avait obéi: le duc alors, voyant toute l'horreur de son crime, et en redoutant les suites funestes, s'abandonna au plus violent désespoir. Bavalan le laissa quelque temps sentir sa faute, et se livrer au repentir; enfin il lui apprit qu'il l'avait aimé assez pour désobéir à ses ordres, etc.

On a transporté cet événement dans d'autres temps et dans d'autres pays, pour des raisons particulières». Voltaire, *op. cit.*, III, 77.

[12] *Ibid.*, p. 77.

ont fait plaisir à la nation. C'est peut-être un nouvel aiguillon de gloire pour ceux qui descendent de ces races illustres. Il me semble qu'après avoir fait paraître tant de héros étrangers sur la scène, il nous manquait d'y montrer les nôtres.[13]

Tancrède was immediately popular, and was the first successful tragedy after the removal of the *banquettes* from the stage.[14] The treatment of chivalry in *Tancrède* was immensely popular.[15] In the first serious consideration given to it in French tragedy, elements of nationalism, didacticism and exoticism helped to make this period more attractive than any other for subsequent writers of national historical tragedy. Interest in medieval history too was a characteristic of the new awakening.

Except for *Zaïre, Adélaïde du Guesclin* and *Tancrède*, in which the only aspects of French national history are in the names of the principal characters, the national history was infrequently used as a source for tragedy in the first half of the eighteenth century. There were two new *tragédies nationales* presented at the Comédie-Française in 1736. They were *Pharamond* (August 14, 1736) by Louis de Cahusac (1706-1759) and *Childéric* (December 19, 1736) by Pierre de Morand (1701-1757). Both have five acts and are in verse.

The events in *Pharamond* take place in Roman Gaul of the fifth century. The principal theme is that of Pharamond's rôle in the unification of the Franks and Gauls into the French Nation. Neither the theme nor events follow history. Moreover, Pharamond was a mythical character.[16]

The action of the play takes place at Rheims in the royal palace. The first act recounts events that transpire on the eve of a pitched

---

[13] Voltaire, *op. cit.*, V, 497-498.

[14] *Les Troyennes* (April 23, 1759), by Châteaubrun, was the first tragedy presented after the removal of the *banquettes*. See: Paul Berret, «Comment la scène du théâtre du 18ᵉ siècle a été débarrassée de la présence des gentilshommes», *RHLF*, VIII (1901), 456-459.

[15] *Tancrède* was acted 384 times at the Comédie-Française from 1760-1920. It was presented thirteen times in 1760. Johannidès, *op. cit.*, p. 103. The scene of the play is laid in Syracuse. The action takes place in 1005. Sicily had been conquered in the ninth century by Saracens. Syracuse had freed itself from their yoke. Norman knights had settled in Salerna a little later.

[16] Louis de Cahusac, *Pharamond* (Paris: Prault, 1741).

battle between Pharamond and Maxime, Roman general and Praetor of Belgium. As the play opens, Ambiomer, chief of the Gallic legions who have come to support Pharamond, is discussing with Arimie, a captive, her choice of a suitor. The beautiful and innocent maiden, the lost daughter of Vindorix, favorite of Pharamond, is deeply in love with Maxime. Pharamond also loves her. Ambiomer is greatly incensed when he learns of Arimie's love. He reproaches her for respecting a tyrant, and recalls how his entire family succumbed from atrocities perpetrated upon it by Maxime. Arimie expresses her hate for Romans, but persists in her love for Maxime. The fact that he had saved her father from certain death increased her sympathy toward Maxime. She does not know where her father is, but at least it is reported that he is still alive. In answer to Ambiomer's violent exhortations in favor of Pharamond as her suitor, Arimie tries to explain:

> Son bras peut à son gré triompher dans la guerre;
> Il peut renouveller la face de la terre,
> Selon sa volonté, transporter les Etats,
> Créér un nouveau peuple et changer les climats,
> Mais toute la valeur de ce chef magnanime,
> Ne peut soumettre un coeur defendu par Maxime.
> (Act I, Scene I)

She regrets this apparent treason, but her heart forbids her to even consider Pharamond.

In an interview with Pharamond Ambiomer offers the services of the best soldiers in the Gallic army. Pharamond is delighted with this demonstration of loyalty. Vindorix joins them to announce uneasy stirrings in Pharamond's army caused by his long absence (at least a month). Pharamond is outraged and vows to punish his soldiers severely. Vindorix chastizes his master for such brashness and defends the soldiers. Segeste comes to announce the arrival of Maxime who has bivouacked in preparation for war against Pharamond. Apparently Maxime plans to avenge the defeat of Varus, one of his cohorts.

In act two Vindorix recognizes in Arimie his long lost daughter. During a conversation with Segeste, Vindorix relates his nightmarish past. Upon being taken prisoner by the Romans, he had seen his son and infant daughter snatched away. In Rome he had been enlisted in the army of gladiators and became very capable in the arena. One day while fighting, he had recognized his son in an adversary. Their happy reunion was short-lived. To show their disdain for such a display, the Romans unleashed a tiger upon them. Just as the tiger was on the point of attacking Vindorix, the son jumped between him and the animal and was killed. Vindorix can never forget the experience:

> Le monstre le déchire, Ah! j'en frémis encore
> Et partage à mes yeux ses membres qu'il dévore.
> (Act II, Scene I)

Ready to die himself, Vindorix was freed through the efforts of the Roman Maxime, who had been touched by the reunion of father and son. Once freed Vindorix had fled Rome and had come to Germany from whence he accompanied Pharamond to France. In spite of the evident good favor he enjoys with Pharamond, Vindorix remains unhappy while thinking of his son and daughter.

Alone with Vindorix, Arimie longs to know of her father's whereabouts. Since Vindorix lends a sympathetic ear to her sorrows, she quickly relates the details of her youth. In the course of her story she mentions Tournai and her father's captivity in Rome during which he served as a gladiator. Vindorix identifies himself, and Arimie exclaims ecstatically:

> O Surprise! O bonheur!
> Je reconnois mon père aux transports de mon coeur.
> (Act II, Scene II)

After the flush of excitement has passed, Vindorix launches into a discussion of the amorous problems faced by his daughter. Arimie swears her eternal filial duty but admits her high regard for Maxime, whom she loves first of all because it was he who freed her father. Vindorix admires his daughter's loyalty: «Ma fille, je te loue, et j'applaudis ta flâme». (Act II, Scene II)

No sooner has he finished than news is flashed of Pharamond's resounding victory over Maxime. Ambiomer gleefully reports Maxime's capture:

> Jour heureux! jour célèbre! ou la Gaule affranchie
> Voit naître une nouvelle et juste monarchie,
> Qui fait un peuple seul des Francs et des Gaulois,
> Et chasse les Tyrans, pour établir les Rois.
> (Act II, Scene III)

In act three Pharamond is depicted as a generous conqueror and madly in love. When the act opens he and Maxime debate the relative merits of their armies. Pharamond feels softness, engendered by too much luxury, brought defeat to Maxime's legions:

> Tout ce que je demande au Ciel qui nous écoute,
> Est de nous garantir de ce poison honteux
> Et puisse-t-il toujours épargner nos neveux!
> Puissent-ils conserver notre heureuse ignorance,
> Et ne jamais subir le joug de l'opulence!
> (Act III, Scene I)

To demonstrate his magnanimity Pharamond liberates Maxime, proclaims the freedom of everyone who lives within his domains, and grants a long leave to his soldiers. Now that war is over he can devote his full energies to the more pressing problem of love. He seeks Arimie to propose that she become his queen. Arimie is flattered but requests that she be allowed to go to Tournai. Shaken by this news Pharamond inquires: «Vous voulez me quitter? O Ciel! est-il possible?» (Act III, Scene V). Regarded as the father of his people, Pharamond is a tyrant for her. Her observations prompt a long harangue from Pharamond on his policy of justice. Maxime meets with his beloved but fears he notices a coldness in Arimie's eyes which perhaps emanates from her disappointment in his defeat. When reassured that he will always be loved, and told of the true reasons for her unhappiness, Maxime promises to pull a new army together. Arimie expresses her displeasure at such a proposal and tells Maxime that Vindorix is her father. They can place their hopes of being united in him. For the present, Maxime must flee.

In act four Pharamond, first willing to marry Gondebaud, the people's choice for the queen, finally chooses to follow the dictates of his own conscience and press Arimie into marrying him. In the meanwhile, Arimie and Maxime have successfully evaded his sentinels. As the act opens Ambiomer promises Arimie all the help he can muster. In an encounter with Pharamond, Arimie is almost forced to admit she does not love him. This arouses Pharamond's suspicions. Vindorix encourages Pharamond to do his people's bidding and marry Gondebaud. The King is willing to sacrifice but had rather have Arimie. Vindorix pronounces his benediction upon Arimie and Maxime. In the last scene Pharamond, whose change of heart complicates matters, would rather be happy than do as his subjects wish. Forced to reveal Arimie's departure, Vindorix is embarrassed but reminds his master that the girl is free to do as she pleases. Unable to control his jealousy, Pharamond declares the death sentence upon the person with whom Arimie is fleeing.

In the fifth act Pharamond recovers his good judgment. Shortly after the act opens Arimie is reported to have been taken prisoner. Her traveling companion escaped. Maxime is not even suspicioned. The royal ire falls upon Ambiomer who, now a prisoner in the palace dungeons, awaits a peremptory execution. All preparations have been made for the marriage between Pharamond and Arimie, and people have already assembled for the ceremony. Worried about her father who vowed to resolve all problems, Arimie has to divert her attention to the more pertinent matter of her pending marriage. When Pharamond enters to conduct her to the wedding chamber, she claims another is her husband. She identifies Maxime as her husband but agrees to marry Pharamond if he will vouch for Maxime's life. Pharamond orders the Roman's immediate execution. Vindorix takes the occasion to defend Maxime. He relates the generosity that had been shown him and explains his questionable conduct in this affair as a means to repay Maxime for his many kindnesses.

Struck by the sincerity of the story, Pharamond renounces his plans to marry Arimie and frees Ambiomer. Vindorix expresses his appreciation. In the closing scene Pharamond states the theme of the play—the importance of having a wise and virtuous minister:

> Mon retour à la gloire est ton ouvrage heureux.
> Un ministre éclairé, prudent et vigoureux,
> Est du Ciel pour les Rois la faveur la plus chère;
> Pour régner sagement il leur est nécessaire
> Dans la paix qu'il procure il met tout son eclat,
> Fait la grandeur du Prince et le bien de l'Etat.
> (Act V, Scene VII)

As was the tendency in all historical tragedies, the principal interest in *Pharamond* is not the depiction of historical events but in the intrigues of love. Nevertheless, love received no analysis, insuring thereby no development of character. Patriotism in the play is its most striking feature. The sepulchral phrases uttered by Pharamond thrilled the French pride. [17]

The first real Franks depicted in French tragedy appeared in *Childéric*, a play in five acts and in verse. [18] It recounts the story of Clovis' valor and eventual reunion with Childéric, his exiled father driven from the throne by the usurper Gellon. As in *Pharamond* historical truth is of the slightest concern. Childéric's exile, the fact that he was the father of Clovis by Bazine, and his return to power after the death of Gellon, had been recounted by Gregory of Tours and Mézeray. The remainder of the plot was invented by the author.

Clovis, although idealistically portrayed, emerges as a strong character in spite of the impossible complexity of action, insipid love affairs and scenes of recognition. He epitomized the spirit of patriotism, a conspicuous element of the play. The frequent references to France doubtlessly stirred the spectators, but not enough to assure success for the play. The first four performances were well attended, but the last three were scarcely warranted. The play was presented later at Versailles, with the queen subsequently agreeing to accept its dedication to her. [19]

Baculard d'Arnaud (1717-1805), a miserable failure as a writer of tragedy, sought his inspiration also in French history. [20] While still at the collège d'Harcourt he composed three tragedies: *Idoménée*, *Didon* and *Coligni*. The last, situated in a period particularly favored by writers of historical tragedy in France, was never presented at the Comédie-Française, but was performed privately at the Hotel de Tonnerre in 1739. [21]

Voltaire's epic treatment of French history in the *Henriade* (1723) had attracted sustained attention to the devastating wars of religion

---

[17] *Pharamond* had only twelve performances at the Comédie-Française, all in 1736.

[18] Henry C. Lancaster, *French Tragedy in the Time of Louis XV and Voltaire, 1715-1774* (Baltimore: The Johns Hopkins Press, 1953), I, 230. *Childéric* was performed only seven times, all in 1736.

[19] Paul d'Estrée, «Un auteur imcompris, Pierre de Morand l'homme et l'oeuvre (1701-1757)», *RHLF*, XVI (1909), 309.

[20] The only biographical study of Baculard is that of Bertran de la Villehervé, *François-Thomas de Baculard d'Arnaud* (Paris: Librairie Champion, 1920).

[21] Clarence D. Brenner, *A Bibliographical List of Plays in the French Language 1700-1789* (Ann Arbor: Edwards Brothers, 1947), p. 29.

fought in the sixteenth century. Inspired by the second canto of the *Henriade*, Arnaud had composed his tragedy. In the *discours préliminaire*, the author outlined events of the massacre on Saint Bartholomew's Day and availed himself of the opportunity to deliver a long diatribe against Catherine de Médicis and Charles IX. His impulsive but caustic remarks mirror a growing trend of the century marked by an impatience with tradition:

> Ceux qui aiment la vérité, la trouveront dans cet ouvrage. La journée de la Saint Barthélemi feroit honte à nos François, s'ils ne la desapprovoient eux-mêmes... Il y a une espèce d'imbécilité à vouloir excuser les fautes de ses ayeux. Il se trouve des superstitions de tout genre; la plus honteuse de toutes est ce respect malentendu pour les siècles précédents; ce préjugé grossier, et cependant si ordinaire, arrête souvent les progrès de la raison. [22]

Turning to the theme of national historical tragedy, Baculard pleads in favor of the genre being divorced from classical rules:

> L'antiquité ne nous opposera jamais un sujet plus tragique que celui-ci. *L'Oedipe* de Sophocle, qui est plein de situations touchantes excite moins la pitié qu'un vieillard de quatre-vingts ans, qu'égorgent avec zèle ses compatriotes. Un François (et il s'en trouve beaucoup) qui ne se piquera point de littérature, verra avec indifférence les tableaux d'Antigone, d'Electre... [23]

Continuing, the author acknowledges his indebtedness for factual information gleaned from the *Mémoires* of Pierre de l'Estoile, Mézeray's *La grande Histoire* and the *Mémoires* of the Président de Thou. Baculard could have very well obtained his facts from the works just cited. However, he used them only as the frame of his tragedy (called *drame* in the 1740 edition). The greater portion of the work is sheer fantasy.

Baculard condemns jealousy as the main cause for the massacre of French Protestants, and not a sincere interest in religion. In a conclu-

---

[22] Thomas Baculard d'Arnaud, *Le Coligni* (Lausanne: Bousquet, 1789), p. 3. The second canto of the *Henriade* is a vivid description of the massacre that took place on Saint Bartholomew's Day.

[23] Baculard d'Arnaud, *op. cit.*, p. 8.

ding paragraph, the author, only twenty-two years old, vaunts the worth of his play:

> ...il n'a fait dans la Pièce que la peinture de la vérité:
> il s'est attaché à démonstrer sous les yeux, que le Fanatisme est également éloigné de la Religion et de la Nature. [24]

The theme, in reality a polemic against priests, brought censorship upon the play, and few copies circulated in France before 1789. Although there are only three acts, *Coligni* bears the stamp of regular tragedy. An extensive commentary interprets the character of prominent persons figuring in the tragedy. Among these are Catherine de Médicis, Charles IX, Gaspard de Coligny, Téligny, Marsillac and Tavannes.

The action takes place in the Louvre on the day and night of August 24, 1572. The Guise family is never mentioned. The Cardinal de Lorraine, brother of Henri, Duc de Guise, is thinly veiled under the name of Hamilton, priest of Saint Cosme. The first act verifies Hamilton's fanatic obsession to rid France of the Huguenots. The first scene is a long monologue in which Hamilton, on the morning of the date set for the massacre, seems to regret his complicity in the affair. Yet when his cohort Bême arrives to declare that all is in a state of readiness, Hamilton demands he be reserved the pleasure of killing Coligny. This act will insure his immortality as he remembers Jacques Clément was elevated to sainthood for his murder of Henri III. This is a flagrant anachronism since Henri III was not assassinated until 1589. In a frenzied oration Hamilton reminds the conspirators of their divine mission:

> Enfoncer sans frémir dans le sein de ces traîtres
> Des poignards consacrés par la main de vos prêtres.
> (Act I, Scene III)

Only Tavannes does not shout in acclamation. An inner voice warns of the consequences precipitated by murder. As he muses, a curtain opens to reveal altars covered with swords. While distributing them, Hamilton, a crucifix in one hand and a sword in the other, enjoins his fellow conspirators to:

---

[24] *Ibid.*, p. 12.

Baignez-vous dans le sang, c'est là l'unique offrande,
Qui soi digne du Ciel, et que le Ciel demande,
Armez-vous de ces traits que Rome a consacrés
Ils ne pourront porter que des coups assurés,
Baisez avec respect ces glaives homicides.
                                    (Act I, Scene III)

Act two presents the protestant leaders and their hopeless predicament. Incited to greater carnage by priests, who rush brandishing crucifixes through the streets, Catholic forces quickly turn Paris into a slaughter house. Their prize victim is Coligny whose guards beg him to flee. Coligny neglects his own safety and resorts to a desperate measure. He will go to Catherine and implore her to order a truce. Téligny, Coligny's son-in-law, resolves to kill Charles IX and Catherine if the admiral is murdered.

Much of act three concerns Coligny's personal greatness. His ability to persuade the Catholic conspirators against further slaughter is uncanny. He knows, however, he must die. To facilitate penetration of the swords of the assassins, he uncovers his chest venerably scarred in battles fought for France. The conspirators are overwhelmed. One throws himself at the admiral's feet; another discards his weapons. They both weep. A shout in unison declares their undying faith in Coligny and their intention to enlist in his following. This touchingly ludicrous and totally fantastic scene is interrupted by the arrival of Hamilton. Enraged by the news that the conspirators refuse to murder Coligny, Hamilton pronounces the death sentence upon them. Coligny promptly pleads for their lives. After much cajoling from Hamilton, Bême is selected as the assassin. Coligny immediately bares his chest. Bême performs the odious task and then turns from Hamilton. Hamilton pierces the dying Coligny with another thrust from his sword. Coligny's last moments are shared by Téligny, also wounded. He is brought in on a stretcher. At first he thinks Coligny is alive but his hopes are shattered by the sight of a bloody pool. In a semi-conscious state, Coligny thinks he recognizes his assassin. When Téligny identifies himself, the admiral is overjoyed and is even happier when he hears the news of his daughter's safety. As Coligny dies, Téligny prepares for death and, as a token of love to his wife, he sends a cloth soaked in blood. Over the dead body of Téligny, the Protestant soldiers assembled swear vengeance on Rome.

Characterized by long monologues and incongruities in its execution, *Coligni* is not greatly inferior to similar plays whose inspiration was drawn from the national history. The entire first act hinges upon Hamilton's determination to murder Coligny. The third act treats of Coligny's murder. It would seem imperative for the author to give some explanation of Hamilton's change of heart of which the spectator is totally ignorant. Hamilton ordered Coligny's murder. The spectator had understood from the beginning Hamilton's wish that he alone would kill Coligny. Other than this salient weakness in the unity of action, Baculard strictly abides by the unities of time and place. The grotesqueness of the scenes in which Coligny bares his chest for the assassins' thrusts, and that in which Téligny sends to his wife a blood-soaked bandage as a token of their love are so ludicrous they tend to produce the opposite effect from that intended. Baculard mastered technically the alexandrine verse, but naturalness is lacking. Each character speaks in a stilted language that prohibits serious development. The total effect of *Coligni* is anticipatory of melodrama.

Baculard's influence in the propagation of national historical tragedy was negligible though his opinions indicate the acceptance of French history as a source for tragedy, made necessary in large part, by the desire of the public for variety. In 1763 Baculard wrote to a friend: «En quête de sujets de tragédie, je voudrais surtout des sujets modernes. L'intérêt des Grecs et des Romains est usé».[25] Again in 1770, five years after the successful presentation of *Le siège de Calais* by De Belloy, Baculard championed the *tragédie nationale*:

> La poésie rentre alors dans toute la dignité de son origine, et l'auteur dramatique devient la dépositaire des fastes de ses concitoyens et le hérault de leur gloire, il les encourage à la vertu, réchauffe les âmes languissantes, en élevant sur le théâtre les trophées de nos ancêtres. C'est ainsi que le spectacle peut devenir utile, et produire de grands effets: il est vrai qu'il ne seroit pas aussi divertissant que l'opéra-comique, Nicolet, les comédiens de bois, etc.[26]

An attempt in drama to insert greater care in the depiction of events treating national history was made by Charles-Jean-François Hénault

---

[25] Villehervé, *op. cit.*, p. 75.
[26] *Ibid.*, p. 117.

(1685-1770) better known as le Président Hénault by virtue of being head of the Académie des Belles-Lettres. The most substantial work of Hénault was the popular *Abrégé chronologique de l'histoire de France,* published in 1744. An excellent handbook, it resumed concisely and authoritatively French history with lucid discussions of events, exterior influences, prominent personages, customs, institutions, and the arts. [27]

Hénault's most famous drama, *François II, roi de France* (1747), was never presented. The work was inspired doubtlessly by the author's thorough knowledge of French history and by the idea of dramatizing historical material for the purpose of making it easier to learn. François II was, therefore, nothing more than a series of historical scenes, exact in every detail. In no way can it be considered a tragedy.

In the preface to his work, Hénault defends French national history as a logical storehouse of material which would interest the enlightened spectator of the eighteenth century. It was unusual to have tragedy seek its inspiration in the national history, but:

> Est-ce que le Cardinal de Lorraine et le Duc de Guise, méditant la perte du Prince de Condé, ne sont pas aussi intéressans que les confidens de Ptolomés délibérant sur la mort de Pompée? Est-ce que Catherine de Médicis ne vaut pas bien la Cléopâtre de Rodogune et l'Agrippine de Néron? [28]

Then turning to the unities, Hénault apologizes because his tragedy does not follow them:

> La règle de vingt-quatre heures n'est pas observée, à la vérité, puisque ce règne a été de dix-sept mois. [29]

There is no unity of action either:

> Comme l'intérêt général de ce Règne est l'ambition des Messieurs de Guise voulant usurper l'autorité sur les Princes du

---

[27] For a detailed study of Hénault, see the biography by Henri Lion, *Le Président Hénault 1685-1770; sa vie, ses oeuvres* (Paris: Librairie Plon, 1903).

[28] Charles-Jean-François Hénault, *Nouveau théâtre françois, Francois II, Roi de France* (no publisher or place given, 1747), p. ix.

[29] *Ibid.,* p. x.

sang, cela ressemble un peu plus à nos tragédies que le règne de François Ier.³⁰

The author defends the historical truth of his play. In the margin of each page, the authority who furnished the facts is cited. Hénault claims he altered no facts nor allowed the intrusion of the slightest anachronism. The introduction of Luc Gauric, a famous Italian astrologer, does not follow fact, but serves to illustrate the suspicious nature of Catherine de Médicis. Luc Gauric never came to France. There are more than twenty-five characters in the play. François II does not appear. The author explains this in concluding the King's young age (sixteen years) kept him from taking any active role in the government.

In five acts and written in prose, the play begins the first of July, 1559. The first act opens in the great hall of the Palais de Tournelles where the body of Henri II lies in state. The aim of the first act is to demonstrate the queen mother's ability at intrigue and her genius in governing. Early in the act, Montmorency, the accidental murderer of Henri II, pays homage to Catherine's political acumen:

> C'est un esprit vaste et profond, une arme ferme et indomptable, et qui, malgré sa roideur, sait se plier, et prendre toutes les formes qui lui sont utiles; elle a les qualités de toutes les situations où elle se trouve, et l'ambition de tous les états.

Montmorency is irritated, nevertheless, that Catherine has forsaken him to place the young King under the tutleage of the Duc de Guise and his brother the Cardinal. The other princes of the blood fear the Guise family. In order to offset their power, the King of Navarre has been invited to court. He had declined the invitation. Catherine is stubborn in her opinion that the Guises are loyal. According to her, the King will rule when the time comes; not she, the Guise family nor anyone else. Catherine determines to play Condé and the Guises against each other for further cementing the monarchy. She wonders when Gauric will come. This is an extraordinary man who had predicted Henri's death, and who will perhaps forecast her future.

The problem of heresy, Spain's threats against France, and Catherine's meeting with Gauric occupy the second act. In a meeting of the

---

³⁰ *Ibid.*, p. x.

Privy Council at the château of Saint Germain, the Cardinal of Lorraine defends the practice of burning heretics. He lauds Philip II of Spain and his severity. The King of Navarre opposes his arch rival and maintains heresy should be the concern of public courts and not of the church. The King of Navarre despises Philip II: «On devrait rougir de donner le nom de zèle à la poltronnerie». (Act II, Scene II). A letter is read from Philip threatening the French with death if they do not obey François II. Excepting the Guise brothers, all the princes are angry that Philip would be so bold. In order to seek a compromise, Catherine charges Condé and Navarre with a mission to Spain. They will accompany the new Spanish queen to her destination.

The scene switches to Catherine's private apartment. She is earnestly beseeching Gauric to advise her in state matters, and to cast a horoscope for her seven children. The astrologer reluctantly responds to Catherine's request. François will die within the next few months. Isabelle will be poisoned. Claude, the wife of Charles II, Duke of Lorraine, will lead a quiet life. Marguerite, whose momentary happiness will be darkened by the Protestant massacre, will lead a life of pleasure and will die naturally (1575). The remaining sons Charles, Henri and the Duc d'Alençon will precede the queen mother in death or die shortly afterwards. This mournful news renders Catherine distraught. Gauric reminds her that nothing can be done: «Le ciel vous punit de votre curiosité, en vous faisant souffrir d'avance tous les morts dont il a semé le cours de votre vie». (Act II, Scene IV)

The terrible reprisals among both Protestants and Catholics is the theme of the third act. The first news conveys a threat against the life of the royal family. This is a rumor circulated by Catholics to instill fear in Catherine and insure some quick action. For the sake of safety, the court moves from Blois to Amboise. The Cardinal de Lorraine marshals his forces for a general suppression of Protestants. Sporadic skirmishes are reported with unspeakable atrocities practiced. Protestants are hanged, drowned or cut to pieces.

In a private conference with the queen mother, Admiral Coligny blames the consuming ambition of the Guises as the cause of unrest: «Les échaffauts et les bûchers ne sont que des trophées exécrables élevés, à l'ambition des Messieurs de Guise». (Act III, Scene X). Catherine is convinced that she should favor the Reformed. New outbreaks of civil war are reported. Chancellor Oliver dies from a heart attack and Condé replaces him in that important administrative position.

Dissension in the Guise family and new measures taken by Catherine are themes of the fourth act. At Fontainebleau the Duchesse de Guise avows her sympathy for the Protestant cause. She too is sorry her husband and his brother have attained such overwhelming power at court. The Duchesse admits her love for the Duc de Nemours (the same as in *La Princesse de Clèves*) whom she is destined to marry three years after being widowed. After the revelation that the Guise family has established an alliance with Philip II, Catherine de Médicis reiterates her supremacy in the struggle for power. In order to formulate additional policies, she calls a meeting of the Privy Council.

In act five the Prince de Condé's death, which would have meant victory for the Guise brothers, is thwarted by the untimely demise of François II. The Duc de Guise, sorely reproached by his wife for having caused the Prince de Condé's imprisonment, enthusiastically proclaims the next move which will be the sudden death of Condé and also that of the Roi de Navarre. News is spread of the King's imminent death from an abscess of the ear. Catherine resolves to guarantee amnesty to the Protestant camp. This will be a strong deterrent to the ambition of the Guise family. The Duke presses for an early decision in his favor:

> Médicis soulagée par mon frère et moi, et ayant pour elle tous les catholiques de la France, ne voit rien qui la contredise. Médicis à la merci des Princes du sang et des Protestants ne peut envisager que des divisions et des orages, et qu'un avenir funeste pour elle et pour la nation.
> (Act V, Scene VIII)

Catherine listens patiently to his harangue and then consults her confidante, the Duchesse de Montpensier. The latter sees the wisest course as a reconciliation with the Roi de Navarre. In the tower which holds him prisoner, Condé contemplates the fickleness of life and uncertainty of future events. His reverie is interrupted by news of the King's death. Condé is freed and prepares to express his thanks to Catherine.

Hénault had been attracted to Shakespeare and his treatment of history. It is evident, however, the Frenchman had no talent at creating dramatic interest. Each scene of the play is an historical event in dialogue. In the preface to *François II*, Hénault expressed his debt to Shakespeare:

> Le théâtre anglois de Shakespehar m'a donné l'idée de cet ouvrage... les tragédies de Shakespehar m'ont fait appercevoir un genre d'utilité auquel je n'aurois jamais pense sans lui. [31]

Although his talent as a dramatic artist was negligible, Hénault was admired for his attitude toward the dramatization of history. The practice of writing history in dialogue received favorable critical comment. The abbé Fréron, editor of the *Année littéraire* from 1754 to 1775, praised the technique of dramatized dialogue as an excellent means of teaching history.[32] Fréron commented at length on the question of poetic figures in French history. He concluded that a character from history should be portrayed on the stage without alteration.

Although Hénault did not contribute any dramatic works that could be classified as tragedy, his efforts to bring historical events into their true perspective were a significant advancement over the old method of liberally mixing fiction with a few facts.

Claimed by its author, Pierre-Laurent Buirette de Belloy (1727-1775), to follow national history as closely as the limits of poetic license would permit, the most successful *tragédie nationale* of the eighteenth century was *Le siège de Calais*, presented for the first time, February 13, 1765, on the stage of the Comédie-Française.[33] Brizard played Eustache de Saint-Pierre, mayor of Calais; Le Kain, Edward III, King of England; Molé, Godefroi de Harcourt, a traitor to France and general of the English armies; La Clairon, Aliénor, daughter of Jean de Vienne, governor of Calais; Paulin, Ambletuse, bourgeois de Calais; Fromentin, Aurèle, son of Saint-Pierre; Dubois, Mauni, English knight; and Dauberval, the Comte de Melun.

In the preface De Belloy contended he was the first to give a tragedy in which the French were genuinely depicted. If by French De Belloy meant bourgeois, then he was correct; if not his claim was in-

---

[31] Hénault, *op. cit.*, p. ii.

[32] A recent article on Fréron is that of Robert L. Myers, «Fréron's theories on tragedy», *The French Review*, XXXI (May, 1958), 504-508.

[33] P.-L. Buirette de Belloy, *Le siège de Calais*, *Chefs d'oeuvre tragiques* (Paris: Firmin Didot, no date).

deed ephemeral. *Le siège de Calais* was a bourgeois play. It is the dramatization of events precipitated by the famous siege lasting from August 1346 to July 1347, delivered to the strategic port of Calais by Edward III of England, and pretender to the French throne. The untold misery of the inhabitants of Calais and their undying patriotism, epitomized by six bourgeois who offered their lives to assure free movement to their compatriots, have inspired eloquent testimony. No one can admire the sculpture by Rodin without reliving that glorious moment in the history of mankind.

Except for the attraction of its subject drawn largely from Froissart, but probably directly inspired by Mme. de Tencin's novel, *Le siège de Calais* (1739), De Belloy's play is lifeless. Cast in the mold of classical tradition with five acts and written in verse, *Le siège de Calais* suffers greatly from the inclusion of the insipid affair, totally a part of the author's imagination, between Aliénor, the daughter of Jean de Vienne, and Harcourt the redeemed traitor. The third act, largely devoted to a discussion between Edward and Aliénor on the Salic Law, proves De Belloy's paucity of talent.

Wishing to obey every convention in tragedy, De Belloy is careful to follow the rule of the three unities. The first act sees Calais reduced to total abjection following the last destructive assault of English soldiers. Eustache de Saint-Pierre, a bourgeois and venerable patriarch of the city, surveys the ruins and muses upon the greatness of human suffering and patriotism. His son, appopriately named Aurèle, has probably been killed in the last skirmish. The citizens of Calais would have never found themselves in such straits if Godefroi de Harcourt, a loyal French citizen until his unjust imprisonment, had not fled, when released, to the English side. De Belloy's patriotic fervor was sharpened by his own forced exile lasting many years. Having been chased out of France upon the instigation of his uncle, De Belloy's sincere evocations of patriotism are praiseworthy, but their effect is spoiled by considerable periphrase resorted to in order not to shock the propriety of audiences. As Saint-Pierre stands musing upon the utter hopelessness, he hears cannons in the distance. Instead of calling them by name, he says: «J'entends toujours gronder ces foudres mugissantes»; and later «... les noirs volcans d'un airain destructeur», or «feux de l'enfer».

Having just learned of her father's capture, Aliénor arrives to relate the battle as she witnessed it from the ramparts:

> Soudain tonne l'airain, jusqu'alors invisible,
> Et ses bouches de fer vomissent dans nos rangs
> Les instruments de mort qu'il porte dans ses flancs.
> (Act I, Scene III)

Aliénor ends her story by alluding to her former lover now turned traitor. She swears an undying hate for him. With his arm in a sling, Aurèle appears much to the surprise and joy of his father. Saint-Pierre, his son, Aliénor, and other bourgeois chieftains turn to the pressing problem of resolving this present untenable position. Edward wants Calais to abjure its loyalty to France. Saint-Pierre states the general reaction to such a request: «Nous mourrons pour le roi, pour qui nous vivons tous». (Act I, Scene VI). Aliénor suggests, and others agree, that Calais be reduced to ashes. Saint-Pierre proposes an evacuation of Calais. In this way lives would be saved and thus dedicated to the greater glory of France. Saint-Pierre then commissions Amblétuse, one of the bourgeois warriors, to convey the message to Edward.

The principal action of act two is woven around Edward's reply to Saint-Pierre's proposal. The fact that all of the population will be left to go free upon the exemplary sacrifice of six bourgeois is horrifying news. Harcourt, whose desertion to the English side was due to his conviction that Edward was the true king of France, will attempt to dispel the stigma cast upon his name. He will use his influence over Edward to encourage him to revoke the harsh sentence pronounced upon the citizens of Calais. Again the desperate bourgeois devise means to escape the English yoke. Amblétuse proposes a fight to the death. Aliénor suggests all women be allowed to take up arms. Saint-Pierre persists in his contention that all should rush to the haven of King Philippe's (1328-1350) bosom. The old bourgeois volunteers as the first of the six to be sacrificed. He is followed by many others. The overwhelming patriotism and sang-froid in the face of death moves the Englishman Mauni to admiration: «Dieu! que ne suis-je né dans les murs de Calais! (Act II, Scene V).

In act three Edward is adamant in maintaining his order. In admiring their spirit, he sees the French as:

> Un peuple doux, sensible . . . une famille immense,
> A qui le seul amour dicte obéissance;
> Qui laisse tous ses droits à son père asservie
> Sure qu'il veut toujours le bonheur de ses fils.
> (Act III, Scene II)

Edward is equally impressed that the bourgeois would be so faithful in their loyalty to the King. Harcourt intercedes for the condemned bourgeois who appear on the stage bound in chains. His demand surprises Edward, who is astonished further to learn of Harcourt's intention to leave the English army. Edward's machinations to rule Calais run aground when he proposes marriage between Aliénor and Harcourt. As new viceroy of Calais, Harcourt will need a bride. Aliénor is ideally suited for this rôle. When confronted, she expresses the attitude of all French toward the English invaders. Edward is not king of France. Furthermore, Aliénor does not love Harcourt. In a long digression unnecessary to the dramatic interest of the play, Aliénor explains the origin of the Salic Law. Her patriotic fervor reaches its highest pitch in paying homage to King Philippe:

> Le Français dans son prince aime à trouver un frère,
> Qui, né fils de l'Etat, en devienne le père.
> L'Etat et le monarque à nos yeux confondus
> N'ont jamais divisé nos voeux et nos tributs.
>
> (Act III, Scene IV)

Although Edward admires the steadfast loyalty to the monarchy as expressed by Aliénor, he is exasperated by her stubborn refusal to marry Harcourt. When she sees Harcourt, Aliénor begs that he intercede for the bourgeois prisoners who now are being whisked to the scaffold. Harcourt has promised he will die also if his overtures to the King are to no avail.

Further plans are devised in act four to free the six bourgeois. The fact that they are in prison enhances the patriotic harangues freely offered by the French. The English are dumbfounded by such unselfish constancy. Mauni, the English general, expresses the attitude of the entire world:

> Votre amour pour vos lois et pour votre pays
> D'un peuple juste et fier enchante les esprits.
>
> (Act IV, Scene II)

Everyone is working for the freedom of these stalwart patriots. Philippa, Edward's queen, has dispatched a message begging for clemency. Mauni has contemplated an audacious plan. Philippe VI has offered a ransom for the freedom of his subjects. Harcourt, in desperation at seeing father and son sacrificed, tries to replace Aurèle. Aliénor confesses she could have saved the prisoners, but to her the price was too great. Nevertheless, she would gladly take the place of anyone among the condemned. In a tirade that was feverishly applauded, Aliénor reminds all kings of their duty even to the lowest subject:

> Un maire de Calais raffermit sa couronne!
> Quelle leçon pour vous, superbes potentats!
> Veillez sur vos sujets dans le rang le plus bas:
> Tel qui, sous l'oppresseur, loin de vos yeux expire,
> Peut-être quelque jour eût sauvé votre empire.
> (Act IV, Scene IV)

Unable to persuade Aurèle to leave the prison, Harcourt swears that the death of these six bourgeois patriots will not precede his own. Forgiving Harcourt for his blindness in following Edward, Saint-Pierre counsels desertion to the French side.

With the introduction of a strange letter from Philippe and the sudden change of heart in Edward, who has remained deaf to all pleas for two acts, the play disintegrates completely in the fifth act. After a brief interview with Saint-Pierre who refuses to accede, Edward receives a letter from Philippe challenging him to a duel:

> Toi, qui t'osant nommer le vrai roi des Français,
> Dans les flots de leur sang fais chanceler leur trône,
> Si tu veux épargner les héros de Calais,
> Je t'offre les moyens d'acquérir ma couronne.
> Viens seul, avec moi seul, par un noble combat,
> Finir tous les malheurs de nos sujets fidèles:
> Notre intérêt n'est point l'intérêt de l'Etat;
> En dignes chevaliers terminons nos querelles.
> (Act V, Scene III)

Upon reading this letter Edward is seized with a fit of rage. Mauni refuses to carry out his sovereign's orders for the execution of the prisoners. In the meanwile Harcourt has freed them on the pretext a message had been received divulging Philippe's ransom payment. Aliénor, struck by this daring action, sees Harcourt as now deserving of her love:

> Cher Harcourt, je te rends et te prouve ma foi;
> Je mourrai ton amante, et mourrai près de toi.
> (Act V, Scene V)

Without provocation Edward's rage changes to ecstatic admiration. He extends complete independence to Harcourt, spares the six bourgeois, and renounces his rights to the French throne.

Sprinkled sparingly with a nice phrase or two, the entire play is bombastic and rhetorical. There is no action to engage dramatic interest. The unnatural reactions of the English to the French spirit of patriotism destroy any verisimilitude. Produced a total of sixty three times since 1765, *Le siège de Calais* was a prodigious success. Because it had been so enthusiastically hailed in Paris, Louis XV ordered a performance at Versailles to take place on February 22, 1765. Extremely pleased with the play, he accorded De Belloy a pension of one thousand *écus* and granted him a gold medal. On March 10, 1765, the author's popularity reached its peak when he was made an honorary citizen of Calais. In the meantime, the King had commanded a free performance for the public. The memoirs of the day mention the eager crowds that flocked to see the play. One remarked:

> Le gratis annoncé a eu lieu aujourd'hui. On ne peut imaginer l'affluence du peuple qui s'est présenté à la comédie. La rue et les entours étoient pleins dès le matin. On a commencé le spectacle à une heure et demie, et il a été écouté avec une attention surprenante de la part des spectateurs. On ne doute pas qu'il n'y eût-là des gagistes qui les avertissoient d'applaudir aux endroits désignés. L'auteur a été obligé de se montrer, il a été reçu avec les acclamations les plus réitérées; on lui a fait l'honneur insigne de joindre son nom à celui du Roi, et l'on a crié Vivent le Roi et M. du Belloy! [34]

The Chevalier de Mouhy reported the ingenuity of some of the patrons, who otherwise would have been turned away, in gaining entrance to the Comedie-Française:

> L'affluence fut toujours si grande, qu'il arriva un jour que partie du Public ne pouvant entrer à la Comédie, les portes en étant trop fièrement gardees, les plus hardis en escaladèrent un jour le balcon avec des cordes, et entrèrent sans qu'on pût les en empècher; tant que les représentations du-

---

[34] Bachaumont, *op. cit.*, II, 167. The first spectacle gratis was given in 1653. See: A. Du Casse, *Histoire anecdotique de l'ancien théâtre en France* (Paris: E. Dentu, 1864), I, 333.

rèrent l'affluence fut toujours si nombreuse, que la salle n'a jamais pu contenir la moitié de ceux qui se présentoient pour y prendre place. Les loges étoient toujours louées quinze jours d'avance.[35]

The play was known all over France, in England, Belgium and Germany. Due to its frenzied monarchal tone, Le siège was frequently acted before soldiers. On July 7, 1765, it was presented before a garrison in San-Domingo, whose governor, Le comte d'Estaing, had it published as the first tragedy printed in French in America.[36] Produced nineteen times, all before Easter, in Paris during the course of 1765, the play earned 60,000 francs. The gross receipts were 62,707 francs, considerably reduced by taxation and the expense of production.[37]

The critics and public were just as ready to criticize Le siège de Calais as they had been to accept it with boundless enthusiasm. Because Dubois, who played the rôle of Mauni, was arrested for having cheated a surgeon, he was expelled from the troupe.[38] Through the connivance of the actor's daughter with a Gentleman of the Chamber, the actors were ordered to continue the play with Dubois in his former rôle. Refusing to play with him, Le Kain, Brizard, Molé, Dauberval and La Clairon were imprisoned. De Belloy, temperamental and giddy with success, claimed the actors were prejudiced. The internecine quarrels of the actors, the absence of La Clairon from the theater, and De Belloy's undiplomatic wrangling with the comédiens prevented the presentation of the Siège from Easter, 1765, to March 1, 1769. It was given ten times in that year, and thirty-two times from 1773-1790. Nine of these performances were in 1789, only one in 1790. The fact that the play was not reproduced again until 1814, when it was played only twice, these being its last performances at the Comédie-Française, defines clearly the antipathy of the public toward the monarchy.[39]

---

[35] The Chevalier de Mouhy also states in the Abrégé de l'histoire du théâtre français, depuis son origine jusqu'au premier juin 1780 (Paris: de Mouhy, L. Jorry et J.-G. Mérigot, 1780) that Dubois had refused to pay for treatments of a venereal disease. III, 81-82.

[36] Marguerite Moffat, «Le siège de Calais et l'opinion publique in 1765», RHLF, XXXIX (1932), 343.

[37] Henry Carrington Lancaster, French tragedy in the time of Louis XV and Voltaire, 1715-1774 (Baltimore: The Johns Hopkins Press, 1950), II, 485.

[38] De Mouhy, op. cit., III, 85.

[39] Joannidès, op. cit., p. 10.

Because of its revolutionary nature, *Le siège de Calais* was destined to be immediately popular. In short, it was a fad. On one hand, a bourgeois was made the hero of a tragedy, and on the other, no classical tragedy had shared more monarchal sentiments than expressed in this play. The bourgeoisie saw the advantage of being elevated to the level of kings and nobles as a further step in the struggle for equality. Louis XV, probably aware of his shortcomings, was gratified by the main theme of the play—the devotion of the people to their monarch.

Although France had not been invaded from 1715-1789, it was forced to sustain a host of wars. Two were fought on the continent. The first, termed the War of Austrian Succession (1741-1748), was fought with Prussia and Bavaria as allies against Austria. The Seven Year's War (1756-1763), the second, was fought with Austria, Russia and a coalition of German princes against Prussia. In America, France and Spain were fighting a sporadic war against the English. France lost on all sides. By provisions of the infamous treaty of Paris in 1763, France surrendered much of her colonial empire in North America, Asia, and in the Indies. The French were humiliated by the defeat. Naturally the government, the court, and the generals were accused. Though ignominious, defeat had not destroyed French patriotism. Louis XV drew his advisers together and ordered a reorganization of the military and naval forces. Soldiers were no longer billeted in the homes of private citizens but assigned barracks, thereby solidifying the forces for purposes of discipline and instruction. Weapons were seriously studied and improvements made. New and modern ships were constructed. The renaissance in the military was demonstrated by the acquisition of Corsica in 1768.

In the intervening years from 1765-1769, the French people had not forgotten *Le siège de Calais*. The transports of patriotism in the play did appeal to them, and their fervent approbation reflected the constant loyalty of the people toward the monarchy, notwithstanding the untiring efforts of the *philosophes* and their sympathizers to bring reform.

De Belloy wrote one other historical tragedy, or *drame historique* as it should be called. Dramas drawn from national history were usually called *tragédies* whether they were in fact because *drame historique* and *comédie historique* were not used before 1789. Enthused with the reception of *Le siège de Calais,* whose popularity was due in large measure to its chauvinistic appeal, De Belloy wrote *Gaston et Bayard* to illustrate French bravery.[40] Known as the French Achilles, Gaston de Foix was a nephew of Louis XII. Bayard, whose abnegation and devotion to duty, earned him the title of *chevalier sans peur et sans reproche,* was nicknamed the French Hercules. Although much older than Gaston, the intrepid Bayard obeyed his superior with evident delight.

The work is termed a five act tragedy and is in verse. Bent on trying to bring within the twenty-four hour rule as many references as possible to the deeds and sayings of Gaston and Bayard, De Belloy altered history with startling flagrancy. The subject of the play is the 1512 conspiracy of Brescia, a town in Italy. The plan, as recorded by historians, was to massacre the French occupation forces of the city. Count Avogare, the leader of the conspiracy, incited the inhabitants to revolt and opened the town to Venetian, Spanish and Roman soldiers.

De Belloy uses this occasion to portray the steadfast friendship of Gaston and Bayard. In the drama Count Avogare is motivated through vengeance for the death of his wife and son. The Count has a daughter, Euphémie, who is loved by Gaston and Bayard. The author's invention, she will be used as the test of friendship between the two soldiers. Another character created by De Belloy is an old man, who, although an ex-patriot, longs to return to the fatherland. His patriotic fervor drives him to reveal the conspiracy. His rôle in the drama is, in reality, a device to resolve otherwise difficult problems, and his inclusion is a striking example of De Belloy's inability as an effective dramatist.

The curtain opens upon a scene in the fortress of Brescia. There are flags, arquebuses, cannons and shot, lances and shields. With a glowing tribute to Bayard's military genius, the obsequious turncoat Avogare welcomes the general who has just arrived from Milan. An experienced appraisal of the situation indicates the state to which the fort has been reduced. Without immediate reinforcements from Gaston, the fortress will flounder helplessly at the mercy of the enemy. The love element is introduced through a reference to Avogare's daughter Euphémie. Bayard's love for her makes him a stronger warrior. A surprise visit from Rovère, Duc d'Urbin, and nephew of Pope Julius II,

---

[40] P.-L. Buirette de Belloy, *Gaston et Baiard* (Paris: La veuve Duchesne, 1770).

(1503-1513) serves to demonstrate Bayard's resignation and acceptance of life. Urbin advances a plan whereby Bayard, whose worth has been overlooked by Louis XII, will be fully recompensed in the forces of Pope Julius. Highly incensed by such a proposal, Bayard is revolted at the idea of fighting for a Pope who is engaged in war for political purposes. Urbin, who had been reared at the court of Louis XII, approves the refusal, but warns of the fort's imminent capture. Altémore, a disguised traitor and accomplice in the machinations of Avogare, is also in love with Euphémie. Gaston's unexpected arrival is announced as a forecast of victory. Avogare swears his hate for the French because they killed his wife and son. He will provide a passage in the walls of the fort to facilitate the arrival of allied forces. The storming of the fortress by Brescian, Roman and Venetian forces is planned for that night.

Act two is almost entirely devoted to Euphémie and her problems of love. She loves neither Altémore nor Bayard. Her heart bleeds for the audacious Gaston, whose reputation had drawn her like a magnet:

> Au récit de sa gloire en tous lieux répandu
> D'un trouble intéressant je me sentais émue.
> (Act II, Scene I)

She argues against her father's treason and implores him to renounce his plan of vengeance. Avogare, recalling the pitiable deaths of his wife and son, grows livid with rage and disowns his daughter. Gaston chances upon Euphémie whose tears induce him to admit his love openly. This admission leaves Bayard dumbfounded. He likewise declares his love: «Prince, j'aime Euphémie, et l'aime avec fureur». (Act II, Scene III). Bayard has sought Euphémie for a long while. He even killed the Spaniard Sotomayor because of her.[41] Bayard departs sorely depressed. Euphémie tells Gaston she loves only him. Their tête-à-tête is interrupted with a note from Bayard challenging Gaston to a duel. The challenge is reluctantly accepted. The duel will be fought within the hour. Avogare anticipates a double death. Left without their two most idolized and capable leaders, the French armies will disintegrate.

Because of his deep friendship for Gaston, Bayard unexpectedly renounces his love for Euphémie. This is the major action in act three.

---

[41] Bayard killed Sotomayor because the latter had forced him into a duel that had nothing to do with love.

Rather than fight his master, Bayard surrenders his sword. Gaston is touched and offers his in exchange. The brief joy felt by Euphémie is quickly dispelled with Avogare's reminder that her fate is in his hands. With news that enemy forces are forming for an assault on the citadel, Gaston and Bayard forget love for awhile. The hapless Euphémie is left to watch the battle from the ramparts. Avogare is sworn to murder Bayard. Altémore is designated to dispatch Gaston.

The miserable failure of Avogare's scheme to murder Bayard and the resultant consequences are treated in act four. From her vantage point Euphémie recounts developments in the battle below. Her account is disrupted by a piercing scream. Bayard has been treacherously wounded by Avogare. With iron from the lance that pierced him still imbedded in his flesh, Bayard appears lying on a stretcher. Avogare is one of the most vociferous mourners. His observations that the enemy will be triumphant stir Bayard to deliver a frantic harangue. The tide of the battle changes abruptly. Told of Bayard's condition, Gaston, imbued with greater vigor, leads his troops to victory.

In the meanwhile, Avogare is angered by Gaston's continued immunity from death. Altémore swears faithfully to perform that deed before the day is over. Urbin, whose sense of honor is unimpeachable, takes it upon himself to tell Euphémie that her father is the enemy agent who bungled Bayard's assassination. Confronted by his daughter, who threatens to divulge the entire conspiracy, Avogare's anger is assuaged only when Euphémie implores his forgiveness. Gaston has learned of his attempted assassination through the intervention of an old denizen. In an ensuing quarrel Euphémie succeeds in preventing the death of either her father or Gaston. Nevertheless, Avogare is arrested forthwith. Euphémie, bathed in tears, begs for her father's life: «Ah! qu'il vive, ou je meurs!» (Act IV, Scene II). Flushed with love, Gaston whispers that not even a hair on Avogare's head will be moved.

The main action in act five takes place in a guard room of the fortress. It is in this act that the old man, mysteriously referred to on several occasions, identifies himself. His information serves to help foil the conspiracy. Until this act, De Belloy has been sparing in his references to *La belle France*. With the old man, ample opportunity is created for chauvinistic declarations. The haunting lines in which the old man pays homage to France were fervently applauded. Through the good graces of Euphémie, the old citizen has been accorded an audience with Bayard and Nemours to whom he relates his past:

J'allai chercher la Gloire au sortir de l'enfance,
Mon bras s'est signalé lorsqu'aux murs de Beauvais,
Une femme a vaincu le Flamand et l'Anglais:
Mais un service ingrat sous un Roi trop austère,
Tourna vers l'Etranger ma jeunesse légère;
De climats en climats j'errai pendant dix ans;
Et depuis trente hyvers fixé chez les Bressans,
Ainsi que tout Français privé de sa Patrie,
Je l'appèle, en pleurant, chaque jour de ma vie.
(Act V, Scene III)

Ashamed of having fought against France, the old man is honored that his sons are now enlisted in its armies. He has undergone many sacrifices to uncover the plot of enemy forces whose plan is to make a surprise invasion of the fortress through subterranean passages. This information was sold to the old man by a Spanish soldier. In order to pay him, it was necessary for the old man to sell his house. Gaston and Bayard promise him a handsome reward. Gaston leaves Bayard in the care of Altémore whose treacherous nature has not yet been broadcast. Just as Altémore prepares to deliver the final thrust that will insure Bayard's death, a tremendous explosion is heard. Avogare's palace, which served as Gaston's headquarters, had been sabotaged. Although wounded, Bayard defends himself valiantly. While watching the unequal fight, Euphémie fainted. Gaston returns at the crucial moment. Through the kindness of Urbin he had been warned not to enter Avogare's palace. The old man and Avogare had been pulverized by the explosion. Saddened by her father's untimely but justifiable death, Euphémie prepares for mourning. Gaston will continue his march through Italy. Bayard will remain a few days longer before departing.

As is the case of *Le siège de Calais*, *Gaston et Bayard* lacks naturalness. The two heroes emerge as little more than impetuous youths bent on adventure. The majority of their brave deeds are only reported. Their primary interest is in Euphémie, a helpless, romantic heroine blanched of all personality. The plot is wasted on this senseless love element. The wooden language of Gaston, Bayard and Euphémie is a strong contrast to that of the fiery Avogare. Through his naturalness and vigor, the villain almost becomes a hero. Other than Euphémie, there is another superfluous character. The ubiquitous presence of Urbin seems unwarranted. To admire an enemy does not involve putting stumbling blocks in one's path to victory. This is precisely the course taken by Urbin. Whenever danger threatens Bayard or Gaston, he is the first to warn them.

The drama was first acted at Paris on April 24, 1771. Le Kain played Bayard; Molé, Gaston; and Mme. Vestris, Euphémie. This was De Belloy's most popular tragedy. Presented twelve times in 1771, it remained in the repertory until 1826 with a total of 163 productions. [42] The receipts were always good. The largest amount received was 4,435 francs collected at the first performance, and never fell below 1,310 francs. [43]

Although particularly admired by the *Journal des Savans*, the most trenchant and appropriate criticism came from Grimm who found De Belloy a man without talent:

> Je suis bien aise que M. de Belloy jouisse de la gloire et surtout des profits de la pièce mais je suis humilié, pour notre goût, du succès de *Bayard*. Je ne saurais nier qu'une nation éclairee, instruite, capable d'élévation, fait un tort réel à sa réputation, en souffrant, sur les théâtres publics, la représentation de ces pompeuses fadaises. M. de Belloy est un porteur de lanterne magique qui expose une suite de figures guindées et en attitudes forcées à l'admiration d'une troupe d'enfans ébahis... [44]

In summing up his criticism, Grimm called De Belloy «un maître faiseur de tragédies». [45]

Michel Sedaine (1719-1797), the stonemason who turned dramatist, wrote one historical tragedy, *Maillard ou Paris sauvé* (1771). [46] Written in five acts and in prose, the work is based on the 1358 revolt instigated by the ambitious Etienne Marcel, provost of the Parisian merchants. Jean II became a prisoner of the English at the battle of Poitiers fought in 1357. The acute situation created by his captivity was aggravated through misunderstandings that arose between the Dauphin (later Charles V) and the Estates-General. Marcel, a powerful member of that body, supported Charles the Bad, King of Navarre. Hostility between Marcel and the Dauphin erupted on February 22, 1358.

---

[42] Joannidès, *op. cit.*, p. 10.
[43] Lancaster, *French Tragedy in the Time of Louis XV and Voltaire, 1715-1774*, II, 500.
[44] Frederick M. Grimm et Denis Diderot, *op. cit.*, I, 485.
[45] *Ibid.*, p. 58.
[46] Michel Sedaine, *Maillard ou Paris sauvé* (Paris: Prault, 1788).

On that day Marcel and a band of insurgents invaded the palace and murdered the marshals of Champagne and Normandy before the prince's eyes. Endeavoring still to displace Charles, Marcel encouraged armed bands of the King of Navarre to invade Paris. His design to open the gates of the city to them was prevented by Jean Maillart, a city alderman. This stalwart supporter of the crown killed Marcel before the Porte Saint-Antoine on the night of July 31, 1358.

Sedaine dedicated his drama to Catherine II of Russia. In the *épître dédicatoire* the author expressed hope that the Russian queen would be more lenient toward its presentation than French opinion. Since the prose publication of Houdar de la Motte's *Oedipe* (1730), it had been ordered that never again could the Comédie-Française present a tragedy in prose. Sedaine agreed with this fiat. «Il y a très peu de sujets propres à la tragédie qui pussent se passer de la pompe des vers et de la noblesse du stile poétique». (p. xv). Sedaine also saw political implications in the rejection of his play:

> Un sujet de l'Histoire de France, présenté à la nation comme Tragédie, sans qu'elle fût écrite en vers Alexandrins, ne pouvoit-il pas être d'une conséquence dangereuse? Devoit-on faire voir aux citoyens de Paris, qu'en 1358 la populace s'étoit révoltée. (p. xiii).

The play was privately presented on the stage of the Duc d'Orléans' theater in the Rue de la Chaussée d'Antin.

To heighten dramatic interest and mitigate the distaste of the conspiracy, Sedaine introduced a touching love problem. Héloïse, the daughter of Maillard, is secretly married to the younger Marcel. Married for more than a year, the couple has had an infant son. The difficulties that keep the two lovers apart stultify interest in the historical events that lead to Etienne Marcel's deah. Whether the little child will be united with his parents is the real problem, not an analysis of the elder Marcel's ambitions or the attempted execution of his evil designs.

Adhering to the unities, the action takes place in the *grande salle* of the Hôtel de Ville in Paris. The fact that the Dauphin is going to call an assembly in the Hôtel de Ville is secondary to Marcel's desire to see his wife. This is the main concern of act one. The young Marcel is delegated by his father to spy on a meeting held at the request of the Dauphin. The unhappy situation that exists in the secret marriage of the two young people is accentuated by the animosity of their parents. Act one closes upon a surreptitious rendez-vous of the lovers. Marcel (fils) is to join his wife at ten o'clock in the evening.

In act two the only allusion to impending events is a report made to his father by the younger Marcel. According to his account of the Dauphin's meeting, a truce is in the offing. The remainder of the act concerns the reaction of Maillard upon learning of his daughter's secret marriage. Only seventeen years old, Héloïse is young enough to wait a year before marriage. During the interval, she will be placed in a convent. Marcel (fils), now twenty-five, is forced into revealing the bold fact of his marriage. Moreover, the child whom Maillard had thought to be the son of a friend is in reality his grandson.

Act three reflects a double conspiracy. The King of Navarre is slated to seize the throne after the deposition of the Dauphin Charles. The second conspiracy is almost as daring. Maillard, who is more bitterly opposed than ever to a marriage between the younger Marcel and his daughter, will be taken prisoner and released only on condition that he honorably permit the marriage. Maillard, who is not only cognizant of his responsibility as a father but also as a first alderman, is aware of recent developments aiming for an overthrow of the government. While searching out clues, he happens upon some of the conspirators and delivers a stern lecture on treason.

Much of the play is enacted in dark recesses of the stage. The emphasis in act four deals with the question of which loyalty is stronger—that of one's love for wife or husband or that to one's country. «Le théâtre est dans l'obscurité; c'est-à-dire, qu'il ne paroît éclairé que par de grosses lampes du centre des voûtes». After a painful scene in which the child is brought onto the stage in his cradle, Héloïse, supposedly ready to leave with her husband to seek safety and peace, reverses her decision upon learning that the conspiracy is set for that night. Instead of leaving dutifully with the younger Marcel, she rushes to her father and relates the terrifying story. Maillard is so absorbed with calling his supporters to arms he forgets his daughter is even married.

The decision taken by Héloïse in act four reaps its vengeance upon her in act five. As the act opens, conspirators designated to capture Maillard surprise the weeping Héloïse. Maillard's forces are successful in quelling the revolt. To assuage their anger, the crowds of people oppressed by Etienne Marcel are tearing the tyrant's body asunder.

The younger Marcel is found with a lance sticking in his back. As Maillard extracts the lance and utters a triumphant cry, his son-in-law dies. The unhappy Héloïse is left alone to mourn her beloved.

As is evident from the brief historical résumé at the outset of this discussion, *Maillard ou Paris sauvé* is a distortion of events made to form the frame for the enaction of a highly emotional and artificial love intrigue. The problem of whether Héloïse should have denounced the conspiracy or trusted in her father, who, as developments intimated, was perfectly aware of Etienne Marcel's moves, presents an intensely dramatic situation. Nevertheless, it came too late in the play to allow elaboration.

The frequency with which the use of national history as an additional field for tragedy was mentioned after 1750 established its acceptance. Known for his *Idée de la poésie anglaise* (1749-1771), the abbé Yart pointed out the efficacy of French history as a rich source in tragedy:

> Ne pourrait-on point introduire sur nos théâtres des caractères qui nous intéressent par eux-mêmes, des passions qui nous fissent sentir les nôtres, des exemples de vertu que nous puissions imiter, en un mot des Français comme nous? On nous représente tous les jours des Grecs, des Romains, des Amériquains et des Turcs, dont les vertus et les malheurs ont je ne sais quoi d'étranger pour nous, bien plus propres à exciter notre curiosité dans une histoire, qu'à emouvoir notre âme dans une tragédie. Nous ne sommes point au-dessous des Italiens, des Espagnols et même des Anglois, qui tient de leur patrie presque tous leurs héros de leur théâtre. [47]

The abbé pursued his discussion by pointing out the difficulties faced in such an undertaking but predicted optimistically that the French were capable of succeeding in such an undertaking. He did not specify what these difficulties were. He obviously was referring to the task of reconciling historical verisimilitude with poetic license. His awareness of the problem was indeed rare in the dramatic criticism of the century. Stentorian enough about changes, the critics were silent on such an annoying solicitude. Their silence manifested a lack of concern

---

[47] Cited by Clarence D. Brenner, «L'histoire nationale dans la tragédie française du XVIIIᵉ siècle», *University of California Publications in Modern Philology*, XIV (1929-1930), 231.

with the course of tragedy, and revealed its true function to them at least as a medium of conveying immediate moral and propagandistic teaching to the public.

As the eve of the Revolution drew nearer, the rising importance of the bourgeoisie was noted in drama with its depiction in major rôles of the tragedy. De Belloy had done much to lower the barrier of discrimination in tragedy against the portrayal of bourgeois characters in major rôles. Yet he was a fervent monarchist. The stage was now set for a man like Sébastien Mercier.

Although regarded with contempt by critics past and present, Louis Sébastien Mercier (1740-1814) achieved vast popularity at home and abroad.[48] The author of several treatises on drama, *Du théâtre ou nouval essai sur l'art dramatique* (1773), with a preface and thirty chapters, contained all his ideas. Mercier was particularly vicious in his attack against the French classical tradition, its form and subject matter:

> On s'imagina toujours faussement qu'on ne pouvait faire une tragédie d'après les Grecs, les Perses, ou les Romains; qu'il fallait absolument des rois pour nous intéresser.[49]

Considering tragedy blanched of its meaning, Mercier turned to the *drame,* a new genre destined to *moraliser les bourgeois.* In order that there could be no deceit in the purpose of the theater, Mercier advocated the moral lesson be understood by the greatest number possible:

> Le nouveau genre appelé *drame,* qui résulte de la tragédie et de la comédie, ayant le pathéthique de l'une et les peintures naïves de l'autre, est infiniment plus utile, plus vrai, plus intéressant comme étant plus à portée de la foule des citoyens.[50]

He felt also that dramatic art not only serves for general instruction and the spread of useful principles but it also cultivates public reason.

---

[48] For a detailed study of Mercier, see Léon Beclard, *Sébastien Mercier, sa vie, son oeuvre, son temps* (Paris: H. Champion, 1903).

[49] Louis-Sébastien Mercier, *Du théâtre ou nouvel essai sur l'art dramatique,* Chapter II, 23. Cited by Francisque Vial and Louis Denise, *op. cit.,* p. 272.

[50] Mercier, *Du théâtre ou nouvel essai sur l'art dramatique,* Chapter VIII. Cited by Denise and Vial, *op. cit.,* p. 278.

«Il est donc temps de peindre les détails et surtout les devoirs de la vie civile...»[51] These ideas paralleled and were inspired by those of Diderot and Beaumarchais. Mercier wrote thirty-one plays. All artistic value in them is destroyed by their longwinded morality.

From the goodly number of Mercier's plays, four pertain to events in French history: (1) *Jean Hennuyer, évêque de Lisieux* (1772); (2) *Childéric Premier, roi de France* (1774); (3) *La destruction de la Ligue* (1782); and (4) *La mort de Louis XI* (1783).[52]

In three acts and in prose, *Jean Hennuyer, évêque de Lisieux* was a mixture of the historical play and the *drame*. Mercier felt that ordinary people should be presented in a serious play. «Mais voir les conditions humaines les plus basses, les plus rampantes! ajoutera-t-on encore, les mettre sur la scène! un tisserand! un ouvrier! un journalier! Et pourquoi pas?»[53] *Jean Hennuyer* portrays the events of history as they affect an humble family of Protestants to be executed by order of the King (Charles IX). Jean Hennuyer, actually a minor character in the play, intervenes to prevent the execution. Saint-Bartholomew's Day was the popular event in French history for writers of propaganda plays such as *Jean Hennuyer*. In writing this drama, Mercier could not have chosen a better time. August 24, 1772, marked the second centenary of the Protestant slaughter on Saint Bartholomew's day. Critics welcomed the play. Grimm said of it:

> De tels ouvrages seraient plus profitables au peuple que toutes les fanfarronades espagnoles des Romains de Corneille et tout le ramage harmonieux et français des Grecs de Racine, quoique l'auteur de *Jean Hennuyer* ne soit pas un homme à comparer à Pierre Corneille ou à Jean Racine.[54]

Written to show the insidious results of fanaticism, *Jean Hennuyer* has, according to Mercier, «l'avantage d'être fondé sur l'histoire et les principaux faits qu'il renferme sont attestés et connus».[55] Through

---

[51] *Ibid.*, Chapter IX, 280.

[52] All of the works mentioned here appeared in the *Théâtre complet de M. Mercier* (Amsterdam: B. Vlam, 1778), except *La mort de Louis XI, roi de France* (Neuchatel: La société typographique, 1783), and *La destruction de la Ligue* (Amsterdam, no publisher given, 1782).

[53] Mercier, *Du théâtre ou nouvel essai sur l'art dramatique*, Chapter XI. Cited by Denise and Vial, *op. cit.*, p. 282.

[54] Grimm, *op. cit.*, II, 303; also Bachaumont, *op. cit.*, VI, 219-220.

[55] Mercier, *Théâtre complet*, II, 287.

his stubborn defiance of a royal decree, an obscure bishop became a hero. The events take place in the little town of Lizieux toward the end of August, 1572. The principal character is Arsène, an humble Protestant and veteran of the religious wars. An air of anxiety permeates the first act. Absent since several days, Arsène (fils) and Evrard had journeyed to Paris where they participated in festivities following the marriage of Henri of Navarre and Marguerite de Valois. Laure, wife of Arsène (fils), is joined by her father-in-law for dinner. On one side of the table is a pitcher of wine and on the other one of milk. As they sit talking of recent happenings and important leaders among whom are Admiral Coligny and Henri de Navarre, a frightened Evrard, Laure's brother, arrives to report rumors of a massacre in Paris.

Abounding in *tableaux muets*, act two reflects the desperation of Protestants whose death has been decreed. Without her husband, the distraught Laure calls upon God to end her days. The elder Arsène also seeks death. Through feigning death in Paris, the son was able to escape and lives to relate the terrible events. Now faced with death in his home, Arsène advances the audacious plan of murdering Jean Hennuyer. That will at least insure safety for the Protestants a few days longer. The old father has a counterplan which involves seeking sanctuary in the Episcopal Palace. As the curtain falls, the Protestant population of Lizieux recommends itself to the mercy of God.

Jean Hennuyer displays true piety in act three. He has already received two communications from Charles IX. In refusing to accept the King's orders, the bishop explains: «Qui ne parle plus en homme ne peut plus commander en Roi...» (Act III, Scene III). Assembled with priests under his jurisdiction, Hennuyer advocates a program of clemency toward all Protestants. The Protestants arrive and request asylum. In attempting to murder Jean Hennuyer, Arsène is foiled by his father. Protestants and Catholics mingle in brotherly fashion. The bishop leaves holding the elder Arsène's hand.

The bishop's magnanimous and daring action of refusing to honor the hateful decree issued by Charles IX served as the historical background for a very mediocre drama. The action is extremely slow, and the language bereft of meaning. In his primary concern to depict *tableaux muets*, the need of restraint escaped Mercier. The result was a melodramatic mixture that contributed little to the growth of historical drama.

In *Childéric 1ᵉʳ, roi de France,* Mercier wrote of the beginnings of French history. The theme of this three act drama in prose is the loyalty of a country's people toward their king. A long historical preface develops Childéric's rôle in the formation of the French monarchy. Exiled from his throne, Childéric sought asylum at the court of Bazin, King of Thuringia. The queen fell in love with the stranger and left her husband. In Mercier's drama the queen is figured as Bazin's daughter; Childéric is depicted as a valiant and noble warrior fully deserving of the princess' love. The action of the play takes place at Tournai in 468. The tomb of Childéric was discovered there in 1653. Mercier states that this is the only known fact about Childéric. All the rest is legend.

The principal concern of action is Childéric's unjust deposition as King of the Franks and his subsequent return. After leaving Tournai, Childéric sought his fortune in Germany. He has returned incognito to place his claim for the throne of France. Tournai is filled with activity. Egidius, who historically was an ally, is featured here as wishing to usurp the throne of France. Although a Roman general, he will proclaim Basine as his queen. Having cast her lot with Childéric, Basine searches for her lover whom she has not seen in several months. Her love is attested by the great respect she holds for Childéric: «Il est né pour commander aux humains, comme a mon coeur». (Act I, Scene V).

In act two opposition is increased against Egidius because he is a foreign usurper. His proud, vain and dictatorial manner is contrasted to the humble and steadfast strength of Childéric. In order to assure his nomination, Egidius spreads the rumor that Childéric has died. Oblivious to warnings from his advisers that the throne is ephemeral, Egidius proclaims his policy of absolute rule. Carloman, a sage French statesman, challenges Egidius' right to the throne:

> De quel droit prétends-tu régner? Toi né dans Rome; toi nourri dans les entreprises de son génie despotique et corrumpu; toi, étranger, et ce nom seul suffit pour te proscrire. Par quelle erreur inconcevable prétends-tu renverser la loi de Pharamond. (Act II, Scene II)

Carloman denies the news that Childéric is dead. Egidius contemptuously forgives the old man. Basine, in Tournai, because she thinks Childéric is there, will lead her father's army in the fight against

Egidius. In a long conversation with the despondent Carloman who is not sure Childéric is alive, Basine shows him a ring given to her by Childéric as a token of his love. With Childéric alive, Carloman is certain liberty will be born again. Childéric arrives presently. After a brief and happy reunion, Childéric, now a mature and moderate prince, admits his love for Basine. The German princess is goaded to action. In a rather amusing speech, she begs for weapons. «Que l'on me donne un casque, une lance, et je combattrai pour la cause des Rois... oubliez-vous ici de quels ayeux je suis née?» (Act II, Scene IV). It is agreed that Childéric will go to the assembly in the temple and reveal his identity. The act closes with Basine's ecstatic praise of Childéric and the French: «Ma tendresse n'est plus alarmée. Il est des Dieux au Ciel, et de grands coeurs en France. Quand j'apperçois son Roi, je vois tous les coeurs voler sur son passage, et la victoire écrite sur son front.» (Act II, Scene IX).

The scene switches to the solemn assembly in the temple. The representatives have just heard Egidius' name proposed for king. Childéric steps to the rostrum to pronounce his intentions:

> Je reviens, mais c'est pour vous arracher à la tyrannie qui vous menace, et sur laquelle vous fermez les yeux. Je porterai sans cesse la patrie dans mon sein; et dans tous les tems mon premier devoir sera, et de venger, et de respecter vos droits. (Act III, Scene I)

It would appear Childéric has only two admirers, Basine and Carloman. His speech is greeted with total silence. Upon his threat to abandon such ungrateful subjects, the delegates acquiesce and swear loyalty. Not satisfied with a peaceful settlement, Egidius declares war. Basine's love has enflamed her fighting spirit. She takes lance and helmet and shouts: «Je vais me jeter dans la foule de ces héros et défendre mon époux» (Act III, Scene IV). While restraining her from such an action, Carloman dispels her doubts of Childeric's prowess in battle. What transpires during the battle already in progress is reported by Carloman from his vantage point on the ramparts. Childéric returns shortly with sword in hand. This occasions a glowing tribute to French bravery and patriotic fervor: «Que la postérité sache ce que peut une nation brave qui combat pour son Roi». (Act III, Scene VI).

The curtain closes on a play whose abundant allusions to the bravery and loyalty of the French, praiseworthy as they may be, are spoiled by the overly ebullient Basine. The love, which she evidently feels toward Childéric, evolves into a travesty. Thereby any attempt at sincerity is destroyed. Such a play was most propitiously written since it appeared during the coronation year of Louis XVI. The work is in reality a harangue in dialogue outlining responsibilities Mercier and France hoped Louis XVI and Marie-Antoinette would heed. The sermon droning out the same ideas with no development tires the reader and leaves no impression. Luckily, the play was never presented.

In a thirty-one page long introduction to *La destruction de la Ligue*, Mercier condemned the last five of the Valois kings. The dramatist planned to correct the untruths related by timid and cowardly historians who had hesitated to reveal stark reality. He saw the reigns of François Ier, Henri II, François II, Charles IX and Henri III as «...règnes détestables et successifs, marqués par tout ce que le crime et le vice ont de honteux et de funeste qui écrasent le Royaume». [56] The most violent attack was leveled against Charles IX:

> Le massacre de la Saint-Barthélemi fut le crime du trône; et ce crime fut médité pendant sept années, entre les deux cours de Charles IX et de Philippe II. Charles IX a signé le massacre de la Saint-Barthélemi dans l'âge où les plus mauvais rois ont eu des vertus et de la sensibilité. Il a tiré sur ses propres subjets, et de coupables historiens ont voulu l'excuser sur son âge... [57]

Mercier claimed the true cause of the religious struggles in the sixteenth century was not the defense of Catholicism, but a sincere expression of the people to overthrow the sons of Catherine de Médecis and establish the Duc de Guise as the new monarch. [58] The untimely murder, in 1588, of the Duc de Guise and the subsequent death of his brother facilitated the way for Henri IV. The gnawing ambition of the Guise family was a source of constant worry to Catherine and her sons, but the defense of Catholicism was the primary

---

[56] Mercier, *La Destruction de la Ligue*, p. ix.
[57] *Ibid.*, p. xvii.
[58] *Ibid.*, p. xviii.

reason for the religious wars. Although he set out to correct untruths, Mercier distorted history to reinforce his own opinions.

La destruction de la Ligue is a four act drama in prose. According to its author the theme is to «faire voir aux hommes combien des idées religieuses mal entendues entraînent d'erreurs politiques, et nuisent à la felicité nationale». [59] His drama purports to be a «tableau fidèle des actions et des préjugés de nos ancêtres braves et trompés». [60]

The action of the play takes place in Paris on March 21 and 22, 1594. Transpiring in the home of the Catholic bourgeois Hilaire, the first act reflects the effects of starvation and differences of political opinion. As the play opens, Hilaire and his son argue over which will eat the last piece of bread. The son will relinquish it to his mother. Their dispute is interrupted by a knock on the door. There is general fright. Mlle. Lancy, a Protestant and the fiancée of the younger Hilaire, has arrived at the behest of her dying aunt. The young girl's father has enlisted in the Béarnais faction. Hilaire's hatred for Protestants incites him to decry their opposition. Other visitors arrive. They are three members of the Ligue and active churchmen. Varade is a rector of the Jesuits; Guincestre is a priest of Saint Bartholomew, and Aubry is priest of Saint-André-des-Arcs. With a warm greeting for Hilaire, they bring news of imminent victory for the Ligue. Taking advantage of the moment, the priests inveigh against printing which produced a deliterious effect upon the world. Hilaire's mother, an old lady of eighty-three years, has listened to their venimous language, and not being able to contain her thoughts any longer, she reminds them of their rich sinecures. She has lost five sons in the religious wars. Death is her only friend. The priests promise to dispatch her before the day is over.

The events in act two take place at the encampment of Henri IV. Mercier strives to show the prince's magnanimity toward fellow Frenchmen and his determination to resolve the devastating conflict between Protestant and Catholic. Henri hesitates in issuing the order to storm Paris. To alleviate the city's famished populace, he commands that bread be thrown over the walls. The bread is refused. Henri has done everything he can to prevent a final assault which will lead to the death of many thousands. He has even learned the catechism and ab-

---

[59] *Ibid.*, p. xxvii.
[60] *Idem*.

jured the Protestant religion. Sully, his trusted adviser, however, has remained Protestant. Henri, whose one aim is to see happiness in all levels of French society, hopes the best suited will reign. A messenger bears the news that Paris, surfeited with the Ligue and its leader the Duc de Mayenne, is clamoring for Henri's bloodless entry within the city's gates. Alone in his tent, Henry weeps.

In act three the scene changes again to Hilaire's house. The grotesqueness of events in this act is epitomized by the death, on the stage, of Hilaire's mother. In desperation to find his daughter, M. Lancy decides to inquire of her whereabouts from Hilaire. Both obsessed with the righteousness of their own cause find enough energy to pronounce long discourses. Lancy had saved Hilaire's family by bringing bread. Shortly after he leaves, the uneasy peace is shattered by soldiers of the Ligue who search for the bread. Overwhelmed with their barbarism, Hilaire shouts: «Tuez-moi sur la place, ou rendez-moi un seul pain». (Act III, Scene V).

The closing scenes of the act are devoted to the agonizing death of Hilaire's mother. Capitalizing on the event, Mercier resorts to one of his favorite devices, a *tableau muet*. Hilaire (fils) returns after a search for bread has proved futile. His relation of the hideous sights resulting from starvation includes the pitiful story of a mother eating her own child. The extremities to which Paris has been reduced, and rumors that Henri has pledged his full support to the city, have rechanneled young Hilaire's political sympathies. He is immediately disowned by his horrified father. Thought to be already dead, the grandmother regains consciousness, and in the semblance of a trance she makes a crystal clear forecast of future events. Then she dies. «Ici se fait un grand silence, les quatre personnages (Hilaire, Hilaire (fils), Mme. Hilaire and Mlle. Lancy doivent former un tableau pathétique». (Act III, Scene VII) M. Hilaire throws himself upon the dead body of his mother and summons the angel of death. The emotion of this pathetic moment is heightened by the whole family's arrest.

In the last act Henri is acclaimed as deliverer and king. The Hilaire family and Mlle. Lancy are imprisoned in the Bastille. The author defends his liberty in situating the last act here. The prison was in actuality the Chatelêt, but the Bastille was chosen by dint of its infamous reputation. In contrast to the boisterous laughter of banqueting guards, the prison is filled with plaintive lamentations. Hilaire rues the day when he blindly chose to follow the Ligue. Subsequently, a screaming mob led by Lancy invades the Bastille. The prisoners are freed, and the guards flee.

In this bizarre work the observations between Hilaire and his wife, while propagandistic, are well constructed. The figure of Henri IV is indeed an unnatural and sorry one. Rather than displaying the jovial character for which he is famous, Mercier transforms him into a wooden puppet emitting maxims. The treatment of the priests, is, as would be assumed, viciously vindictive. Their fanaticism is so intense they become grotesque demons obsessed with the desire to stamp out all opposition. Attenuated by style, satire is an effective means of pointing out need for refom. If there is no style, the subject under consideration becomes distorted even to the point of nausea. *La destruction de la Ligue* produces that result.[61]

La mort de Louis XI, written in prose, is not divided into acts but scenes, fifty of them. Like Henri IV and Jeanne d'Arc, Louis XI has become a legendary figure.[62] In Mercier's time Louis XI was regarded as a sombre religious fanatic given to intrigue and persecution. The opinion contains only some truth. Louis did much to consolidate the power of the monarchy and contributed more than any other king before him to the unification of France.

In Mercier's play Louis XI is a senile old fool afraid of death. Through a series of excellently drawn tableaux, in which Mercier manages to catch the spirit of the age, Louis' eagerness to cheat death is unfurled. Peasants, doctors, monks, court intriguers and plain people are colorfully and accurately depicted. In this respect, Mercier made a significant contribution in improving historical drama. The events of *La mort de Louis XI* take place at the château of Plessis-lès-Tours. The year is 1483 just prior to the King's death. The drama has two parts. The first strives to portray the irascible, tyrannical and superstitious nature of the dying king. The second involves a complete change in character and his eventual death.

In order to discourage assassination attempts against Louis, harsh security measures are being enforced at the castle. Silence of night is

---

[61] It is not known whether this play was ever presented.

[62] The best treatment of Louis XI and his reign is found in Pierre Champion, *Louis XI* (Paris: Champion, 1927). The edition of Mercier's drama is that which appeared at (Neuchatel: La société typographique, 1783).

broken by the unexpected arrival of a courier who bears important news for the King. After being thoroughly searched and having his papers appraised, the courier receives notice his majesty will see no one until morning. The courier is none other than Mobourg, an expatriot and now a representative of the Spanish court in Madrid. Mobourg had defected to Spain because of the unjustified murder of his father by drowning. Until the King summons him, Mobourg is requested to wait in a designated guard room. There he chances upon a former friend, Guillaume Tonnard, now eighty-eight years old. The two cronies pass their time in recapitulating events transpiring since Mobourg left France. In scene two Tonnard deplores conditions existing under France's last three kings. Charles VI was insane. Charles VII was:

> prince sans force et sans âme, une servante d'auberge (Jeanne d'Arc) vint montrer à la tête de ses armées les vertus qui lui manquoient. Enfin, il s'enferma dans une tour et y mourut de faim de peur d'être empoisonné par la main de son propre fils.

Louis XI is also insane. He has hallucinations that Plessis-lès-Tours will be attacked by an unseen enemy. For that reason, 18,000 soldiers are bivouacked in the area. Louis is also ostentatious. He spends astronomic sums to create a menagerie. Mobourg's mission is to collect pay for Valencian dogs, Sicilian mules, and Barbary lions. The most lugubrious aspect of Louis' character is the great secrecy shrouding his fatal illness. Tonnard and Mobourg reach the simultaneous conclusion that all monarchs are degraded or perverse.

In response to an order from his physician, Louis has left his chambers to enjoy the early morning air. Disguised as a captain, the King makes his appearance sitting on an armchair enclosed within a strange box resembling somewhat that in which a sentry stands. As peasant women pass by on their way to work, the King inquires if they have heard any rumors about his health. The public belief that he is dying is loathsome to the weak King. He beseeches the saints in heaven to spare his life. Back in his heavily guarded quarters, Louis awaits an interlude of entertainment which will consist of cats chasing rats. This will suffice for his hunting exercise.

The tenor of the play becomes even more grotesque with the arrival of canons and monks bearing relics earnestly sought by the King.

Louis pays a handsome price for each relic. An unexpected guest is an envoy from the court of Bajazet at Constantinople. Hearing of Louis' malady, the sultan wishes to offer a few relics. An argument ensues in which the sultan's good intentions are questioned. Louis chastizes the envoy: «Retirez-vous, et dites à votre maître que je ne veux point de ses présens; je n'accepterai jamais son amitié et son alliance, qu'en cas qu'il veuille se convertir à la foi catholique». (Scene XV).

The next several scenes are devoted to the Dauphin and the consequence of Louis' unrealistic policies toward his son. The Dauphin's tutor and brother-in-law, the Comte de Beaujeu, reports to the King:

> Votre majesté sera satisfaite. Il est dans la plus parfaite ignorance, et quand même il lui viendroit l'idée de s'enfuir et de se révolter, il n'a aucune capacité pour se faire écouter de qui que ce soit. Soyez persuadé, sire, qu'il n'éblouira et ne séduira personne par ses connoissances; il est bien tel que votre majesté le désire. (Scene XIX).

To this report, the demented Louis replies: «Les connoissances lui seroient inutiles; il n'est pas fait pour entrer dans les affaires de mon vivant; il faut qu'il ignore tout ce qui se passe dans mes états». (Scene XIX).

Intermediate scenes accentuate the King's obstinacy in not following his doctor's orders, the scandalous conduct of the Princess Jeanne and her forced marriage with the Duc d'Orléans (later Louis XII), the hostility between the King and the magistrature, and his disregard for friendly relations with foreign powers.

In this first part of the drama, the thread of unity is that of hate. Unconcerned with verisimilitude, Mercier chose his situations and pieced them together. In the second part, the ever approaching death of the King and an atmosphere of gloom create an attitude of pity. Frequent references in the first part to the Saint Homme de Calabre serve to give unity to the two parts. Louis XI had awaited the arrival of the hermit François de Paule. His universal reputation as a wise man who had wrought many miracles in curing the sick prompted Louis' appeal. François de Paule is admirably drawn. His humility and freshness are a welcome relief from the haughty and stuffy Louis whose whole reign is characterized as one of suffocation typified in the closed windows and doors of Plessis-lès-Tours. Contrary to Louis' wildest dreams, François de Paule cannot prescribe a sure cure for the King's bodily ills:

> Des avis charitables et des prières, voilà tout ce que je puis vous offrir. Roi, vous n'avez que peu de tems à vivre, et le jour du jugement approche. Interrogez votre conscience; elle vous fera sentir ce que vous avez. (Scene XLI)

The Kings's confidence changes to anger; yet François de Paule perseveres. He enumerates Louis' most appalling practices. Among these are prisoners in cages, heavy taxes and an untold number of murders. The saintly François reminds Louis that the only recourse to salvation is through a visit to the prisons. Upon his return, the once great King renounces his sins and dies. The grandees of the realm stand before his bier. Charles VIII is proclaimed King. The difficult problem of naming a regent is immediately broached with unsatisfactory results. Left alone in death, Louis reminds all of their inexorable fate.

As a note to the last scene Mercier expressed regret at not being permitted complete freedom:

> On auroit pu tracer ici une dernière scène d'une terrible vérité, mais on l'abandonne à l'imagination: la sépulture d'un monarque haï! Il est des choses que le poète sent, mais que les règles de l'art et les convenances lui défendent de peindre. J'ai regret que le goût timide de mon pays m'ait interdit ce dernier et vigoureux tableau, qu'il m'a fallu sacrifier. [63]

Perhaps because of its form, *La mort de Louis XI* is far superior to other historical dramas of Mercier discussed above. Although of a definite inferior caliber, the superiority is due to the marked absence of any love interest. There is, as in the other historical dramas of Mercier, no Laure, Mlle. Lancy or Basine to monopolize the action with maudlin shenanigans. With Mercier, whenever love is an element in his plays it becomes the principal preoccupation and sight is lost of the main theme which, according to him, is the dramatization of a past period in French history. With the exception of Louis XI and church representatives, who are depicted too grotesquely to be

---

[63] Mercier, *La mort de Louis XI*, p. 176.

convincing, characterization in *La mort de Louis XI* is miraculously achieved. François de Paule is particularly well drawn. His simple, direct language and a manifest disinterest in corruption and ambition transform him into an admirable personage.[64]

The influence of the *drame sérieux* on the formation of the *tragédie nationale* was of great consequence. Little by little the intent and form of tragedy were transformed by theorists and dramatists who fought with greater determination to break with tradition. Every vestige of not only the old social order but also of the literary order was odious to the iconoclasts. The *tragédie nationale* is the link between the *drame sérieux* and regular tragedy. Mercier struck the chord that was to echo through the pages of every subsequent drama drawn from national history, and thus made this form of art a trenchant weapon for hacking away the walls of the old order. There was little concern, however, for the face of new institutions that would ineluctably replace the old ones.

Among the first of a long series of distinguished theatrical performances given under the direction of Mlle. Montansier in her refurbished theater at Versailles was *Gabrielle d'Estrées* by Edme Billardon de Sauvigny (1736-1812).[65] Presented for the first time on January 28, 1778, the play is a tragedy, has five acts, and is in verse.[66]

A long preface written in defense of Gabrielle d'Estrées (1573-1599) and against her many detractors precedes the work. Freed by divorce in 1599 from the shackles of a fruitless marriage with Marguerite de Valois, Henri IV entertained the prospect of marrying Gabrielle d'Estrées, his beautiful and honored mistress. He hoped to have in his second wife a woman who would bear him sons. Gabrielle, first married to Liancourt, had separated from him at Henri's insistence to become the Marquise de Monceaux in 1596 and the Duchesse de Beaufort the following year. Living in the Hôtel Schomberg near the Louvre, her activities were officially connected with those of the King. During her liaison with Henri she had born him three children

---

[64] *Jeanne d'Arc* (1789), the last drama of Mercier drawn from national history, was never published and seems to have been lost.

[65] Edme Billardom de Sauvigny, *Gabrielle d'Estrées* (Paris: Robustel, 1778).

[66] For an interesting treatment of Mlle. Montansier and her exploits in the theater, see Louis Péricaud, *Histoire des grands et petits théâtres de Paris pendant la Révolution, le Consulat et l'Empire* (Paris: E. Jorel, 1908).

of whom one was a son. In 1599 she was pregnant for a fourth time.

Besides being deeply in love with Gabrielle, Henri wanted his wife to be French, not a foreigner mainly interested in political intrigue. He made his designs known, but public opinion was not at all favorably disposed toward his marrying no less than a princess. Moreover, the public disliked Gabrielle violently, and her name was sullied by every unthinkable appellation.

When the news of Henri's projected marriage reached Rome, Pope Clement VIII went immediately into seclusion. He judged the French king's wishes unreasonable and unworthy. He was distressed also over the religious problems that could arise from such a union. Aware of the opposition in France to the King's marriage, Clement warned of the dire consequences that could arise over succession to the throne which perhaps would fall into the hands of a heretic, and thus 25,000,000 souls (the population of France at the time) would desert the Christian community.

Anxious to fulfill his desires, Henri exerted all the pressure he dared to extract a pontifical dispensation. In desperation he even threatened to marry without the Pope's blessing. The negotiations opened by him and the preparations almost completed for the marriage in Paris were brought to naught by Grabielle's sudden death during the week of Easter, 1599. Evidently strain caused by the Pope's delay and threats of harm from all sides brought about a miscarriage. Gabrielle died two days afterward. Overwhelmed with grief and by the sudden turn of fortune, Henri ordered his beloved interred, on April 20, 1599, with all the pomp becoming a princess of the blood. No sadness swept through the streets of Paris; instead, its inhabitants breathed a sigh of relief. The King and France had just escaped a great peril. Among those who celebrated this miracle was Sully.

For his play, De Sauvigny took the facts and wove a highly dramatic intrigue with Sully as Gabrielle's closest friend. The author interprets Gabrielle's rôle as requiring her, through the maneuvers of Sully, to renounce any desires of marrying Henri. Warned of the political consequences that would ensue, Gabrielle chose the less glamorous of two decisions: (1) to ignore Rome and become queen of France, or (2) refuse to marry Henri. The choice of the latter demonstrated an unselfish move on her part and hastened her death. Without Henri there was no reason for her to live. Gabrielle, universally admired as the most beautiful woman in France, thus became, for De Sauvigny at least, a martyr and heroine.

De Sauvigny's sentiments toward Gabrielle were expressed in a poem, which precedes the play, honoring beautiful women of whom she was an outstanding example:

> Pour plaire, pour être adorée,
> Et pour enchaîner la faveur,
> L'adresse qu'elle s'est permise;
> C'est de régner avec douceur,
> Toute la peine qu'elle a prise,
> C'est de laisser agir son coeur. (p. xiii)

Several pages of the preface were devoted to a brief history of the theater of Versailles. The author also included a letter, dated March 12, 1778, and written by Mlle. de Montansier, in which she extended an invitation to dramatists to bring their plays to her newly appointed theater. De Sauvigny congratulated Mlle. Montansier and her troupe for their sensitive interpretation of his play:

> Ma pièce a été jouée avec beaucoup d'ensemble et sans déclamation. Le plus grand nombre des Actrices d'aujourd'hui semble ne faire cas que des rôles de morgue et à passions fortes, c'est-à-dire que leur jeu ne diffère de celui des hommes que parce qu'il est plus forcé. (p. viii)

He was particularly lavish in his praise of Mlle. Pitrot for her knowing interpretation in the rôle of Gabrielle.

The theme of the play is Gabrielle's lack of ambition to become queen as opposed to her profound love of Henri. In the first act, assailed by rumors that Henri will be forced into a political union with an Italian princess, relatives and friends of Gabrielle try to influence her to press Henri into declaring a quick marriage. The play opens at a moment when Gabrielle is pressed by her aunt, the ambitious and scheming Marquise de Sourdis, to insist on marrying Henri at the earliest possible moment. Although she is aware of the King's love for her, Gabrielle has no desire to become queen, and moreover there is little chance for her to even be considered. All that counts in her relationship with Henri is their love. She states as much:

A l'objet de mes feux je m'abandonne entière;
Je ne sens que par lui la joie et le bonheur,
Et si je veux régner, c'est au fond de son coeur.
(Act I, Scene I)

When informed that there are competitors for Henri's hand and that he is disposed to do what is politically expedient, Gabrielle is very unhappy. Nevertheless, she is destined to love him regardless of any future event. A celebration in honor of Henri increases the Marquise de Sourdis' fears of seeing her niece replaced by another. Gabrielle momentarily believes Henri does not love her. Her aunt resolves to call upon her agent, Zamet, now at the court of the Médicis, for information concerning their intentions. She attributes to Sully the scheme to discard Gabrielle, and states her plan to eliminate him by bringing about a change in Henri's affections.

The distress caused by the fear that Henri does not love Gabrielle is dispelled in the second act by his unqualified declaration of being unable to live without her. The Marquise de Sourdis seems to have been successful in plotting Sully's downfall. Henri arrives at Gabrielle's apartment and is greeted by the latter's aunt who launches into a long explanation of Gabrielle's present delicate state and offers reason why the King should see her niece no more. She then accuses Sully of conspiring to turn Henri against Gabrielle. According to reports, Sully is presently in Florence negotiating arrangements which will cancel the marriage between Henri and Gabrielle. Henri is abashed at such a vicious attack against Sully, but even so, if there is any truth in this story he will foil the entire attempt by hastening his marriage. When confronted by Henri, who bids her to prepare for the wedding, Gabrielle doubts his sincerity. Enraged at the thought of his friend acting behind his back, Henri orders Sully's immediate seizure. Gabrielle defends Sully declaring his motives, whatever they be, are always in the best interests of the State. If the people want Marie de Médicis or anyone else as their queen, then Henri should heed their wishes. Now that Sully has returned from his mysterious trip, Henri should at least hear his side of the story. Admiring Gabrielle's courage and kindness, Henri commands an audience with Sully.

Sully's political astuteness and admirable diplomacy are the main concern in act three. In the interview with Henri, Sully praises the King in his successful efforts to bring all elements of the population together. Henri circumvents the issue of marrying someone else other than Gabrielle but concludes he should be allowed to choose his mate. Sully, on the other hand, believes a political marriage assuring peace with Spain, Italy and the League would be wiser. When told that Gabrielle was his only defender among a host of detractors, Sully is appreciative of her friendly attitude. This encourages Henri to extol Gabrielle's many virtues:

> Ce n'est pas la beauté que j'idolâtre en elle.
> Quelle âme fut jamais plus sensible et plus belle?
> (Act III, Scene IV)

Misinterpreting Sully's expression of gratitude toward Gabrielle, Henri is reassured that his trusted minister approves. Sully replies that he did not say he thought Henri should marry her. Conscious always for the need of peace, Sully is somewhat afraid of Rome's reaction to such an unorthodox move as proposed by Henri. To show his disapproval of the projected wedding between Henri and Gabrielle, Sully tears into shreds the announcement declaring the King's intentions.

In act four Sully is denied the right to remain at court, but will be appropriately rewarded for his past services. Before his departure, the minister succeeds in seeing Gabrielle and persuades her to refuse Henri's proposal.

Still convinced that Sully has thwarted the ambitions she entertains for her niece, the Marquise de Sourdis cajoles Gabrielle to join the ranks of those who wish to heed his hasty departure. Gabrielle maintains her calm reassurance that Sully has always had a good reason for his actions. Nevertheless, frightened by a strange premonition of disaster, she dispairs of happiness with Henri:

> Le Trône, l'Univers, que font-ils à mes yeux?
> Je n'aime que pour toi ce jour que je respire.
> Ton Coeur est tout mon Bien, ma gloire, mon empire.
> (Act IV, Scene III)

During a visit made to deliver presents to Gabrielle, the King admits he ordered Sully exiled but at the same time the act was done with no ill feelings.

Before departing, Sully pays a surprise visit to Gabrielle and shows the excommunication papers issued for her. He explains:

> Cette soeur des Valois, en sa haine obstinée,
> N'a rompu qu'à ce prix son funeste hyménée
> Et Rome dont vos feux allarmoient le courroux,
> Ordonne qu'à jamais Henri renonce à vous.
> (Act IV, Scene VII)

The excommunication papers are only a suggestion of the unhappiness in store for France should Gabrielle persist in her plans to marry Henri. Sully then proposes a compromise by which Gabrielle would renounce her claims to the throne, but in the process she should convince the King that the decision to deny her is his own idea. Shocked by the boldness of Sully's proposal, Gabrielle consents, nevertheless, to leave the court but not before she extracts a promise of fidelity to Henri.

In the last act Gabrielle fulfills her vow to Sully, renounces Henri, and dies. At the beginning of the act she faces her lover amid a crowd of well-wishers, and, pale wth emotion, she tells him there is an obstacle to their marriage. She reiterates her eternal love for him, however, as a parting gesture. Sully comes to impart the news that Rome has refused to sanction the proposed marriage. Henri then tells Sully there is no need to announce that fact. He has already decided not to marry Gabrielle. Very thankful for her action, Sully is now afraid she will commit suicide. His fears are substantiated by a report that during a visit to Zamet, an agent of the Marquise de Sourdis, Gabrielle was seized with a fit. Relating the tragic event, the messenger said:

> Tout-à-coup elle tombe en un sombre délire
> Le frisson la saisit et ses sens sont glacés:
> Mon oeil la méconnoît dans ses traits effacés:
> Le ciel à ses tourmens égale sa constance.
> (Act V, Scene XI)

After hearing the report the King rushes to Gabrielle's bedside. Helpless in the knowledge that she has only a few moments to live, Henri orders Zamet cast into prison. In her dying gasps, Gabrielle tells her lover that fate wished her death, not Zamet:

> Le ciel vouloit ma mort...
> Je me meurs...
> (Act V, Scene XII)

Stunned by the rapidity of events and overwhelmed with grief, the King declares mourning throughout France.

With only the principal theme of the play historically true, the exposition of most of the facts contributing to the dénouement is drastically distorted. There is no mention of the unities, although the action could have easily transpired within twenty-four hours and in the Louvre. The liberty taken in interspersing historical events occurring over a space of several years, either before the present moment or later, detract from the force of the plot. The language of the play is by far its most praiseworthy element. Only on rare occasions does the author resort to periphrasis and then only because he wishes to characterize a personality. Such is the case in the second act when the Marquise de Sourdis explains reasons for her niece's indisposition. In general the language of all characters is surprisingly natural and straightforward. Having set out to show that beauty can go deeper than the skin, De Sauvigny naturally presents Gabrielle in a sympathetic light. In spite of the unalterable pressures to force her into intrigues, motivated by the haughty and thoroughly vicious Marquise de Sourdis, Gabrielle remains outside their realm. Her tranquil mien is undisturbed because of the reassurance of Henri's undying love. When, at intervals throughout the play, threats arise to shock her tranquillity, Gabrielle reacts to them with disarming honesty. She stands as an excellent example of abnegation. Her nobility is demonstrated in the pristine denial of her most ardent wish which, of course, was to marry Henri. The admiration sustained for Gabrielle from the beginning is somewhat lessened by the contrived ending. The immediate reasons for Gabrielle's death are nebulous. The spectator is encouraged to think she was poisoned by Zamet; yet evidence points to a strange but fatal paralytic seizure to which she was subject. No previous indication of her unstable health had been made.

Henri IV is also depicted as a sympathetic, constant lover and honored king. The decision to accede to the wishes of his people rather than to his own and therefore not marry Gabrielle is naturally commendable. Nevertheless, the awareness of historical fact regarding Henri's relations with Rome and Gabrielle negates for the spectator the sincerity which the author wished evidently to convey.

Sully is the real protagonist in the play. An historical knowledge of his open and hostile opposition to the royal union destroys his authenticity. The author's scheme of permitting Sully to persuade Gabrielle not to marry Henri belies historical fact to such an extent that the spectator is disgusted rather than moved, as was intended, to admiration by the minister's astute and tenacious diplomacy. Unfortunately, the distortion of a far too familiar story destroyed an otherwise worthy drama.

From the more than two hundred tragedies performed at the Comédie-Française in the years between 1700-1789 about twenty-five were inspired by French national history. Many serious dramas were drawn from the national history but they were not presented publicly. During the period mentioned above, tragedy had relinquished its sovereign position, enjoyed in the seventeenth century, as the most outstanding literary genre and had disintegrated into almost total oblivion. In their efforts to give tragedy renewed vigor by opening up new fields for it to explore, writers inadvertently brought about its death. Voltaire one of the most prolific writers of tragedy during the century although a classicist in style, was influential in introducing elements foreign to classical tragedy. His sanction of the use of French national history as a new and rich field to exploit for the sources of tragedy met with decided success. After the middle of the century, French history was frequently used as a basis for tragedy. In fact, *Le siège de Calais*, the most successful tragedy of the period, was drawn from French history. There was no particular period favored by dramatists who drew from French history; however, the Middle Ages rose in popularity because of Voltaire's efforts in adapting to drama aspects of the history of that period. The Massacre of Saint Bartholomew's Day inspired two works, *Coligni* of Baculard and *Jean Hennuyer* by Mercier. The sudden popularity of the *drame sérieux* influenced many dramatists to write in prose; the most outstanding of these was Mercier.

The growing importance of the *tiers état* was reflected in the *tragédie nationale* through the choice of situations in which the protagonists belonged to that class. The most notable work among this group was the perennially famous *Siège de Calais*.

Much of the dramatic material written in the sixteenth and seventeenth centuries and lying within the category of the *tragédie nationale* dealt primarily with the religious controversies among Protestants and Catholics. By nature highly propagandistic, these writings were replaced in the eighteenth century by dramas whose aim was evidently a criticism of the monarchy, the nobility and the clergy; thus the function of the *tragédie nationale* to serve as a primary vehicle of propaganda was strengthened. Important among such dramas was *Louis XI* by Mercier.

CHAPTER IV

THE *TRAGÉDIE NATIONALE* FROM 1789-1800

The decade from 1789 to 1800 was one of the most turbulent periods in French history. Every facet of the social structure underwent drastic change. In the field of drama, tragedy, as its precepts were understood and followed from the middle of the sixteenth century to the advent of the Revolution, was totally distorted. Dramatic materials bearing the stamp of tragedy were vehicles of propaganda. Censorship was absolute. For fear of losing his head, no one dared write except in the popular political vein. This was more than difficult as politics changed colors like the chameleon. With the public as censors, a tragedy applauded one day would be censored the next.

Historical tragedy and propagandistic writings, allegedly tragedies, distinctly separate in the sixteenth, seventeenth and eighteenth centuries, were fused during the Revolution into one powerful weapon to be wielded at will against the enemy. In fact, tragedy disappeared except in form. From the more than two thousand dramatic works written during the decade, there were less than fifty which were termed tragedies. About forty of these were drawn from contemporary events. Indeed, the stage had become a veritable laboratory in which the slightest incidents from contemporary life were transformed almost instantly to form the plot of tragedies, *drames* and comedies.

Out of this sea of productivity, hardly any name is known today. Fame, however, came to Marie-Joseph de Chénier, remembered more readily because of his unfortunate brother André rather than for his own talents as an author.[1]

---

[1] Dropping the particule in his name only in 1789, Marie-Joseph de

In five acts and in verse, *Marie de Brabant, reine de France* was the first of two new tragedies drawn from French natonal history and presented in 1789. Written by Barthélemi Imbert (1747-1790), a minor journalist born in Nîmes, *Marie de Brabant*, was presented only six times. The premiere occurred on September 9, 1789. [2]

Since its publication in 1744, Hénault's *Abrégé chronologique* was one of the most dependable sources for French history. Imbert leaned heavily on Hénault for the thread of his plot. The daughter of Henri III, Duc de Brabant, Marie had married Philippe III (1245-1285) in August, 1274. Philippe, the pious and honest but credulous son of Louis IX, after the death of the Queen Isabelle d'Aragon, had taken Marie as his second wife. Pierre de la Brosse, a valet de chambre and barber to Louis IX, had quickly demostrated an amazing influence over Philippe. The court was sharply critical of La Brosse and finally succeeded in bringing about his downfall through an accusation that he had poisoned the Dauphin. Marie had been accused of the same crime by La Brosse and imprisoned for some time.

The diabolical machinations of La Brosse to consolidate his power with the throne sustain the principal interest of the play. An interesting and amusing touch is the great concern of Jean, Duc de Brabant, with his sister's honor. There are two parallel love plots. The first, that of the King and Queen, is noble, beautiful and tragic. The second, fiery and young, between Eléonor, a relative and lady-in-waiting to Marie, and the handsome commoner D'Arméry, nephew of La Brosse, is dissimulated with difficulty.

The first act reveals the fiendish scheme of La Brosse to rid himself of Marie. As the play opens, the Queen and her brother are speak-

---

Chénier, the youngest of four sons, was born in Constantinople on August 28, 1764. His father, the French Consul General, brought Marie-Joseph as a young boy to Paris. There, the boy knew, through contact with them in his mother's salon, many influential people of the day. In 1781 he entered the army to become an officer. He had always been devoted to the theater and time free from duty gave him an opportunity to pursue his interest. He wrote his first tragedy, *Azémire*, in 1786. Ashamed of the play, he refused to include it in the *Recueil* of his theater published in 1801. Seeking to satisfy an ambition, Chénier combined political and literary careers. Without interruption, he was a member of all the legislative bodies in France from 1792-1801. He died in Paris on January 10, 1811.

[2] The edition consulted for this study was that published in Paris by Prault, 1790. *Pierre de la Brosse,* a morality play dating from the year 1278, treated materials similar to those in *Marie de Brabant.*

ing of their long separation. She has been married seven years and during that time has seen little of her family except the young and innocent Eléonor, a cousin. Marie has only praise for the King: «Philippe est... sage, religieux, sensible». (Act I, Scene I). She also loves the Dauphin, her stepson. Happiness would prevail at court if Pierre de la Brosse could by some magic be whisked away. Marie is afraid of him. Although all is apparently calm, she has a premonition of evil. The uxorious Philippe lauds his wife's patience and understanding toward the Dauphin, who is to be presented soon to his subjects. Expectation is shattered by an officer's anouncement that the Dauphin has been poisoned. Overcoming the initial shock, the King's reaction is one of anger toward subjects who would dare murder their Prince. La Brosse, probably the agent of the poison, although this is never revealed, confides in the King that, obnoxious as it may sound, the Queen would benefit more than any other from the Dauphin's death. Her elder son would then be in line for the throne. In a conversation with a friend La Brosse reveals he has sworn vengeance on Marie because of some unforgiveable discourtesy: «D'un déplaisir mortel elle a blessé mon coeur». (Act I, Scene VIII). The reader never learns of what this *déplaisir mortel* is constituted. Consuming ambition has made La Brosse a fanatic. The act ends with his stated intention of bringing tragedy to the royal house:

> Et que ce jour décide enfin après le roi,
> Qui doit régner ici de la reine ou de moi.
> (Act I, Scene VIII)

Act two pits Philippe against his wife. In carrying out plans to ruin Marie, La Brosse ushers in an old man whom he has bribed and who claims he overheard Marie plotting the death of her stepson. On the basis of this accusation the King orders the Queen's immediate arrest. Marie wanders through the palace; all eyes avoid her; she asks herself why and determines to demand some explanation of the King. In two very beautifully executed scenes, Philippe, confronted by his wife, cannot bear the thought that she is guilty, and yet he refuses to listen. In accordance with popular demand he has ordered the Queen's execution but hesitates because of his love:

> Quels combats déchirants! A son aspect, mon coeur
> Tresaille tour-à-tour de tendresse et d'horreur.
> (Act II, Scene II)

Act three shatters the reader's first hope of a truly fine drama. The old man who had come to accuse Marie has died. With no witnesses alive the King doubts the veracity of such a story. La Brosse, not dismayed, decides the only way to assure the Queen's quick death is through pitting Philippe against the Duc de Brabant. The latter accuses La Brosse of treason, who in turn challenges the Duke to a duel. Philippe is gratified to know such an old man as La Brosse will fight for his King. The Duke claims Philippe, only interested in divorce, has caused the Queen to be falsely accused. When the King learns this, he consents to see his wife. In a rather sorrowful scene Philippe tells Marie even if she were innocent, he could do nothing because he is at the mercy of the ignorant mobs who demand her death. This is totally incongruous with the pasty Philippe, who, although a tool at the mercy of La Brosse's fiendish ambition, certainly displayed more affection for his wife than the author permits here. The weakness of acceding to the public's wishes was also unnatural.

That La Brosse would go to any extent, even treason, to satisfy his ambition is depicted in the fourth act. Treason to one's country is unpardonable. Even the British ambrassador to whom La Brosse has sold state secrets warns of this. It is indeed strange that the ambassador who had bought state secrets from La Brosse would then issue a warning. To prove an otherwise useless point the author seems to be fascinated with heaping one more odious deed upon La Brosse. Preparations for the Queen's immediate execution continue. Almost drowned out by noises from the mob demanding her death, Marie plaintively begs her husband to kill her now but asks him to be kind to the Princes. The curtain closes on the two sons who, with arms outstretched, rush toward their father.

Act five depicts La Brosse's perdition. Marie, still awaiting death, is assured by Eléonor that the name of Brabant will be hailed again soon. On a darkened stage, La Brosse is filled with apprehension. The longer Marie lives, the less his star has its chance to shine. Suspecting that Arméry has been working against him, La Brosse resolves to murder his nephew. Pitiful cries issue from the wings. The King rushes out to discover what has happened. La Brosse, with perfect sang-froid, informs all that he has just killed Arméry. The deed was a most necessary one. According to him, Arméry had been consorting with the Queen. Marie passes, surrounded by guards and funereal torches, on her way to her death. Arméry, not fatally wounded as his uncle thought, arrives on the scene to produce a letter from the English ambassador in which La Brosse's treason is mentioned. Arméry will marry his beautiful Eléonor; La Brosse will be executed, and the King says to Marie: «Reine, il me reste encore mon peuple et votre coeur». (Act V, Scene XII).

Unlike many of the tragedies written in the latter years of the eighteenth century which conformed rather rigidly to the rules of classical tragedy in all other aspects except the three unities, *Marie de Brabant* adheres strictly to them. Those of time and place are particularly noted. All of the action takes place in a central room within the royal palace. The author is careful to note that the fifth act *se fait dans la nuit*.

There is little characterization in the play. Excepting Pierre de la Brosse, all of the characters appear as automatons. Every action is initiated by the fiendish La Brosse. The author's enthusiasm pushed him to create a grotesque portrait of the barber who had been elevated to such a high position. The constant allusions to de la Brosse lead the reader to think the author had contemplated naming his play *Pierre de la Brosse, intrigant par excellence*. Indeed, Philippe and his Queen are blanched beside this energetic agent of the devil whose heinous deeds culminated in the attempted murder of his nephew. The blows from La Brosse's sword, skilfully placed, must have wounded Arméry rather critically for the spectators are treated to sustained lamentations from the wings. Yet, D'Arméry appears shortly as a *deus ex machina* to deliver the English ambassador's letter. Although the audiences of 1790 were scarcely offended by blood, Imbert did not permit D'Arméry to appear naturally with his clothes spotted.

The number of presentations (six) does not reflect the good taste of dramatic audiences during the period, but rather acts as a barometer to indicate the waning popularity of tragedy and of the monarchy. Although vastly inferior to *Charles IX* in characterization and execution of plot, *Marie de Brabant* surpassed Chénier's tragedy in versification.

Marie-Joseph Chénier made his electrifying début in the field of tragedy with *Charles IX ou la Saint Barthélemi*. Presented at the Comédie-Française on November 4, 1789, the play was at once popular. Unknown before its performance, Chénier became overnight the idol throughout France of sympathizers in the Revolution. His fortunes, nevertheless, were not to remain so flattering. Censored by the

Comité du Salut Public for outspoken opinions on tyranny appearing in *Timoléon* (1794), he was virtually forced to cease activities as a dramatist. He was as equally unpopular with Napoleon.[3]

Of his tragedies, eleven in number, three had their sources in French history: *Charles IX* (1789), *La mort de Calas* (1791) and *Fénelon* (1793). The most important by far is *Charles IX*. The performance of this play on November 4, 1789, was an important event in the annals of the Comédie-Française. Just as the fall of the Bastille on July 14, 1789, marked symbolically the political end of the *ancien régime*, so did *Charles IX* bring the French Revolution to the stage.

Disappointed in the reception of *Azémire*, presented once at Fontainebleau in November, 1786, Chénier began work on *Charles IX*.[4] His sources were abundant. Besides the detailed account of the massacre that took place on Saint Bartholomew's Day contained in the work of the historian De Thou,[5] and the French translation of the biography of Coligny in Latin printed by the Elzevire brothers, Chénier availed himself of previous dramatic works on the subject.[6] Nathaniel Lee, an Englishman, had written a play in 1690 which he called *The Massacre of Paris*.[7] Louis-Sébastien Mercier and Baculard D'Arnaud had exploited materials on the same subject in writing *Jean Hennuyer, évêque de Lizieux* (1772) and *Coligni* (1739). The most important single influence on Chénier, however, must have been one of his favorite works, the *Henriade* of Voltaire.

The *Discours préliminaire* to *Charles IX* is a manifesto of the *tragédie nationale*. In choosing to write on the well-known event from French history, Chénier expressed his opinions not only toward the use of that field as a source but also on the purpose of tragedy. What he

---

[3] For a detailed study on the life of Chénier see A. Liéby, *Etude sur le théâtre de Marie-Joseph Chénier* (Paris: Société française d'imprimerie et de librairie, 1901).

[4] It was not until the third performance that the subtitle *ou l'école des rois* was added in place of *ou la Saint Barthélemi*. See Henry Lumière, *Le théâtre français pendant la Révolution* (Paris: E. Dentu, 1894), p. 27.

[5] Le Président J.-A. De Thou, *Historiarum sui temporis...* (Paris: M. Patieson, 1607).

[6] *Vie de Gaspard de Coligni* (1518-1572) (Leyde: Bonaventure et Abraham Elzevire, 1643). Written by Jean de Serres or François Hotman, the biography in Latin was entitled *Gaspariso Colinii, castellonii, magni quondam Franciae amirallie, vita* (no place, 1575).

[7] Nathaniel Lee, *Dramatic Works* (London: F. Clay, 1734), III, 289-347.

said in defense of the political role of tragedy was echoed through the years of the Revolution:

> ...les tragédies d'un peuple libre, d'un peuple éclairé, devraient toujours avoir un but moral et politique; et les principes de la morale et de la politique ne sauraient changer. [8]

Reinforcing his argument with examples from antiquity, he compared the sources of tragedy in the Greek theater and those of the French. He showed that because of frequent references to the Peloponnesian Wars, *Oedipus at Colonnus* of Sophocles was more interesting to Greek audiences. He found strictures applied by Richelieu on literature prevented the natural development of the *tragédie nationale* in France:

> Les malheurs de la France, occasionnés presque toujours par la faiblesse des rois, par le despotisme des ministres, et l'esprit fanatique du clergé, auraient nécessairement rempli de véritables pièces nationales. Le gouvernement n'était point assez raisonnable pour les permettre, et les Français n'étaient pas encore capables de les sentir. [9]

Chénier erroneously considered himself the author of the first *tragédie nationale*. He paid homage to Voltaire who had done important groundwork in preparation for his own play with mention of French names in *Zaire* and *Adélaïde du Guesclin*. [10] Interest in tragedy had encouraged Chénier to introduce celebrated events from French national history:

> J'avais cru qu'on pouvait rendre notre théâtre plus sévère encore que celui d'Athènes; j'avais cru qu'on pouvait chasser de la tragédie ce fatras d'idées mythologiques et de fables monstrueuses, toujours répétées dans les anciens poètes. J'ai du moins saisi la seule gloire ou il m'était permis d'aspirer, celle d'ouvrir la route et de composer le premier une tragédie vraiment nationale. [11]

Without citing other authors and *tragédies nationales,* he attacked De Belloy's acquiescence in serving the vanity of several powerful houses

---

[8] Marie-Joseph de Chénier, *Theatre* (Paris: Foulon et Cie, 1818), I, 100.
[9] Chénier, *op. cit.,* I, 83.
[10] *Ibid.,* p. 90.
[11] *Ibid.,* p. 92.

in the nobility and certainly that of the King. The result, then, of *Le siège de Calais* was far from being historical nor did it follow in the path of common sense.[12]

Chénier dramatized events of the massacre because he considered it the most tragic of all events from modern history. Sensing opposition to his choice of subject, he maintained there was no indecency in showing a French king on the stage at the same time guilty of homicide and perjury. To him Charles, then twenty-two years old, was a hypocrite. In the choice of subject, Chénier had selected, under the guise of historical tragedy, a propitious moment to indict the present government:

> Le massacre de la Saint-Barthélemi n'est point le crime de la nation; c'est le crime d'un de vos rois; et il ne faut point confondre vos rois avec la patrie, malgré les maximes d'esclave qu'on vous débite à vos théâtres, dans vos prétendues pièces nationales; c'est le crime de Charles IX, de sa mère, du duc de Guise, du Cardinal de Lorraine; c'est le crime du gouvernement.[13]

Nevertheless, Chénier dedicated his play to Louis XVI. The events of this ignoble period as recorded by historians were closely followed by Chénier. However, he accorded important rôles to the Cardinal de Lorraine and Michel de L'Hôpital. The Cardinal was in Rome on a mission at the time of the massacre and Hôpital had ceased his function four years before. Chénier revealed his belief as to how history was to be used in explaining these incongruities:

> ...il serait absurde d'exiger d'un poète qui compose une tragédie nationale la scrupuleuse exactitude d'un historien. Dans une tragédie, il suffit de ne faire agir des personnages que d'une manière conforme à leur caractère connu.[14]

As Chénier depicted them, Catherine has no other passion but to deceive and command—governing her son, but in turn herself governed by the De Guises. Cardinal de Lorraine and his nephew, the Duc de Guise, are proud, audacious and despicable; Charles IX is feeble

---

[12] *Ibid.*, p. 93.
[13] *Ibid.*, p. 98.
[14] Chénier, *op. cit.*, p. 99.

and consequently easily swayed; Admiral Coligny is full of hate but is patriotic; L'Hôpital is eminently virtuous; and Henry IV is young but respected.

Charles IX was received by the Comédie-Française on September 2, 1788.[15] Of course, the play had to be read privately before public presentation of it was definitely decided. The reaction to one of the private readings was noted by the Marquis de Luchet:

> M. Chénier a lu (le 13 janvier 1789) chez M. le vicomte de Ségur une tragédie intitulée *Charles IX*. Mme la duchesse d'Orléans et M. le prince Henri ont assisté à cette séance fort longue, et fort nombreuse. Personne n'a été emu; beaucoup ont baîllé, et tous se sont écriés que c'etait admirable.[16]

After it had been received by the Comédie-Française, *Charles IX* was quickly censored. Chénier immediately began a personal campaign against Suard, the royal censor, calling him an agent of tyranny. Persisting in his course of demanding that the tragedy be presented, Chénier procured the aid of friends in distributing brochures advertising his composition. Eventually, the pressure became so great as to require the ruling of Bailly, mayor of Paris, who felt censorship should be maintained.[17] The negative response spurred Chénier to present his problem before the municipal assembly where he declared himself in favor of the total abolition of any form of censure. Following his impassioned plea, permission was granted for the presentation of the play.

With such publicity *Charles IX* was guaranteed notoriety, but additional interest was generated due to polemics among the actors of the Comédie-Française concerning the distribution of rôles. Saint-Phal refused to play the rôle of Charles IX in preference to that of the King of Navarre which he considered more consistent and more important. This refusal on the part of Saint-Phal opened the way for Talma to play a serious rôle. Although a member of the troupe since 1787, he had been given only minor parts:

---

[15] Liéby, *op. cit.*, p. 33.
[16] Cited by Edmond and Jules de Goncourt, *Histoire de la société française pendant la Révolution* (Paris: Bibliothèque Charpentier, 1914), p. 45.
[17] Liéby, *op. cit.*, p. 40.

Reçu depuis peu de temps, cet acteur ne jouait que trés rarement, ou s'il paraissait quelquefois sur la scene, c'était pour remplir des rôles accessoires dédaignés par les premiers sujets (acteurs). [18]

The interpretation of the vacillating king was Talma's first gigantic step as a tragic actor.

Saint-Phal, although ostensibly refusing to play Charles IX because the rôle was not important enough for him, probably did not accept for political reasons. It was during the months from September, 1788, to November, 1789, that the first signs of discord among members of the Comédie-Française were evident, leading, of course, to inevitable schism between those who supported the monarchy and those in favor of the new *régime*. Talma was the leader of the *avancés* or the *escadre rouge* as he and his cohorts were called by the old guard. He had as his ardent supporters Dugazon and Mme Vestris, sister of the latter. The conservative faction or *les noirs* was much more numerous. Along with the leader, the fiery Naudet, there were Larive, Saint-Prix, Saint-Phal, Fleury, Dazincourt, Florence, Champville, Mesdames Emilie and Louise Contat, Raucourt, Devienne, Joly and Langue. [19] The political importance of the Comédie-Française was reflected also in its change of name to the Théâtre de la Nation after the Easter recess of 1789. However, the actors kept the title of *Comédiens ordinaires du Roi* until the King's ignominious flight to Varennes (June, 1791).

Just as Jean-Louis David in painting and Marie-Joseph Chénier in literature embodied Revolutionary principles so did Jean-Baptiste Talma on the stage. Since the theater served the same purpose as other media of communication do today, especially newspapers, radio and television, Talma was an extremely important figure in the rapid growth of the Revolution. Before discussing *Charles IX*, its reception and influence, a brief sketch of Talma's life up to November, 1789, will emphasize his import not only as an actor but will also serve as a key to an accurate appraisal of him.

François-Joseph Talma was born in Paris on January 15, 1766. [20] His father, valet de chambre to an Englishman, had greater aspira-

---

[18] Etienne and Martainville, *op. cit.*, I, 48.
[19] Welschinger, *op. cit.*, p. 524.
[20] François-Joseph Talma, *Mémoires* Ed. Alexandre Dumas (Paris: Hip-

tions. He studied dentistry assiduously with the intention of setting up his own practice. When his employer left France, Talma's father enrolled his son in a private school and followed the master. After his studies, Talma joined his father in London where the latter had already begun the practice of dentistry. Young Talma became an apprentice to his father but had little interest in the work. He was devoted to the theater, and, responding to a desire to act, had joined a small group of devotees.

Talma left London sometime in 1785 and returned to Paris where he too exercised the trade of his father. During the next eighteen months while continuing in dentistry, he took courses at the *Conservatoire de déclamation (L'Ecole royale dramatique)*. Dugazon, Fleury, and Molé —all very celebrated actors in their own right— were his teachers. He succeeded in being added to the troupe of the Comédie-Française and made his début on November 21, 1787. His first rôle was that of Séide in *Mahomet* by Voltaire. Of the young actor, the *Journal de Paris* said: «Le jeune homme qui a débuté hier par le rôle de Séide annonce les plus heureuses dispositions; il a, d'ailleurs, tous les avantages naturels».[21]

During the two years at the Comédie-Française before *Charles IX*, Talma had become, through a mutual interest in antiquity, a very close friend to the painter Jean-Louis David. Talma's natural audacity was made apparent by his interest in historical exactitude of costume. This was an aspect of tragedy that had been all but neglected.

Talma was named *sociétaire* on April 1, 1789. As was the tradition, the newest *sociétaire* was scheduled to give the *Discours d'ouverture* following the Easter closing. Talma, in this capacity, delivered the discourse which, strangely enough, was written by Marie-Joseph Chénier. Filled with allusions to the crisis faced by the nation, Chénier had put into the speech much of his personal feeling toward the prejudice against *Charles IX*.

Briefly stated, events leading to the Saint Bartholomew's Day Massacre were precipitated by the peace of August, 1570, which conceded

---

polyte Souverain, 1849). Most of the remarks relating to Talma's life are taken from the above. A fairly informative biography is that of Alfred Copin, *Talma et la Révolution* (Paris: Bibliothèque des Deux Mondes, L. Frinzine et Cie., 1887).

[21] Copin, *op. cit.*, p. 17.

full amnesty to the Protestants with the right of public worship extended to them under certain restrictions. [22] Their power was increased when Admiral Coligny arrived at Blois on September 12, 1571, to confer with Charles IX on state problems. Coligny's main contention was that France's inner turmoil would be lessened by a foreign war to be waged in Flanders against Spain. Charles appeared very interested in the scheme. It never reached fruition because of intrigues in the court against Coligny. Finally, it appeared that the marriage of Henri de Navarre and Marguerite de Valois, sister of Charles, solemnized on August 21, 1572, would end the struggle between Protestants and Catholics. This was not the case. While returning to his house in the Rue de l'arbre sec, on the night of August 22, 1572, Coligny was shot by Maurevel, the King's assassin, as he was called. Two bullets struck Coligny; one severed the first finger of the right hand, the other wounded him in the left arm. This unfortunate incident resulting from the tense atmosphere of thousands of Protestants in Paris, a Catholic city, led to the catastrophe which started on Sunday, August 24, and lasted that day and the following two days. The news spread from Paris to the Provinces, and every city had its own Massacre. This scourge brought death, some say, to upwards of 100,000 souls. Conservative estimates set the figure at 20,000.

Cast in the mold of a classical tragedy, *Charles IX* would be an excellent play if Chénier had not allowed his political opinions to color historical verisimilitude. Since, as in the Greek tragedies, the events were already known, the main interest of the audience was vested in character. In the first act the author skilfully portrayed every major character in the play. The action takes place in Paris at the Louvre. As the curtain rises, Coligny and the young Henri de Navarre are deep in conversation about their homelands. Coligny is at court only at the behest of Jeanne d'Albret (died June 9, 1572), Henri's mother, who wanted the Admiral to remain a close adviser to her son. By lambasting court life Coligny establishes the tone of the play—censure of the monarchy: «Parmi les courtisans je viens sans confiance». (Act I, Scene I). Attempts on his life did not frighten him because he would continue serving France. He expresses his undying hate of the

---

[22] For a detailed study, from which my comments have been taken, see Henry White, *The Massacre of St. Bartholomew* (New York: Harper & Brothers, 1868).

De Guise family. Henri, on the eve of his wedding to Marguerite de Valois, has a foreboding of evil to come, suggested by blood-colored dice that he had thrown during the day. He had rather return to his native Béarn where the active life draws a sharp contrast to the *mollesse* of the court at Paris. Michel de L'Hôpital is very happy with the prospect that at long last the devastating wars will end with the marriage of Marguerite to Henri.

After the prelude in which Coligny is depicted as a man of great valor, Henri as young but wise, and L'Hôpital as a pillar of virtue, the diabolical characters of Catherine, Lorraine, De Guise and Charles are all the more striking. Catherine enters whispering to Lorraine:

> Flattons nos ennemis; ne nous trahissons pas
> Ce jour verra la paix, cette nuit leur trépas.
> (Act I, Scene III)

Act one ends with the treaty between Protestants and Catholics signed and sealed by the King's gift of an ancestral sword to Coligny.

Catherine's deceit and her son's vacillation in the face of positive action overshadow the entire second act. As soon as the treaty binding all parties together is signed, Catherine, alone with Charles, pushes for the murder of Coligny and all Protestants in Paris. If he thinks a king has friends, he should remember: «...un roi n'a point d'amis». (Act II, Scene I). Every action in appearance friendly is done only through self-interest. Catherine bids her son to be particularly chary of Coligny for he would relish being master. Demonstrating his easy persuasion, Charles replies in what would seem a totally unwarranted fashion that he too is convinced of Coligny's consuming ambition: «Je l'ai souvent pensé, je le sens, je le crois». (Act II, Scene I).

Lorraine chastizes the King for not purifying France in doing the will of the Eternal. He means, of course, the annihilation of every living Protestant. Charles shows sings of greatness when he observes that the flow of blood hardly seemed to fit the will of the Eternal. Lorraine remonstrates that Charles will have to answer for his deeds. This frightens the King into saying exactly what his mother and Lorraine wanted: «Je répandrai le sang de ce peuple perfide». (Act II, Scene II.)

The scene switches to Coligny and his preoccupation with peace through war with Spain in Flanders. Charles is sincerely fond of Coligny, and promises to follow the good advice of his trusted friend. The admiral cautions Charles concerning a leader for the French forces. Neither Retz, Guise nor Tavannes could be trusted because they were all in league with Philip II of Spain. The new leader would be none other than the young Henri of Navarre. One army, led by Coligny, would cross the Pyrenees and another, under Henri, would march into Belgium. Charles accepts the plan. Coligny closes the interview with fatherly advice to the young King:

> Evitez les malheurs des rois trop complaisans;
> Ne laissez point sans cesse au gré des courtisans,
> Errer de main en main l'autorité suprême.
> Soyez roi de France et non de votre cour.
> (Act II, Scene III)

When with the Catholic faction Charles does not possess strength necessary to withstand their crushing determinism. After thanking Coligny for his good advice, the King turns to say: «Je le hais dès l'enfance». (Act II, Scene IV). It develops that Henri is not to be massacred. If that should be allowed, then it would be the same as Catherine sacrificing her own daughter. The massacre is set to begin at midnight. Charles is filled with terror, but does not contradict his mother's will.

Act three pits the liberal and honorable L'Hôpital against the arch conservative and bigoted Lorraine who entones the wrath of God upon the rebels:

> Un seul (culte) doit réunir nos peuples et nos rois,
> Et tous les protestans sont ennemis des lois.
> (Act III, Scene I)

Lorraine apostrophizes L'Hôpital for his policy of appeasement. Charles has been persuaded to revoke the edict of 1562 permitting Protestants freedom of worship. Actually the first peace between Protestants and Catholics was concluded in 1563, the second in 1568 and the third in 1570. It is now the moment for all people to be united under the banner of Catholicism. Only L'Hôpital abstains in his approbation. The act ends with Charles, typically unsure, postponing the final decision a little longer.

Act four begins with Charles who, alone in meditation, wonders what he should do. He decides the initial order sanctioning the massacre should be revoked. Catherine, in the meanwhile, has already dispatched orders sealing the death of Coligny and consequently of all Protestants. In a fit of anger Charles insults his mother who immediately threatens to leave. He begs her to stay. Coligny reveals he has been accused in a plot to murder the King. This rumor was circulated by the Catholics. Coligny and De Guise in a rare display of histrionic acrobatics release all the anger pent up over the years against each other. The clock strikes and Lorraine blesses those in his presence charging them to commit barbaric acts: «Couvrez-vous saintement du sang des criminels». (Act IV, Scene V). The bells of Parisian churches heighten the impact of his charge.

The fifth act opens with Henri and L'Hôpital securely locked in an apartment of the Louvre. Although they have not been told verbally of the massacre, the tolling of bells announces Coligny's murder and the slaughter of Protestants. L'Hôpital predicts the horror with which subsequent generations will read of this event and entones the moral lesson of the entire play:[23]

«Le crime est sur le trône; il est temps de mourir». (Act V, Scene II). The triumphant assassins enter Henri's chamber. Powerless, Henri lashes out at Catherine:

> Cet art, à nos Francais si longtemps étranger,
> De flatter sa victime avant de l'égorger,
> Que ne le laissiez-vous au fond de l'Italie?
> (Act V, Scene III)

The last scene of the play shows the King crazy from fear and self-reproach:

---

[23] Chénier contended later this play was a condemnation of civil war, not of the monarchy. The following is cited from a letter recorded by the Goncourt brothers in their notable work, *La société française pendant la Révolution*, p. 147:

> En peignant la rage des guerres civiles, cette tragédie ne peut qu'en inspirer l'horreur. En peignant un roi perfide, sanguinaire et bourreau de son peuple, cette tragédie doit faire aimer plus que jamais le gouvernement d'un monarque second père du peuple et restaurateur de la liberté française, digne héritier de cet Henri IV, dont j'ai voulu présenter la jeunesse à l'amour d'une nation généreuse et libre. (Quoted from *Catalogue d'autographes*, 8 avril 1884.)

> Et je suis tout couvert du sang de mes sujets
> J'ai trahi la patrie, et l'honneur, et les lois
> Le ciel en me frappant donne un exemple aux rois.
> (Act V, Scene IV)

The curtain fell on an audience already greatly excited by recent events—notably the fall of the Bastille, the march to Versailles by the women of Paris, and work of the National Assembly, particularly the abolishment of all hereditary titles. Every seat at the Comédie-Française had been sold out in advance. All printed editions of the play were expended as soon as they appeared.[24] The receipts, upwards of five thousand *livres* for the first six performances, never fell below three thousand after a series of twenty-three performances in two months.[25] The play was presented a total of thirty-six times in this and the following year. It was last presented at the Comédie-Française in 1900.[26] The first thirty-three performances passed unhampered by censorship. It was finally imposed, upon the insistence of the clergy, by the King himself.[27]

The plot, as conceived and executed by Chénier, is indeed powerful. Although there is no action, interest is maintained through characterization. The depiction of Charles IX as a mercurial madman, at times great, at others weak and hypocritical, reveals true dramatic talent. Nevertheless, Chénier allowed his political sympathies to exercise ascendancy over the restraint of art. History proves that of all the party, Charles was the least guilty and the most to be pitied. The use of the Alexandrine posed no unusual problem to Chénier. Only the speeches of Charles, however, contain any true mastery.

Critical opinion was universally favorable. Chénier was hailed as a genius, *Charles IX* as a welcome addition to the otherwise monotonous bourgeois dramas of the day. Besides the audacious theme of showing a French king ordering the massacre of his people, the tragedy had more laudable qualities. The foremost, and that which added to the interest of the play, was the total absence of a love element, an aspect which had hampered the growth of the *tragédie nationale*. Ché-

---

[24] The Frères Goncourt, *L'histoire de la société française pendant la Révolution*, p. 48.
[25] Lièby, *op. cit.*, p. 54.
[26] Joannidès, *op. cit.*, p. 20.
[27] Copin, *op. cit.*, p. 39.

nier had formulated his opinion toward the use of love in historical tragedy from an observation made by Voltaire many years before. «Si l'amour n'est pas tragique... il doit régner seul: il n'est pas fait pour la seconde place.» [28] A further innovation, whose need was sorely apparent in the long, prosaic *tragédies nationales* preceding *Charles IX*, was the suppression of confidents. Chénier found them «froids et parasites qui n'entrent jamais dans l'action». [29] The performance of the play was further enhanced by a serious attempt at historical exactitude in costume. The *Journal de la mode et du goût* contained an interesting commentary:

> Charles IX a les cheveux noirs, sans poudre; il porte des moustaches et au menton un petit bouquet de barbe à l'escopette; fraize de gaze blanche à gros plis, manteau de velours noir galonné d'or, pourpoint de satin blanc à petits carreaux galonné d'or et à deux rangs de boutons d'or. [30]

Theatrical events of the year 1790 were dominated by the quarrel over *Charles IX*. However, one of the first tragedies presented in the early months of that year was *Louis XII, père du peuple*. This laconic drama was written by Charles Ronsin (1752-1794), a *capitaine d'honneur* of the Parisian guards. Presented at the Comédie-Française on February 12, 1790, disturbance in the theater was so great, the play could not be performed in its entirety. The author explains in the *avertissement* why he thought the work should be published:

> La représentation de cette tragédie ayant été fort orageuse, et le Public n'ayant pu l'entendre, et par conséquent la juger, l'auteur a cru devoir la livrer à l'impression. Il est loin de croire qu'un ouvrage composé en un mois, puisse être sans défauts; mais il se flatte que tous les bons François applaudiront aux sentiments qui l'ont porté á traiter un sujet qu'il avoit cru propre à ramener le calme dans les esprits, en proscrivant la fureur des exécutions populaires, et dans lequel il offroit à ses Concitoyens une occasion de rendre un hommage éclatant au jeune Héros qui défend notre liberté avec

---

[28] Voltaire, *op. cit.*, III, 182.
[29] Chénier, *op. cit.*, I, 102.
[30] Cited by Frères Goncourt, *Histoire de la société française pendant la Révolution*, pp. 48-49 from *Journal de la mode et du goût*, by Lebrun, April, 1790.

autant de sagesse que de courage, et à un Roi qui, en venant habiter parmi nous, a rempli si dignement la promesse qu'il avoit faite de n'être qu'un avec son Peuple.[31]

The clemency of a benevolent monarch is the theme. Events in the play supposedly center around the return of Louis XII to Lyon after a six month absence on an expedition to Italy.[32] While the King was away an unscrupulous minister misused power that had been delegated him. This drama, in which there is no tragic action, is in three acts and in verse.

The first act centers around Louis LeMore, Duc de Milan, captured by the Chevalier Bayard and imprisoned at Lyon. The Duke comes forth from his cell. After a long soliloquy which reveals the Duke has been in prison six months, and has not talked to anyone during that endless period, Montale, a common laborer, comes to share the dungeon life. Ronsin seizes every opportunity to remind his audience that Louis XII, evidently meant to be Louis XVI, is known as *Le père du peuple*. Even the Duc de Milan recognizes this fact although it does not help him any:

> François, vous voyez tous un Dieu dans votre Roi.
> Père de ses Sujets, c'est un tyran pour moi.
> (Act I, Scene II)

Montale appropriately defends his King, and tells why he is in prision. He led a revolt against Héroët, Louis' finance minister, who has been exploiting the populace with unduly heavy taxes. Héroët ordered a quick execution for Montale. This rash action is halted by the venerable Bayard whose stature Ronsin unwittingly depicts as even greater than the King's. Bayard is surprised to see the Duke treated as a common prisoner and promises to initiate a change of status for him immediately. Reticent in accepting Bayard's aid, the Duke proclaims proudly:

> La nuit de mon cachot m'inspire moins d'effroi;
> J'en préfère l'horreur à cette cour barbare.

---

[31] The edition consulted: Charles Ronsin, *Louis XII* (Paris: L. Potier, 1790).

[32] For a treatment of Louis XII see Théodore Godefroy, *Histoire de Louis XII, roi de France, père du peuple, et des choses mémorables advenues de son règne, depuis l'an 1498 jusques à l'an 1515*. (Paris: A. Pacard, 1615).

The entire first act abounds in incongruities. First, it is difficult to surmise why the Duke should play a major role in an action which has little to do with either Louis or Héroët. To this is added the presentation of the Chevalier Bayard who claims he did not know anything about the Duke's imprisonment. Bayard had been at court during these six months. Why had not he known the whereabouts of such an important man as the Duke? Further, why had Bayard not thwarted Héroët's tyranny?

The action of the second act switches to the vestibule of a palace. This act signals the return of Louis from his Italian campaigns. He finds his subjects, while enthusiastic in their welcome, are not the happy lot he left behind: «J'ai vu sur tous les fronts une ombre de tristesse». (Act II, Scene III). Bayard tells the King of great injustices perpetrated by Héroët. To show his democracy, Bayard suggests Montale be allowed to relate Héroët's atrocities. Montale, the laborer, embodies the spirit of those loyal monarchists who not only at the beginning, but throughout the Revolution, struggled to effect a reconciliation among dissident factions working for the permanent abolishment of the monarchy. A great percentage of the monarchists were from the ranks of the peasantry. Montale is by far the most interesting person in the play. His fervent devotion to his King and to justice is obviously sincere:

> Nous vivons dans un temps de désordre et d'horreur,
> Ou des adulateurs, les maximes infâmes,
> Des venins du mensonge ont infecté les âmes,
> Et traitent lâchement de peuple révolté
> Un peuple ami du trône et de la liberté.
>
> (Act II, Scene IV)

Greatly impressed with Montale, the King relegates to him the duty of freeing the Duke. Meanwhile, Louis promises justice to all. A touch of spectacle is added when Bayard orders the bourgeois militia groups to swear their fealty. The martial music was doubtlessly included by the author as a concession to the growing revolutionary spirit.

Act three resumes a principal theme of the play—the equality of man. Confronted by the King and Bayard, Héroët epitomizes that indifference to humanity so characteristic of power-crazed men. Louis reminds Héroët of the equality of all men, and Bayard adds his sanction to the King's words with even a stronger statement:

> Sire, je dirai plus: le simple agriculteur
> Qui dans ses longs travaux vieillit avec honneur,
> Vaut bien le chevalier qu'illustre son courage;
> L'un féconde la terre, et l'autre la ravage.
> (Act III, Scene IV)

Louis orders Héroët bound in chains to await a final sentence. Montale, whose generosity of soul is another of the themes in the play, is consistent when he begs Louis not to permit Héroët's death. This request astounds all present. The King is so moved, he deems exile an appropriate punishment for the criminal.

The mobs cry for Héroët's death. Louis charges them to leave the heavy burden of justice with the throne. Awed by the presence of the King, the mobs kneel in obeissance. This action prompts Bayard to pronounce the final moral dictum:

> Profitez, ô Louis, de cet exemple auguste;
> Que le meilleur des Rois soit aussi le plus juste.
> (Act III, Scene VI)

Louis will remain at home to govern his subjects. All France will unite together for the common good.

Although its intentions are worthy, the play is a fiasco. There is no action, no analysis of character, nor beautiful poetry. The speeches are long and bombastic. The plea to remain calm and obedient to the King in the face of a crisis was laudable enough, but it fell on deaf ears already atuned to dissolution of the monarchy. The play has only one characteristic typical of classical tragedy. Apparently Ronsin thought the choice of subject and the fact that his play was written in verse qualified *Louis XII* as a tragedy. There is no attention paid to the unities, not even to that of action; there is no tragic event; the most outstanding character is a man of the people, and there are only three acts. The play is nothing more than a propagandistic sermon in dialogue. The author took a popular king, fabricated a purely imaginary incident during his reign, and placed it within a modern frame. Such an ambition is even difficult for a literary giant; Ronsin is small even among dwarfs.

Although *Charles IX* had been censored following its thirty-second presentation, Chénier, Talma and their followers had not ceased in their efforts to have it reinstated. The audiences were particularly restive and, imbued with revolutionary fervor, they clamored for their favorite play, or manifesto as it was. The composition of theatrical audiences in 1790 has been aptly described by Etienne and Martainville:

> Le parterre de la Comédie-Française présentait chaque jour en raccourci, le tableau d'un peuple en révolution qui, tout étonné d'avoir recouvré ses droits, en fait un usage souvent peu raisonné. Les comédiens ne pouvaient établir aucun ordre dans leur répertoire. Une piece etait mise à l'etude et le parterre mutin, ou remué par des gens intéressés, réclamait à grands cris la représentation d'un autre ouvrage, auquel les reglements n'assignaient qu'un rang postérieur. Enfin, le théâtre et le parterre semblaient être les camps de deux armées ennemies; mais on doit dire, à l'honneur des loges, qu'elles gardèrent la plus exacte neutralité.[33]

The internal political quarrel in the Comédie-Française did little to improve the situation. Talma and Naudet were actively engaged in an altercation. Such a schism between two of the leading actors only served to leave the whole company at one another's throats. An unruly public demanded the founding of a new theater in which true tragedies of the Revolution could be presented by actors untarnished by sympathy in the monarchy. The idea of a new theater, separate from the tainted Comédie-Française, gained subtantial support each day. The receipts of the one theater were indeed small. The fact that another was a growing reality filled the entire company with consternation. Such was the state of affairs when Dazincourt, an ardent monarchist, gave the traditional address at the Easter closing on March 20, 1790. In his address, skilfully worded, Dazincourt made an appeal to the audience not to be impatient with works that were already committed for presentation. He promised unflagging devotion among the actors. He alluded to public opposition that had been manifested toward the company and to the internal disturbances which hindered its efficiency:

> Une jalouse cupidité dont nous ne nous permettrons pas de dévoiler le secret, et qui voudrait s'élever sur nos débris,

---

[33] Etienne et Martainville, *op. cit.*, I, 89.

a cherché constamment, depuis des mois, à fatiguer et décourager notre zèle.[34]

The speech was evidently written to express the hope of seeing a spirit of solidarity once again in the Comédie-Française. Reason, however, was not to prevail.

Following the Easter recess the doors of the Comédie-Française opened again on April 12, 1790. In order to encourage increased attendance, Naudet announced a new plan by which less solvent citizens could enjoy the theater more frequently. Six hundred seats at a very moderate price were to be reserved for the benefit of the poor.[35] During the ensuing months, a decree issued on January 13, 1791, permitting the establishment of any number of theaters in Paris superseded the need of such an innovation.[36]

In the meanwhile, the two camps in the Comédie were becoming more hotile. Talma, exempted by ironclad rules from playing important rôles, was anxious to place himself again in the limelight. This meant reinstating *Charles IX*. To this end Talma resorted to circulating several petitions in his favor, but was unsuccessful in getting any response from the authorities. His efforts were rewarded when the Comte de Mirabeau, his friend and the famous representative from Provence, requested of the Comédie-Française that *Charles IX* be given on July 14 in commemoration of Bastille Day. Mirabeau was received cordially by actors at the Comédie and assured the play would be presented only upon public demand. Not satisfied with his reception, Mirabeu led a delegation to the Comédie on July 21, 1790.[37] As the curtain rose on *Epiménide*, in which was depicted the reaction of a man who had awakened after sleeping many years, there was a concerted request that *Charles IX* be presented. Naudet appeared quickly to inform the audience that *Charles IX* could not be played any time soon. Saint-Prix (Cardinal de Lorraine) and Mme. Vestris (Catherine) were sick. This announcement seemed to calm the audience. However, Talma, judging this was his moment, rushed on the stage to say that Mme. Vestris could play although somewhat

---

[34] *Ibid.*, p. 92.
[35] *Ibid.*, p. 95.
[36] Welschinger, *op. cit.*, p. 98.
[37] Béatrix Dussane, *La Comédie-Française* (Paris: La Renaissance du livre, 1921), p. 90.

indisposed. Saint-Prix, who was suffering from erysipalis could not be expected to appear. His rôle would be read by Grammont. The enthusiastic response of the audience assured immediate presentation of *Charles IX.* The performance was impeded by a noisy and restless house. It was summer. The receipts were small. Chénier took the occasion to accuse the actors of being prejudiced against him. If they were not, they would have postponed presenting the tragedy until autumn.

Smarting from this insult and exasperated with Talma's iconoclastic actions, the actors among the conservative and more established element of the company voted to expel the fiery inferior from their ranks. Bailly, the mayor of Paris, tried to placate ill feelings with compromise. He suggested the Comédie reinstate Talma. The actors held to their previous decision. Finally, on September 16, 1790, the situation exploded, resulting in extensive damage to the theater and an attempt on the lives of the actors, saved only by armed intervention from the police.

The conservative actors naturally lost a hopeless but valiant battle. On September 28 Talma was reinstated in full standing. *Charles IX* was presented without incident to a full house the next day. Had the actors not accepted Talma, the Comédie-Française was to be closed indefinitely. This sort of pressure was so distasteful it moved Contat and Raucourt to resign. Mlle. Contat penned a letter to the remaining actors in which she severely condemned Talma.[38]

Talma had this time become the incarnation of the Revolutionary spirit. If there had been any doubts before where his sympathies lay, they were dispelled by public admission of his unqualified endorsement of the Revolution. In a letter he wrote to a M. de Coupigny on December 25, 1790, Talma said:

> Que de siècles, mon ami, se sont écoulés depuis votre depart! Il me semble être dans un monde imaginaire. Que de choses nouvelles pressées, accumulées dans ce court espace de temps! Oh! mon ami, que d'abus détruits, que de préjugés vaincus, quelle foule d'institutions bizarres anéanties! Quel triomphe pour la philosophie.[39]

---

[38] Henri Lumière, *Le Théâtre Français pendant la Révolution* (Paris: E. Dentu, 1894), p. 66.

[39] Copin, *op. cit.*, p. 62.

One of the most celebrated heroes of French history is Jean Calas. It is not so much what he did that has made him famous but rather what was done to him. His martyrdom in 1763 at the hands of fanatics and his subsequent exoneration through the efforts of Voltaire epitomized the spirit of tolerance so characteristic of the period of enlightenment. The first tragedy treating Jean Calas was presented at the Comédie-Française on December 18, 1790. The moderate, Jean-Louis Laya, was the author of *Jean Calas*.[40] As part of the preface to the play, Laya included Voltaire's *Traité sur la tolérance* in which the Calas affair was fully discussed. Laya professed not to have altered any of the principal facts as stated by Voltaire.[41]

On October 13, 1761, the Calas family, whose father, Jean, was a prosperous Huguenot shopkeeper in Toulouse, had its life abruptly changed by the suicide of one of the sons, Marc-Antoine.[42] His death was precipitated most likely by disappointment in not being able to become a lawyer because of his religious upbringing. The boy was naturally morose and given to melancholy. There is no information which would indicate his ever wishing to become a Catholic.

The father was accused by fanatic mobs of having murdered his son because the latter wanted to abjure the family's faith. This appears totally incongruous. An elder son, Louis, had become a Catholic two years before. Further, a faithful servant to the family was a fervent Catholic. Lastly, and most obvious, Calas was sixty-eight years old. It would seem unnatural that he could overpower a vigorous and resisting youth. The entire family and a guest were accused of being accomplices in the crime.

In spite of the overwhelming evidence in his favor, Calas was tried and found guilty by a vote of eight to five. The sentence was death on the wheel. The two daughters of Calas were forced into a convent, his two sons banished forever, and all the Calas property confiscated by the crown. The sentence was carried out on March 9, 1763.

Voltaire heard about the injustice indirectly from a friend who had stopped off at Ferney for a visit. When he heard the story, Voltaire

---

[40] Jean-Louis Laya, *Jean Calas* (Paris: Maradan et Perlet, 1791).
[41] *Ibid.*, p. v.
[42] *Le traité sur la tolérance* is found in Volume IV, 13-115, of the *Oeuvres complètes* of Voltaire.

did not believe French justice could go so far amiss. Nevertheless, after little investigation, he discovered the horrible truth. This spurred him to work for the rehabilitation of the Calas family. Although much has been written on the case, *Le traité sur la tolérance* contains the most lucid statement of opinions. Voltaire's interest and influence resulted in a review of the case by the Parlement de Paris. By its pronouncement handed down on March 9, 1765, the entire family was cleared. This was the second anniversary of the father's execution.

Although it reflected growing animosity toward the clergy, and was by any standard acerbic in its attack against Catholicism, *Jean Calas* was not a popular play. There were only seven performances of it at the Comédie-Française, three in 1790 and four in 1791.[43]

In addition to the inclusion of an historical *précis*, Laya expressed appreciation to the actors who participated in the play's first performances. He was particularly generous in his praise of Vanhove who took the rôle of Calas. Other prominent actors were Mlle. Thénard (Mme. Calas), Fleury (LaSalle), Mlle. Joly (Jeannette), Saint-Phal (Lavaisse) and Mme. Petit (Rose).

Written in the traditional form of a tragedy with five acts and in verse, the action takes place in Toulouse. The first two acts are in the apartment of M. Calas. The action of the play begins a few moments before the death of Marc-Antoine Calas. He is presented as an erstwhile gambler who has fawned upon the kindness of his sixty-eight year old father. As the play opens, the audience seees an apparently peaceful bourgeois scene. M. and Mme. Calas, their daughter Rose, her admirer Lavaisse, and Jeannette, a family retainer, are in the sitting room. Lavaisse is reading from a book on religion. He interrupts his reading from time to time with a comment on the preponderant ignorance of Catholics at Toulouse. What appeared to be a peaceful scene is soon dissipated as Calas unfurls the family difficulties. Of the five children, three are still at home. Louis, an elder son, renounced Protestantism two years previously. After leaving home he opened a business of his own; at present he finds life very hard. To show that he has no prejudice against Louis, the father sends him a tidy sum each quarter to help underwrite expenses in the tottering business adventure. Antoine is a boy of talent, but very melancholic.

---

[43] Joannidès, *op. cit.*, p. 60.

Lavaisse reminds Calas that Antoine, an inveterate gambler, had lost at cards that very day. That would explain in part his lugubrious mood. Calas is anxious to get his daughter Rose married. Antoine had excused himself during the time that Lavaisse was reading. Calas' remarks are interrupted by loud cries. Calas, Lavaïsse, Jeannette and Rose rush out to find Antoine who has hanged himself from a rafter in the family store.

Act two shows the force of militant prejudice and depicts the stalwart valor of Jean Calas in the face of false accusations and imminent death. Laya further presents the hideous picture of mob violence sanctioned by the jurists of Toulouse. As soon as Antoine's body is found, the father is immediately jailed and accused of murdering his son. The accusation is substantiated by a prevalent belief among Catholics «que la religion protestante ordonne aux pères et mères d'étrangler leurs enfans, quand ils veulent se faire Catholiques». (Act II, Scene III). This is the first mention of why Antoine probably committed suicide. In the course of her lamentations, Mme. Calas reveals that she was born an English citizen. She is frightened by the news that *Le capitoul* (member of a judging body) wishes to speak with her. This same *capitoul* harbors an overpowering hate for Jean Calas. Many years before in London, *le capitoul* had insulted a Protestant woman. Calas defended her. The *capitoul's* accusation was rejected. Since that time, the jurist has been waiting for an occasion to reap his vengeance. He reports the entire family and Lavaisse have been accused of complicity with Calas. Mme. Calas suggests the Catholics of Toulouse are preparing to commemorate the Massacre of Saint Bartholomew's Day. The sacrifice of this family's blood constitutes a suitable libation to a Catholic God.

The third act mirrors the corruption of lawyers and judges. The scene switches from the Calas home to the courtroom. The *capitoul*, who is the presiding judge, vows vengeance on the family in the name of Catholicism. The hopeless eloquence of LaSalle, who speaks in defense of justice and not necessarily for Calas, falls on deaf ears. Jeannette appears as a character witness for Calas. Instead of waiting until questioned, she throws a purse of money on the table and testifies that *le capitoul* had personally bribed her to accuse Jean Calas of murdering his son. This surprise information prompts LaSalle to demand the testimony be written into the record. In such a compromising position, *le capitoul* offers to leave the chair. The offer is rejected by all the other judges except LaSalle.

Act four takes place in Jean Calas' cell. It reveals further the inhumanity of mob violence illustrated here by the statue erected of a son with a finger pointing toward his father, and the caption «c'est toi père inhumain». The last wish of Jean is that Lavaisse marry Rose. Upon learning that he has been condemned to die, Jean is happy in the thought that his family will be free. He refuses offers of freedom from LaSalle and Lavaisse. *Le capitoul* enters to inform Calas that the scaffold is now ready.

In the last act Laya, attempting to depict sorrow, succeeds only with a caricature. As the act begins, Mme. Calas, in her own cell, ponders her husband's fate. Her reverie is interrupted by Lavaisse who brings the sad news. The *capitoul* comes to free Mme. Calas and Rose. The distraught ladies see the sad sight of Jean «les mains et les pieds chargés de chaînes; il est soutenu d'un côté par un religieux, de l'autre, par le geôlier qui se retire dès qu'il est entré». Calas wishes to speak to his wife and daughter both of whom have fainted. The last scene relates Voltaire's efforts to clear the memory of Jean Calas and the eventual rehabilitation of the remaining members of his family. While busy with this project, Voltaire brought the mother and children to live with him. This was an element added by Laya.

Regarding the last four scenes, Laya noted that «MM. les comédiens ont préféré de baisser la toile après le départ du père. Il me semble pourtant que l'arrivée de M. de la Salle est ce qu'il porte un peu de consolation dans l'âme du spectateur que cette situation douloureuse vient de froisser».

In a strange mixture of a *drame sérieux* and a tragedy, Laya was not concerned with the essential details of the Calas affair which, it seems to me, were the reasons that led to Marc-Antoine's death and that of his father, and not the fabricated charges of hate in a judge. Further, the love element is very much out of place. It occupies such an important position as to relegate Calas's fate to secondary concern as illustrated in his preocupation with Lavaisse and Rose and not with the injustices perpetrated upon him. Because of the saccharine treatment of love, which keeps him busy, Laya succeeds in no wise to depict character. LaSalle's concern for justice appears forced. *Le capitoul* is an unfortunate addition. The poetry in the play has no distinction. It would seem more natural for the characters to have spoken in prose. While obviously disregarding the unity of place, Laya was much concerned with that of time. This resulted in the unfortunate circumstance of ineffective presentation. The untold suffering born by Calas and his family during the months in prison were telescoped into a very short time; and moreover, there is no mention of the hardships they had to bear.

Adhering more closely to historical fact, a less pretentious play on the same theme as Laya's was *Calas ou le fanatisme* presented on December 17, 1790, on the stage of the théâtre des Variétés.[44] Written by Auguste Lemierre d'Argy (1762-1815), the work is simply called a *drame*, has four acts and is in prose. The tack taken by d'Argy is quite different from Laya's treatment. The primary concern in d'Argy's play is keeping intact the good name of the Calas family. The author, conscious of the three unities, and yet proud of his freedom, is explicit:

> La scène est à Toulouse: l'action dure 15 jours: Le premier et second actes se passent dans la maison de Calas; le troisième dans la Salle de l'interrogatoire et le quatrième dans la prison.

It is evening. As the play opens, the spectator is treated to a scene typical of bourgeois family life. The family circle is broken only by the absence of Louis. Marc-Antoine, his brother Pierre, and the sisters Rose and Anne-Rose are at home with their parents. Mme. Calas is absorbed in her sewing. The daughters prepare to go out for a few hours. The father, who had encouraged Marc-Antoine to also become a merchant when doors to the legal profession were closed to him because of his faith, dictates a business letter. Marc is totally distracted. The lack of response in his son fills the old father with anguish. To establish a change of mood, Calas sends Marc to mail an important letter. Lavaisse, a friend of Marc, has just arrived from Bordeaux. Jean Calas discusses Marc's gloom and dispair. It seems Marc has given himself over to gambling because he is bored by having to work in the family dry goods' store. To help dispel his boredom, Marc continued to study law. Jean thinks his son would

---

[44] Lemierre d'Argy, *Calas ou le fanatisme* (Paris: Bureau des Révolutions, 1791).

do well to leave Toulouse. With this in mind, he proposes a trip abroad.

Unlike Laya's play in which Marc does not appear, d'Argy adds a very interesting touch. Called out on a business mission, the father leaves Marc alone. One of his favorite works in literature is *Hamlet*. The page most worn is that of the soliloquy *être ou ne pas être*. This is not a gratuitous fact. The youth seemed to have spent much of his time reading about suicide. Afraid that his father does not love him, Marc is prompted to suggest that he is going on a long trip. Of course, this is an allusion to his approaching death. The first act ends when the family retainer, Jeanne, a fervent Catholic and accredited historically for having been instrumental in Louis Calas' conversion to Catholicism, suggests the same course to Marc. He replies that he is consumed with fire and runs from the room.

The second act depicts the reaction produced on members of the Calas family as they learn of Marc's suicide. As a prelude to the avalanche of misfortune, we are introduced to one of the judges, M. David. One of the current scandals in Toulouse is the unsolved murder of a M. Sergi's daughter. The spectator learns later that the judge, David, has a son who actually killed Adélaïde Sergi for reasons of jealousy.

Having gone into his store, Calas discovers his son's body hanging from a rafter. The father's first thought is not to inform the police. Such news would do harm to the family's reputation. A friend, Caseing, advises him to inform the police immediately. Mme. Calas is more distressed about what people will say than with the fact that her son is dead. When confronted by the authorities, who quickly surround the house, Calas claims at first that his son died from a heart attack. He later changes the story to convey the truth.

The act ends with a strange and unheeded exchange between David and his son. The father has already insulted the Calas family, calling them all heretics. The younger David does not share his father's opinion.

Much of act three continues the struggle between David and his son. Now in the courtroom, David (fils) implores his father not to condemn Calas, obviously an innocent old man. Without any satisfaction from his father, the son decides to save Calas. The trial begins with a long speech by Calas attesting his innocence. The ordeal has been too great for him. He faints appropriately. Both LaSalle and the younger David defend Calas' innocence. The boy proclaims: «C'est une injustice affreuse, et le ciel en prendra vengeance». (Act III, Scene V). In a moment of exultation, the young David admits that it was he who murdered Marc-Antoine. This stunning news halts the trial. Demonstrating his inherent nature of a generous man, Calas extends his sympathy to the older David who naturally refuses to listen.

The freedom enjoyed by Jean Calas following the dramatic confession of the young David is short-lived. The last act finds Jean Calas, ten days after the trial, again in his cell. His lamentations are unending. Nevertheless, as he is taken away to be executed, he continues to protest the injustice of his sentence.

After the first two acts, the audience is dragged into a lachrymose secondary plot. The author becomes so involved with the problem of Davis (fils), he almost forgets to return to the main theme of his play. The melodramatic performance of the half-crazed David destroys any illusion that d'Argy is vitally interested in presenting the Calas family. The action of the play is passably motivated, yet the author scarcely succeeds in piecing the scenes together logically. In fact, the drama seems to end without the audience knowing the whereabouts of anyone except Jean Calas. After his confession, nothing more is known of David (fils). It is presumed he denied Antoine's murder, was freed through the influence of his father, and subsequently admitted the murder of Adélaïde Sergi.

D'Argy reveals no talent in characterization. Quite human in the opening scene before his arrest, Jean Calas turns into a mouthpiece against fanaticism. Unlike other serious plays of the period in which the speeches are endless, d'Argy introduces very short dialogues which stimulate the spectator's interest. Nevertheless, that interest is quickly dispelled for the action hits an impasse.

Another play emerging from the mass of propaganda that flooded the scene in 1790 was *L'attentat de Versailles ou la clémence de Louis XVI*.[45] This work directed against Necker, LaFayette, Philippe Egalité—Duke of Orleans, and Mirabeau, is relegated to the tragic genre only because of its form. There are five acts in verse, but there is

---

[45] Genève: 1790. Neither author nor publisher is given.

no tragic action as such since the coup d'état instigated by Philippe d'Orléans and his followers is foiled.

In an *avertissement*, the author, obviously a royalist who preferred to remain anonymous, defends the use of material taken from a contemporary event:

> J'offre à mes concitoyens une pièce vraiment nationale, dont le sujet n'a point été puisé dans les annales obscures de l'histoire, mais pris sur le temps même.
> J'ai vu et j'ai voulu consacrer un des plus extraordinaires et des plus affreux événements dont un Français puisse être le témoin dans sa patrie.

The event to which the author is referring was the march on Versailles, October 5, 1789, by the women of Paris and the King's return to Paris the following day. The attack made upon Versailles was supposedly incited by Mirabeau or the Duc d'Orléans. Neiter Orléans nor Mirabeau had been needed to inspire the march on Versailles. It was the spontaneous act of the Parisians. [46]

For some of the scenes the author virtually copied suitable passages from classical authors. One notable example, patterned on Athalie's dream from the play by Jean Racine, is the account by Marie-Antoinette of a dream foretelling the projected coup d'etat of the Duc d'Orléans. The author happily admits the plagiarism:

> J'en ai même souvent pris des vers entiers, imité beaucoup d'autres et presque toujours rappelé chaque scène par un des premiers vers de celle contre laquelle j'osois me proposer de goûter.

The array of characters includes the King, Queen, Dauphin, Duc d'Orléans and his wife, Necker, Mirabeau, LaFayette and Barnave. Necker's name has a peculiar spelling—*Nekre*. The author claimed: «On s'est permis d'écrire son nom comme on le prononce pour la facilité et la douceur de la versification».

The entire action takes place at Versailles. As the first act opens, two deputies, Calonne and Duruey, are discussing the lamentable state

---

[46] An excellent general study on the French Revolution is that of J. M. Thompson, *The French Revolution* (New York: The University Press, 1945).

in which the monarchy is now languishing. Both echo the opinion that Necker is a diabolical agent sent to effect destruction:

> Un étranger sorti d'une secte ennemie
> En un vaste désert a changé ma patrie.
> (Act I, Scene I)

There is an anachronism here. Necker had been dismissed on July 11, 1789. Necker is depicted as a proud, vain man with a consuming ambition to be another Richelieu. One person who has similar ambitions is the Comte de Mirabeau.

In act two we are witness to the ambitions and machinations of Mirabeau and Philippe d'Orléans. Mirabeau realizes that his influence upon the King will be felt only if Marie-Antoinette, Philippe d'Orléans and Necker are destroyed:

> Sans femme, sans ministre abhorrant nos Etats,
> Le timide Louis va me tendre les bras.
> (Act II, Scene I)

With these three individuals gone, Mirabeau will be forced to contend only with La Fayette:

As a part of his scheme, Mirabeau flatters Philippe d'Orléans into thinking they are on the same side. According to Mirabeau, Philippe will soon be king of France. In a curious scene, the perfidious Duchesse d'Orléans weeps because she has heard her husband has enemies. They would prevent him from becoming king. Mirabeau tries to console the lady, but does warn Philippe that some doubt his ability to rule as king.

Marie-Antoinette presents herself as a helpless, lachrymose heroine in act three. In the company of Calonne and the Marquise de Tourzel, the Dauphin's governess, the Queen recounts a frightful dream. With the addition of a few names and places, the dream is lifted textually from Athalie's tirade, act two, scene five, of Racine's *Athalie* in which the phantom of Jezabel predicts her daughter's downfall. Marie-Antoinette confesses her fright:

> Un songe qui m'effraie, et par-tout me poursuit,
> Vient troubler mon repos et le jour et la nuit.
> J'errois dans les détours du parc de Trianon,
> Seule au déclin du jour, dans un sombre abandon,

> Quand je vois près de moi s'élever de la terre
> Un spectre, je veux fuir; grands Dieux! c'était ma mère
> Dont la main soulevant ses longs habits de deuil,
> Présente à mes regards la tête de Choiseuil,
> Mon coeur, malgré mes sens, vers tous les deux m'entraîne.
> Tremble, me dit le Duc, ô malheureuse Reine!
> D'infâmes assassins redoute le courroux;
> On en veut à tes jours, à ceux de ton époux,
> D'Orléans... A ces mots les éclats du tonnerre
> Dérobent à mes yeux, et Choiseul, et ma mère,
> Et le Roi s'empressant à mes lugubres cris,
> De cet affreux sommeil vient tirer mes esprits.
> (Act III, Scene II)

The scene changes and Necker comes to confer with the Queen. She interpellates him severely: «Vous ne parlez jamais que de votre mérite». (Act III, Scene III). In an ignominious scene Necker and his wife discuss the eventuality of being forced to flee. She would be satisfied absconding with the treasures her husband had already appropriated. He cannot flee. Supreme power is almost in his hands.

Act four shows the conspirators in a strategic meeting. Philippe promises all his followers an important position in the government if the plot to unseat Louis is successful. Mirabeau has capitalized on the situation to set off a revolt in Paris which supposedly supports Philippe, but in actuality favors himself.

Necker fears all is lost. The Queen informs him that the King, no longer lethargic, will assume full control.

In act five the conspiracy is revealed, and the royal family saved. Calonne has intercepted important letters which reveal the conspiracy of Orléans, Necker and others. As the act opens, would-be assassins are attempting an invasion of the royal apartments. The first violent attack against La Fayette shows him as demonstrating a real lack of interest in the royal family's welfare. As mobs attempt to storm the palace, La Fayette is asleep. Calonne expresses his contempt for the erstwhile leader of the King's guards:

> Elevé dans Boston au mépris de nos lois,
> Washington lui montra comme on trahit ses Rois.
> Docile à ses leçons, jaloux de sa mémoire,
> La révolte est pour lui le chemin de la gloire.
> (Act V, Scene II)

Only the guards are faithful to the King. They repulse the assassins. In a very bizarre scene, the foolish Duchesse d'Orléans rushes in to beg clemency of Louis. She claims ambition caused her husband's reckless plot. Philippe then arrives to throw himself upon the mercy of the King.

In the meanwhile, assassins have succeeded in forcing their way into the Queen's bedchamber just at the moment when she was getting up. She appears in disarray. La Fayette, the French guards, and deputies of the Estates-General are also there. In the last scene of the play Mirabeau refuses to give up hope although his present ambition seems thwarted as the troops surround the royal family.

There is no evidence that this play had either a public or private performance. The author, evidently opinionated, took an event and twisted the real facts to depict his own interpretation. To him vultures had surrounded the throne and were readying themselves to light upon the debris. Aware of increasing danger, Louis XVI rose to defend his rights as the legal monarch. Necker, Mirabeau and La Fayette are distorted almost beyond recognition. There is little characterization. The episodes are too melodramatic to be convincing. The language is bombastic and unnatural.

Clovis, a *tragédie nationale* dedicated to the Confederation, also appeared in 1790. Written in five acts and in verse, the work was by an anonymous author.[47] In the preface he salutes the Revolution as a great event:

> Le soulèvement universel d'un peuple qui chasse ses tyrans et qui change la forme de son Gouvernement, est l'un des plus grands événements dont l'Histoire puisse faire mention, et le plus grand spectacle que le théâtre puisse offrir aux regards et à l'instruction des Hommes.

He also defends the choice of his subject which he finds excellent. Clovis was the founder of the French monarchy; he fought against the Romans, and he was the first Christian king of France. Then there is a brief sketch of the historical details. Clovis' intimate union with Gondebaut, King of Burgundy and his subsequent marriage with Clo-

---

[47] (Paris: n. p., 1790).

thilde increased his power and paved the way for his acclaim as the King of all Gaul.

The action takes place at Rheims in Gondebaut's palace. Although the theme of the play is the conversion of Glovis to Christianity and the expulsion of Roman armies from Rheims, the love interest between Clovis and Clothilde assumes the primary rôle.

The first act introduces two essential problems. The princess Clotilde must soon choose a husband. Although she has already been promised to Clovis, Syagrius, a Roman general, has also placed his claim for her hand. Besides Clotilde's dilemma, the Romans and Franks are fighting for control of Rheims. Should Clotilde decide in favor of Syagrius, then Clovis would wage war; and if she should select Clovis, Syagrius would fight. In any event Clotilde promises Gondebaut she will do her duty as a loyal and obedient daughter. Clovis is deeply in love with Clotilde:

> Ses yeux avoient lancé leur étincelle,
> Et des feux de l'amour embrase tous mes sens
> (Act I, Scene III)

When he sees her, his praise cannot be enthusiastic enough. Clotilde is a queen. She also loves Clovis, but has hesitated in revealing her real sentiments because of her suitor's pagan beliefs. The one criterion of her marriage to any man is that he must be Christian. Clovis has little sympathy for any religion in which those who look for another life despise this one too much. Clotilde rises to the defense of Christianity.

Clovis succeeds in freeing Rheims, which gladly joins the Frankish confederation. Defeated in war and love, Syagrius reminds Clotilde that Clovis is a pagan. Clotilde, trying to placate the two rivals, warns that her love can be had only with the promise of peace.

In act two Clovis is approved as King of the French forces. As the scene opens, Lisois, a Frankish general, has returned from an expedition to Paris whose willful capitulation attests to Clovis' widespread popularity. Clovis, aware of Clotilde's admonition, ponders the meaning of Christianity. Lisois confesses he is a Christian, but not yet baptized. Clovis defends paganism with examples of great and powerful men who never knew Christianity. Lisois maintains, however, Christianity instills a new, unknown fire in man.

In the course of an assembly composed of representatives from several tribes, it is decided Clovis will be the leader of all French forces. This, of course, entails a long diatribe against Roman tyranny as contrasted to Clovis' generosity.

Act three centers around Syagrius' consuming jealousy and anger at being rejected. He proposes the stratagem of kidnapping both Gondebaut and Clotilde. With them in his power Rheims will be taken by surprise. He attempts once more to entice Clotilde with threats and promises. He reveals a secret ambition of severing Gaul from Roman domination with the intention of becoming its first monarch. Clotilde begs that her final decision be postponed another day. Syagrius is too anxious. Clotilde must come with him now. To this command Clotilde utters a plaintive cry: «O ciel, daigne envoyer Clovis à ma défense». (Act III, Scene I). Enraged by Clotilde's supplication, Syagrius drags her and her father away. Clovis comes to the rescue with a small band of soldiers. During the fracas Syagrius, left alone, has his dagger raised to pierce Clotilde's breast. She utters a cry, falls on her father's shoulder, and he succeeds in turning the blow. Before Syagrius has the time to overpower Gondebaut, Clovis returns to place his rival and enemy in irons. The Roman forces have retreated. Clotilde's Christian goodness takes full sway. It is her wish that Syagrius not be punished but set free to return to his camp. Clovis accedes to her wishes but does not understand why Clotilde shows no righteous indignation. She does not seek to explain because: «Vos yeux (ceux de Clovis) restent couverts des bandeaux de l'erreur». (Act III, Scene VI)

In act four it is learned that Clovis has been converted to Christianity. A miracle revealed God to him. His priests arrive to warn against fighting the Romans who have assembled for a decisive battle. Just as the priests of Jupiter were sacrificing a victim to the gods, a lightning bolt struck the celebrant's knife and the pretended victim was left free to flee. Clovis defies his priests, and asks Clotilde to bless him. She gives him a sword and shield, thus confirming her love and faith in him.

Much of the fifth act concerns the battle between the Romans and the Frankish confederation. The Roman army is 10,000 men strong. The horrors of the battle are recounted by Gondebaut and others who watch from the city's ramparts. A messenger reports the Franks have been conquered. Gondebaut hastens to remind his daughter she should be prepared to accept Syagrius as her husband. With hopes dashed of ever seeing Clovis again, Clotilde is overjoyed to hear that the French have really won an impressive victory. Clovis, with head bared, had disappeared into the thick of battle. Clotilde's lamentations are interrupted by Lisois who reports a miracle. In the midst of battle a luminous cross descended from heaven saying:

> Adorez cette croix qui vous montre sa gloire,
> François, c'est l'étendard du Dieu de la victoire.
> (Act V, Scene IX)

With Syagrius beheaded and the Roman force routed, Clovis appears among all the splendor and pomp that his admirers could assemble. The attempt at spectacle is the one distinguishing trait of this tragedy. This is noticeable from the beginning of act two upon Lisois' return from Paris made spectacular by captured Roman standards with the eagle reversed. Next, an impressive assembly is held in Rheims to decide the city's fate. The stage directions are elaborate. Deputies from the Frankish confederations, German allies, Parisians, the Rheims senatorial body, and ambassadors attend this meeting. The delegates have a particular seat in which they remain until the arrival of Gondebaut. As he enters the hall, the entire assembly stands. He takes his seat beside Clovis and Syagrius. At the end of act four, Clovis and his army, fully armed, pass in review before Gondebaut and Clotilde. Appropiate music is provided.

The most spectacular scene occurs at the conclusion of the play:

> Clovis arrive porté sur un pavois, entouré de drapeaux et d'aigles romaines renversées. Une pique est dans sa main droite. Le connétable de France porte devant lui son épée nue. Deux François sont à ses côtés. L'un porte son bouclier froissé, et hérissé de traits; l'autre son casque, également froissé, et auquel il ne reste que quelques lambeaux d'aigrettes. Les prisonniers les plus distingués son derrière lui, tête nue et dans les fers. Plusieurs François portent les pièces de l'armure de Syagrius, sa lance et son épée. On en forme un trophée au fond de la salle. Les Français arrivant sur plusieurs rangs, en poussant des cris de triomphe et de joie et portant les drapeaux de leur nation. Une musique guerrière les accompagne.

The author had obviously incorporated into his play the Revolutionary enthusiasm for spectacle and fanfare, but was insouciant of how such could be simulated on the restricted stages of Parisian theaters.

The author's attempt to present what seemed to him a *tragédie nationale* was spoiled by the senseless love intrigue. As in other tragedies of this type, the author demonstrates his hesitation in breaking away from the classical pattern in which the analysis of emotions, most frequently those evoked by love, was the main concern. In this play the author's inability to present a forceful analysis of the love of Clotilde for Clovis naturally resulted in a melodramatic production in which the episodes are pieced together without art.

The author's ability to characterize is defunct. Clotilde, who should have emerged as a strong, determined woman yet maintaining her femininity, is little less than an anemic heroine spouting maxims, blanched of meaning, in defense of Christianity. The robustness and verve, with which the author strived to characterize Christianity, are totally absent. Instead, Clovis' remarks in favor of paganism have a greater ring of sincerity and are thus more effective. Clovis' conversion is unexplained. The reader is forced to think the conversion was effected through love for Clotilde, and not from any deep-seated personal convictions. The author's ability as a poet is nil. The verses are a string of platitudes without any cohesion. The action of the play is largely episodic.

The year 1791 was indeed a gloomy one for the Comédie-Française. On January 13 a decree issued by the Assemblée Nationale declared any citizen free to establish his own theater. Naturally, an infinity of bad actors and inferior authors mushroomed overnight.

In 1673, at the death of Molière, there were five theaters in Paris: (1) Le Palais-Royal, (2) L'Hôtel de Bourgogne, (3) Le Marais, (4) La Comédie-Italienne, and (5) L'Académie royale de Musique. These did not include the *spectacles forains,* important to the development of drama but forced, by pressure from the recognized theaters, to practice arts not classified under the heading of literature. From 1680 to 1791 there were only three theaters subsidized and recognized by the state: (1) La Comédie-Française, (2) La Comédie-Italienne, and (3) L'Opéra. During the period from 1791-1799 more than fifty theaters had their beginning and demise.[48] In Paris alone, at the end of 1791 there were thirty-five theaters.[49]

As a natural result of differences in political sympathies, Talma and his followers left the Comédie-Française and established themselves in the Théâtre-Français de la rue de Richelieu (Palais-Royal). Talma and his troupe made their debut here on April 27, 1791, with *Henry VIII* by Chénier.[50]

With the departure from the Comédie-Française (Odéon) of Talma, Mme. Vestris, Grandménil and Mlle. Desgarcins, the ranks of those actors who specialized in tragedy were so depleted, it was mandatory to present comedy on most occasions. Further, the Comédie-Française was so pressed for funds, it was forced, in order not to close, to resort to various schemes among which was an agreement with the Comédie-Italienne permitting the fusion of declamation and music.

Whereas the Comédie-Française sprinkled now and then its traditional repertory with a new play, Talma's theater became «le temple de la Révolution».[51] As the Revolution weaved its course, a continuous cabal was installed at the Comédie-Française (Théâtre de la Nation), that din of aristocracy. Each word, each gesture were a pretext for vociferous protestation and even rioting. The fact that the Théâtre de la rue Richelieu specialized in plays of a revolutionary nature was not the sole reason for a marked superiority over the Théâtre de la Nation. Talma's affinity for exactitude in costume was enthusiastically sanctioned by his colleagues and hailed by critics. Etienne and Martainville reported:

> Cette partie de l'art dramatique, trop longtems négligée, et si nécessaire à l'illusion, dut tous ses progrès aux recherches et aux dépenses que faisait ce théâtre, non seulement pour les ouvrages nouveaux, mais encore pour les tragédies anciennes l'exactitude de costume ne contriuba pas peu à l'enthou-

---

[48] Jules Bonnassies, *Le théâtre et le peuple, esquisse d'une organisation théâtrale* (Paris: Armand le Chevalier, 1872), p. 54.

[49] Frères Goncourt, *Histoire de la société française pendant la Révolution*, p. 162.

[50] After August 10, 1792, this theater became Le Théâtre de la Liberté et de l'Egalité. The name was again changed on September 30, 1792, to that of Théâtre de la République.

[51] Dussane, *op. cit.*, p. 94.

siasme du public, qui, peu d'années avant la révolution voyait encore les acteurs du Théâtre Français jouer des Grecs et des Romains avec des manteaux de soie.[52]

Because it appealed to their emotions and to their pocketbooks, the Parisian populace flocked to the Théâtre de la rue Richelieu. The prices were appreciably lower than at the Théâtre de la Nation.[53]

From among the mass of dramatic writing that emerged in 1791, there are two plays worthy of our consideration. The first, *Jean Calas*, written by Chénier, was drawn from national history and the second, *Les victimes cloîtrées*, illustrates graphically prevailing attitudes characteristic of propagandistic writings.

Jean Calas ou l'école des juges was presented on the stage of the Théâtre de la rue Richelieu on July 7, 1791.[54] Termed a tragedy, the work is in five acts and in verse. Whereas Laya placed major emphasis in his play on a love affair and Lemierre concentrated on the theme of vengeance, Chénier deprecated monarchs, lawyers and intolerance in religion.

The first act is in the form of a diatribe against absolute monarchs and intolerance in religion. The action transpires in the city of Toulouse during the trial of Jean Calas and his family for the death of Marc-Antoine Calas. The jurist LaSalle, who is the mouthpiece of the author, monopolizes the action. Having met his friend Clérac, the presiding judge at the Calas trial, LaSalle immediately broaches the ephemeral problem of innocence. He supports the family's complete ignorance of events that precipitated Marc-Antoine's death:

---

[52] Etienne et Martainville, *op. cit.*, II, 116.

[53] Prices quoted are the following: Premières loges, loges d'avant-scène and balcons—4 livres, 4 sous; galeries, loges grillées, secondes et orchestre—3 livres; amphithéâtre, troisième loges et parquet—1 livre, 10 sous; rotonde, 2 livres; quatrième loges, 1 livre. See Théodore Muret, *L'histoire de France par le théâtre, 1789-1851* (Paris: Amyot, 1865), I, 96.

[54] The new Théâtre de Monsieur opened on January 6, 1791. Prices for the seats there were: Parquet—3 livres, 6 sous; première galerie—3 livres; deuxième galerie—48 sous; troisième galerie, 24 sous. See Louis Pericaud, *Histoire des grands et petits théâtres de Paris pendant la Révolution, le Consulat et l'Empire* (Paris: E. Jorel, 1908), p. 114.

Marie-Joseph Chénier, *op. cit.*, I.

> Je les crois innocens, et je ne puis songer
> Qu'un frère en sa fureur ait égorgé son frère,
> Ou qu'un fils ait péri sous la main de son père.
> (Act I, Scene I)

In return, Clérac vilifies all Protestants and delivers a long harangue in honor of Louis XIV, whose order, in 1685, to revoke the Edict of Nantes drove thousands of Protestants from France. LaSalle feels differently:

> Louis, cet ennemi de toute liberté,
> Plus flatté que chéri, plus craint que respecté,
> Imprimant à l'Europe une terreur profonde,
> Obtint le nom de grand par le malheur du monde.
> (Act I, Scene I)

Their conversation is interrupted by the sudden arrival of Louis Calas, the son of Jean who had become a Catholic. Louis requests that LaSalle help him establish his father's innocence. A boisterous mob calls for Louis' death. By means of a sermon on love, a companion known only as «Le Religieux» entices the crowd to silence.

Act two, which transpires in a courtroom, is a recapitulation of events during the night on which Marc-Antoine Calas committed suicide. It is also in this act that the author establishes the partiality of the judges. Only LaSalle maintains it is better to have judged wrongly than unwisely.

Six months have passed since Jean Calas and his family were imprisoned. Intensely happy to see his family again, Jean is saddened when ordered to recount events leading to his son's death. In spite of LaSalle's eloquent testimony in his behalf, an air of gloom hangs over the assembly.

The despondency and presentiment pervading act three are heightened by a violent storm. The author notes that its violence should increase in proportion as the moment draws nearer when Jean Calas will learn his fate. As Jean Calas awaits the pronouncement of a sentence, whose contents he knows presage no good, he pleads with his son, Louis, to protect Mme. Calas. Driven to frenzy in the knowledge that nothing can be done for his father, Louis delivers the supreme blow to Catholicism:

> C'est un culte barbare, injuste, sanguinaire;
> C'est la religion des bourreaux de mon pere.
> (Act III, Scene IV)

As the act closes, Clérac hands down the death sentence. He bids all to tell Jean Calas goodbye.

In act four Mme. Calas and her children bid the father adieu. Within his prison cell Jean Calas has received calmly the news that he is to die. He refuses to confess to «Le Religieux» and declares that only God can be his confessor. Disconsolate from the news that she and the children are free, Mme. Calas wishes to die with her aged husband. In spite of LaSalle's continued entreaties to the judges in favor of Calas, his death is certain. As the jailer prepares Calas for execution, the latter predicts the shame with which the good name of France will be sullied because of such an odious crime.

Act five casts doubt upon the sagacity of the sentence. The action takes place in the same public square as that of act one. Overcome with grief, Mme. Calas asks LaSalle's advice about what she should do next. He counsels a trip to Voltaire whom he calls:

> Un illustre vieillard, fléau des fanatiques
> Courez vous prosterner aux genoux de Voltaire.
> (Act V, Scene III)

Convinced throughout the trial of Calas' guilt, Clérac is assailed by doubts now

> S'il était innocent?...
> Ciel! j'étais convaincu, je doute maintenant.
> (Act V, Scene V)

Interspersed with Clérac's reiterations of doubt, and lamentably louder, Mme. Calas summons the wrath of God upon the unjust judges who brought death to her husband. In the last scene, decrying the judgment of his condisciples, LaSalle defends Jean Calas' innocence and voices the hope that France, through this example, will become an asylum to the unfortunate.

Chénier was guilty of taking advantage of the political tenor of the times, and inserted in his works, at every possible occasion, opinions professed by the public. Thus Jean Calas is filled with vitriol directed against tyranny, corruption in law courts and intolerance in religion. In this long sermon there is no development of character, little action, no interest, the language is totally flat, and the repetition of the essential theme is exasperating.

Driven finally by necessity to produce plays similar in theme to those offered at the Théâtre de la rue Richelieu, the Comédie-Française (Odéon) presented a scabrous play on March 19, 1791. This was the infamous *Victimes cloîtrées* in five acts and in prose by the actor-author Monvel.[55] The principal theme is an attack on religious orders. A civil constitution of the clergy promulgated in July, 1790, had been violently opposed by many clergymen. Their refusal to swear allegiance to the new constitution invoked the wrath of sympathizers in the Revolution. With this surge of hate the oldest institution in France was left tottering. A discussion of *Les victimes cloîtrées* has been included as a reflection on the disjointed times. It was one of the most popular plays of the decade.

The first act, whose action takes place in a French provincial town, sets the scene of a very grotesque drama. Eugénie St. Alban, deeply in love with the young and dashing Dorval, had been left behind by her parents who went away on a visit to Paris. During their absence. Eugénie had fallen sick, supposedly died, and was buried by her mother's confessor, Le Père Laurent, head of a nearby Dominican monastery. To drown his grief, Dorval had entered Père Laurent's monastery. He is scheduled soon to take the final vows which will sever all contacts with the outside world.

As the play opens Francheville, a brother of Mme. St.-Alban, is to return presently from an absence of two years. Praising his master, who was elected mayor while he was away, Picard, an old family retainer, anticipates Francheville's arrival. Having heard that Francheville was to return, Père Louis, a monk in Laurent's monastery, has rushed to see the mayor. His nervousness and allusions to Dorval and the monastery create an air of mystery. Neither Louis nor Picard is pleased with Père Laurent. Picard seizes the occasion to praise accomplishments of the Revolution among which were the abolishment of despotism. Not being able to wait any longer for Francheville, Louis hesitates to impart his message to Picard and in turn requests

---

[55] C. Monvel, *Les victimes cloîtrées* (Paris: Chambon, 1796).

that Francheville come to the monastery as quickly as possible. As the act closes Francheville greets his servants and prepares for the arrival of Mme. St-Alban.

The main concern in act two is the sharp contrast drawn between the serenity of Francheville's personality and that of his simpering sister. Mme. St.-Alban is a slave to Père Laurent, detests servants, and the Revolution. Chided by her for bearing the colors of the Revolution, Francheville retorts that under the *ancien régime*: «Je n'ai voulu rien être parce que je ne pouvois être qu'un instrument de despotisme». (Act II, Scene III). Their argument is brought to a close by the arrival of Père Laurent who has come at the bidding of Dorval. The diffidence with which his sister regards Père Laurent incites Francheville to deliver a long diatribe against monks. Dorval arrives to demand some explanation of why he was not permitted to marry Eugénie. His eyes fall upon Eugénie's portrait above the mantle and all the love he bears for her is so great he faints. Having regained consciousness, he resolves never to see any of them again. Unkindly disposed to the monkish life, Francheville decides to dissuade the youthful Dorval. His decision is reinforced by a letter from Père Louis imploring him to come quickly before Dorval is released into the hands of his cruel enemy.

Act three unfurls the evil workings of Père Laurent's mind. The scene changes to the monastery. Having been notified of Francheville's request to visit Dorval, Laurent is furious:

> Ce Dorval qu'Eugénie m'a préféré, ce Dorval que je déteste, il est à nous; sa raison égarée nous l'assure à jamais. Que demain il s'enchaîne au pied de nos autels, que sa fortune immense devienne notre bien.
> (Act III, Scene I)

In a trance Dorval enters and feverishly clamors for the day when he will join Eugénie in paradise. In spite of the reasons advanced by his friend Francheville outlining why he should renounce monastery life, Dorval persists in his previous decision.

After Francheville's departure, Père Louis succeeds in reaching Dorval and brings surprising news. During a conflagration that destroyed part of Laurent's apartments Louis had discovered in some papers the startling evidence that Eugénie, who had refused to heed Laurent's amorous attentions, was not dead but imprisoned in the convent separated from the Dominican monastery only by a thin wall. Overwhelmed, Dorval faints. Laurent and his aids put Dorval in chains. Père Louis barely escapes the same fate.

Any attempt in act four to depict reality is overshadowed by the grotesqueness:

> La scène est double et le théâtre représente deux cachots, celui du couvent des religieuses est celui des Dominicains. Le cachot des Religieuses et éclairé par une lampe de terre, posée sur une pierre. Tout le meuble consiste en un paillasson vieux et déchiré, une petite cruche d'huile, une cruche de grès, un pain bis, et une pierre pour servir de traversin et de siège à la prisonnière.
> Le cachot des Dominicains est, au lever du rideau, plongé dans une obscurité profonde. On y voit deux tombes en pierre noire, avec un anneau à chacune pour lever la grande pierre qui la couvre. Au fond de chaque cachot une petite porte de fer.

As the curtain rises, Eugénie, clothed in rags, wasted and pale, waits for death. Every few seconds she thinks there is a sound from the other side of her wall. Imbued with the shightest flicker of hope, she walks around the cell, but too weak to withstand the strain, she faints.

Securely locked within his cell, Dorval looks hopelessly about the domain of death. He discovers the remains of two men and a note written in blood telling of a means to escape by digging through to an outer wall which is in reality Eugénie's cell. He proceeds to follow instructions. Soon rocks are loosed and fall into Eugénie's cell. Encouraged by the noise, Eugénie rushes to the wall to beg for help. Upon seeing that Dorval is her deliverer, she faints. Their reunion appears to be spolied. Shouts from without suggest the arrival of Laurent and his followers. As a last ditch stand, Dorval prepares himself for battle with a poker, and Eugénie picks up two stones. Luckily the noise was made by Francheville, Père Louis, and the national guard. Due thanks are expressed to Père Louis whithout whose help the lovers were doomed to certain death. It is assumed that Père Laurent was torn asunder by the angry mob.

Monvel's offering is nothing more than high melodrama. The vindictive Père Laurent fills the rôle of villain; Eugénie and Dorval are helpless pawns in his hands; Père Louis and Francheville are intrepid heroes. Only the comic character, so evident in melodrama, is missing here. The success of the play depends on horrible episodes of which the most striking is that of Eugénie in her cell. She had resisted Laurent to preserve her honor and her love for Dorval. The inhuman conduct attributed to the monks was highly unrealistic and thus any pretence at reality is false. The savagery with which Monvel criticized monastic life is a slight indication of the madness rampant in 1791.

As for all France, the outstanding event of the 1792 theatrical year centered about the events of August 10. On that day, an immense mob assembled around the Tuileries. The royal family fled for safety to the hall of the National Assembly. The Swiss guard of the palace, finding it impossible to keep back the mob, opened fire. Casualties were high. The rage of the people knew no bounds. Being joined by the national guard, they broke into the palace and murdered all who were found in it. This affair furnished a new charge against the King. The Swiss were said to have fired by his orders, and thus he was accused of making war against the people. Louis' enemies took advantage of this excitement to procure his suspension from the office of king, and the commital of the royal family as prisoners to the old and gloomy Temple.

The circumstances discussed above, and apprehension of the populace, upon learning of fresh advances made by allied armies indicating an imminent invasion of the capital, led to the ignominious September massacres. In Paris alone several thousands were put to death. The city counted a population of about 600,000 souls in 1792. [56]

At intervals throughout the year all theaters remained closed. However, they were ordered, for the first time, to discontinue the traditional Easter recess. [57] As the Revolution gained momentum, plays not expressing any particular sympathy with it were completely suppressed. This, of course, meant that most classical plays received the hatchet. Likewise, free showings of plays, chosen by the government became more frequent. [58] Since the theaters remained closed more

---

[56] Edmond et Jules de Goncourt, *Histoire de la société française pendant la Révolution*, p. 206.

[57] Henry Lumière, *op. cit.*, p. 104.

[58] Plays named were *Brutus* (Voltaire), *Guillaume Tell* (Lemierre) and *Caius Gracchus* (Chénier).

often than not, there was little opportunity for new works to be presented. No historical tragedy was written during the year. The financial situation of all theaters was deplorable. From March to June, 1792, the Comédie-Française (Théâtre de la Nation) had an expenditure of over 86,000 *livres*. During the same period a debt of 58,000 *livres* had accumulated. [59]

In 1793, the most turbulent year of the Revolution, there were no less than 250 plays presented on the stages of Parisian theaters. The arrest on September 3, 1793, of the actors of the Comédie-Française and the closing of that institution's doors marked the end to 113 years of continuous existence.

On January 21 Louis XVI was beheaded. All theaters, accustomed to closing for special occasions, remained open on that memorable day. According to accounts, the receipts at the Comédie-Française showed 106 tickets were purchased at an expenditure of 197 livres, 18 sous. [60]

During a time when fear discouraged any act of naturalness, the Comédie-Française remained audaciously aristocratic. The increasing power of the Jacobins, however, pointed to an inexorable end for the *comédiens*. With the presentation on January 2, 1793, of *L'ami des lois* by the liberal Jean-Louis Laya, difficulties between the actors of the Comédie-Française, and the government came to a head. [61] This thinly veiled satire of the Jacobins drew enthusiastic applause from full houses. Critics noted it as a milestone in the annals of the theater. But more important still was the plays's theme indicating unequivocally that France was afraid of the Jacobins; and, although powerless to oppose them with arms, expressed its distrust by attending the performances of a play which attacked the outspoken extremists. Etienne and Martainville have an account of the crowds that flocked to see the play:

> Avant trois heures du soir, toutes les rues voisines de la Comédie-Française étaient encombrées de spectateurs accourus de divers points de la capitale. Tous les passages contre l'anarchie excitaient le plus vif enthousiasme, et l'auteur, démandé à chaque représentation, venait recueillir les applaudissements d'un public au comble de l'ivresse. [62]

---

[59] *Ibid.*, p. 95.
[60] *Ibid.*, p. 106.
[61] Jean-Louis Laya, *L'ami des lois* (Paris: Maradan, 1793).
[62] Etienne et Martainville, *op. cit.*, III, 48-49.

Incensed by such an expression of independence, a decree was issued by the Commune requiring immediate withdrawal of the play.[63] Censorship became absolute after the incident over *L'ami des lois* and resulted in an order promulgated on August 2, declaring that henceforth in twenty Parisian theaters, three times per week, dramatic works would be presented «...qui retracent les glorieux événements de la Révolution et les vertus des Défenseurs de la liberté».[64]

During the altercations between the Comédie-Française and the government, the Théâtre de la rue Richelieu was much in vogue. Chénier was still the favored author. On February 9, 1793, his play *Fénelon ou l'école des juges* was presented.[65] Containing five acts and in verse, the work is preceded by a long preface. Chénier opened by reproving those people who maintain that philosophy and liberty were English inventions. He defended the theater as a threshing floor for politics and morals, traced the use of national historical drama in Spain and England, and concluded with a thrust at his detractors.

One of the figures from French national history most admired during the Revolution was Fénelon (1651-1715), archbishop of Cambrai (from 1695). Known for his strictness, yet broad, liberal philosophy, Fénelon was remembered most readily as the author of *Télémaque* (1699), where the adventures of the son of Ulysses in search of a father are made into a political novel to act as a guide to the Duc

---

[63] An analysis of the play will indicate its nature. Versac, a friend of the *ancien régime*, has a daughter whose hand is sought by three rivals. The first, Nomophage, hypocritically patriotic, is favored by Mme. Versac; the second is Dorlis, formerly a nobleman, now ardent supporter of the Revolution and yet a partisan of order and justice; the third, Filtos, is a young man innately atuned to virtue but has been fiendishly blinded into admiring anarchy. To further his cause Nomophage engages the services of Duricrâne and Claude, violent journalists whose special talent is to stir up unrest. In order to render Dorlis powerless, they accuse him of complicity in an affair that is suspiciously unrevolutionary. Inicited by the journalists, mobs ransack Dorlis' house, search for him, and finally surround Versac's house. Realizing the crowd is almost beyond control, Forlis pleads that justice be allowed to intervene. His force and sincerity prevail; the crowd is calmed. Forlis is proclaimed a hero. Nomophage is placed in chains, and Dorlis marries Versac's daughter.

Although there is little intrigue, the audiences saw striking resemblances between certain characters and leaders among the Jacobin group. Everybody recognized Robespierre in Nomophage, and Marat in Duricrâne.

[64] Welschinger, *op. cit.*, p. 503.
[65] Chénier, *op. cit.*, II.

de Bourgogne, eldest son of Monseigneur, and heir apparent to the throne of France. Abounding in maxims against absolutism, *Télémaque* was seized upon by revolutionists as a veritable constitution left unheeded by Bourbons tottering to their fall.

Chénier's work is little more than a melodramatic episode illustrating Fénelon's tolerance and sense of justice. The end result is a violent attack against religious orders. The action takes place in Cambrai at a convent. The demoniacal obsessions of an abbess to force Amélie, a young girl reared from infancy in the convent, to take vows against her wishes are considered in the first act. As the scene opens, Amélie converses with a friendly nun, Isaure. Plagued by doubts concerning her future if she should choose to remain in a convent, Amélie is haunted by strange, human-like sounds she has heard. Isaure, very perturbed, cautions Amélie not to mention having heard those sounds. Now that an air of mystery is created, the author proceeds to develop the sadistic tendencies of the abbess. The convent is preparing to receive a new prelate who is none other than Fénelon. In the last minute preparations for the archbishop's arrival, the abbess remembers to congratulate Amélie for the step she is about to make. Amélie implores the abbess to allow her a few days more. A premonition that she will see her parents prompts Amélie to make her request. The abbess replies that Amélie is only an ungrateful wretch, and moreover there is no possibility of seeing her parents. They are dead. Before leaving the abbess warns Amélie that any resistance will mean severe punishment. The mystery of the lamentations heard by Amélie is cleared in the last scene. Isaure, an inhabitant of the convent for the past fourteen years, has had the unpleasant task of carrying bread and water to a female prisoner locked within the convent's subterranean prison. After hearing this story, Amélie begs Isaure to lead her to this prisoner.

The visit and its revelations are the concern of act two. In the dark dungeon a pale Héloïse deplores the unlucky fate which placed her here. She has managed to keep alive these past fifteen years by remembering her husband and daughter and hoping that she can see them before death comes. When confronted by Amélie, Héloïse recounts the story of her life. From an illustrious family in Provence, she had flaunted her independence by marrying a man whom her father disfavored. In search of a wealthy German for a son, the father required Héloïse to accompany him on a trip to Germany. During a halt in Cambrai, Héloïse admitted she was already married and pregnant. Beside himself with rage, the father left her with the nuns. A month afterward the child was born. Héloïse refused to become a nun and was cast into the dungeon in which she now awaits death.

The account of Héloïse's wasted life encourages Amélie to speak of her burning desire to see her parents. Héloïse recognizes her daughter:

> ...O mon bien, mon trésor!
> Viens, c'est moi, c'est ta mère!
> (Act II, Scene III)

Amélie's one obsession is to free her mother. The task will be made easier by an appeal to the new prelate.

Fénelon's arrival and his meeting with D'Elmance are unfurled in act three. Upon arriving in Cambrai, one of the first people Fénelon meets is D'Elmance, a boyhood friend and husband of Héloïse. When queried as to why he is in Cambrai, D'Elmance answers that Héloïse's father admitted, on his deathbed, he left her in Cambrai. For the past twelve years, D'Elmance has waited patiently to see his wife again. Fénelon listens to the story and weeps. Amélie arrives. D'Elmance is struck by the resemblance between her and Héloïse. After listening to the thread of Amélie's story, Fénelon rushes with her to the convent.

In act four Héloïse is freed. As she sits in her dungeon, a strange happiness pervades the air. Isaure, who has been a benevolent friend these many years, arrives to assure Héloïse that Amélie escaped from the guards. However, women torturers are preparing their implements for Héloïse. Accompanied by the abbess, whom Héloïse has not seen for the past fifteen years, the torturers are ready. Their work is mercifully stopped by Fénelon, who apologizes to Héloïse for not having come sooner.

The occasion is made clear for a long criticism of religious intolerance. This is the concern of act five. In lauding Fénelon, D'Elmance observes:

> Les ministres de Dieu déshonorent ses temples.
> De sanglans tribunaux consacrent leurs succes,
> Des François à leur voix égorgent des François:
> Sur les rives du Rhône, au pied des Pyrénées,
> Ils dépeuplent encor nos villes consternés

A leurs crimes nouveaux épouvantent nos yeux
Mouillés des mêmes pleurs qu'ont versés nos aïeux.
(Act V, Scene II)

In the closing scenes Fénelon consents to officiate at a second marriage of D'Elmance and Héloïse.

This fabricated incident from Fénelon's life is characteristic of melodrama. Although less gory in detail than *Les victimes cloîtrées*, the grotesque element is heightened by the sex of the torturers. An exception among those of his calling, Fénelon is depicted as a kind and generous man. His meeting with D'Elmance, Amélie's arrival, and the alacrity with which Fénelon acts to stamp out the sadism of the abbess appear too contrived to be convincing. Even though the language of the play is sugar-coated, it is too disgusting to be natural.

The ironclad grip that censors maintained over the presentation of plays exercised a detrimental influence.[66] One of the stipulations forbade the use of titles other than *citoyen* or *citoyenne*. This posed a serious problem in that the substitution of *citoyen* for such words as *baron, duc, marquis* or *comte* destroyed rhyme. Further, most plays were totally reworked to suit the whims of the censors who were *sans-culottes* themselves or else catered to them. Every concession was made in the staging of plays. Greeks, Romans, Venetians and Gauls appeared with the tricolor very much in view. Phèdre, declaring her love for Hippolytus, had her chest amply covered by a tricolor streamer.[67]

Paméla ou la vertu récompensée, an inferior five act comedy in verse, written by François de Neufchâteau, and presented at the Comédie-Française (Odéon) on August 1, 1793, was the source of the entire company's arrest, with the exception of Molé, and the subsequent closing of that theater.[68] Still smarting from the blow at their reputation achieved by *L'ami des lois*, the Jacobins chose this moment to seek their revenge. Because of allusions in *Paméla* to the right of free choice in religion, a Jacobin sympathizer was spurred to report

---

[66] For a study of censorship in the theater see Victor Hallays-Dabot, *Histoire de la censure théâtrale en France* (Paris, Dentu, 1862).

[67] Etienne et Martainville, *op. cit.*, III, 142.

[68] Welschinger, *op. cit.*, p. 58.

the subversion.[69] Neufchâteau reworked the play and deleted passages he thought could in any way be offensive. The play was presented in its new form on September 2. The author had not reworked the play to the satisfaction of Jacobins, and during the night of September 3 twenty-eight members of the troupe of the Comédie-Française were committed to prison. To the Madelonnettes went Dazincourt, Fleury, Bellemont, Vanhove, Florence, Saint-Phal, Saint-Prix, Naudet, Dupont, Champville, LaRochelle, Marsy, Gérard and Alexandre Duval; to Sainte Pélagie: Mesdames LaChassaigne, Raucourt, Suin, Louise and Emilie Contat, Thénard, Joly, Devienne, Petit-Venhove, Fleury, Mézeray, Montgautier, Ribou and Lange.[70]

In prison the actors and actresses were treated with deference. Most were allowed to go free provided they promised to join the troupe in the rue de Richelieu; others were freed because they had been active in the Revolution. Although most of the above list were released shortly after their incarceration, seven were condemned and remained in prison eleven months.[71] Their lives were saved only through the efforts of one Charles de Labussière, an amateur actor and a clerk in the employ of the Committee of Public Safety. Able to gain access to the dossiers of those detained and lists of the condemned, Labussière held a very important position. By means of a very devious but risky method he saved over eight hundred lives from

---

[69] The line most commonly objected to was spoken by Andrews, an advocate of religious tolerance:

> Chaucun prie à son gré; les amis, les parents
> Suivent, sans disputer, des cultes differents.

Drawn from Richardson's *Pamela,* the play by Neufchâteau is an imitation of *Pamela nubile* of Goldoni. Lord Bonfil, passionately in love with his servant Pamela, tries in vain to seduce her. Unsuccessful, he schemes either to place her in the service of his sister, Lady Davers, marry her, or send her back to her parents. He finally decides to marry her. When Bonfil announces his intention to marry Pamela, Andrews, Pamela's father, reveals that he is really Count Oxpen, a Scottish chieftain with a price on his head. However, unknown to him, a friend has succeeded in obtaining his pardon. Count Oxpen gladly offers his daughter to Lord Bonfil and they are left to make preparations for a hasty marriage.

[70] Lumière, *op. cit.,* p. 192.

[71] Dussane, *op. cit.,* p. 104. Mlle. Joly, Dupont, LaRochelle, Vanhove, and Mme. Petit-Vanhove were freed to join Talma. Dazincourt, Fleury, Louise and Emilie Contat, Raucourt, and Lange were scheduled to receive the guillotine on 13 Messidor (July 1, 1794). Muret, *op. cit.,* I, 85.

being snuffed out by the guillotine. As soon as he learned the names of those scheduled for execution, he would set about destroying all evidence of their existence; thus, in the confusion lives were saved. He would return to his office at night and in the darkness:

> prend à tâtons les pièces et les fait détremper dans un seau d'eau; il les malaxe, les réduit en bouillie, cette bouillie en pelotes; il glisse ces pelotes dans ses poches; au petit matin il se rend aux bains du Pont-Royal, émiette les pelotes en boulettes dans sa baignoire, et lance les boulettes à la Seine par la fenêtre de sa cabine. [72]

Other clerks searched in vain for the lists. Fortunately Labussière was allowed to channel his ingenuity in other directions after the ninth of Thermidor (July 27, 1794). [73]

It goes without saying that Talma and his colleagues were severely criticized because they refused to intervene in the quarrel between the Comédie-Française and the Jacobins. The simple truth is that they feared for their own heads.

During the reign of Terror, theaters were sullied more than ever by the presentation of revolutionary plays, disgusting as well as immoral. To satisfy the insane desires of terrorists, the Théâtre de la rue Richelieu presented, on October 18, 1793, *Le Jugement dernier des rois*, a prophecy in one act by Slyvain Maréchal (1750-1803), a vociferous atheist and revolutionist. [74]

The play's success was beyond even the expectations of its author. Of all the works presented during the Revolution, *Le jugement dernier des rois* is not only the most revolting but also serves to illustrate the remarkable degradation of dramatic art during the period. Talma apologized for even belonging to the company which condescended to present such a monstrosity:

> La reine Marie-Antoinette avait porté sa tête sur l'échafaud le 16 octobre, et le 18 octobre, nous donnions, rue de Riche-

---

[72] Dussane, *op. cit.*, p. 104. The story of Labussière's efforts to save innocent victims from the guillotine appears in all treatises concerning the theater during the Revolution.

[73] For an explanation of the Revolutionary calendar consult Claude Boto, *Calendrier de la Révolution* (Paris: Imprimerie Nouvelle, 1928).

[74] Sylvain Maréchal, *Le Jugement dernier des rois* (Paris: C. Patris, 1794).

lieu, une pièce où par bonheur je ne jouais pas, et qui était intitulée le *Jugement dernier des Rois*. Aujourd'hui que le temps, en passant sur toutes les terribles passions de cette époque, les a refroidies, je me demande comment on a poussé l'oubli des convenances à un pareil point. Cette pièce du *Jugement dernier* était quelque chose d'odieux. Lorsque j'en parlai au comité, l'on me montra un ordre du Gouvernement; devant cet ordre il fallait s'incliner: c'est ce que nous fîmes. [75]

An old man, victim of a despotic king of France, has been living in oblivion for twenty years on a deserted volcanic island. Alone with his thoughts, the old man outlines the history of crimes committed by kings. He carves out in the rock the two most cherished words he knows: *liberté, égalité*. His isolation is ended with the sudden arrival of a band of strangers. These are the *sans-culottes* of all the countries of Europe. Overwhelmed with joy, the old man embraces those he recognizes as being French. He then inquires of their visit to this forsaken island. He learns that Europe is free, thanks to France from whose soil the flower of liberty has sprung. Now that republics are established in all European countries, each has sent a *sans-culotte* to a general convention. The convention's principal item of business is to pronounce the exile of every tyrant. The place of exile chosen is none other than this volcanic island. All the oppressive tyrants will appear here with the exception of one «dont la France a fait justice». This is an obvious reference to Louis XVI who had been guillotined on January 21, 1793.

The old man considers himself signally honored. He assures his visitors that no more appropriate place could be chosen. He even cites the existence of a volcano «qui, d'un moment à l'autre, peut exterminer tous ces tyrans». On a leash the tyrants are led one by one across the stage. We see the kings of England, Prussia, France, Naples, Spain, Poland, Catherine of Russia and Pope Pius VI. After having jeered them sufficiently, the *sans-culottes* withdraw but not before warning their unfortunate victims that they are at the foot of a very active volcano.

---

[75] François-Joseph Talma, *Mémoires* Ed. Alexandre Dumas (Paris: Hippolyte Souverain, 1849), IV, 32-33. No evidence has been preserved showing an order was issued for the presentation of the play. The rôle of Pope Pius VI was taken by Dugazon; Michot that of Catherine; Baptiste (cadet) played the King of Spain.

Seized with fright, the sovereigns unleash their emotions in a general fray. Some box; not adept in that art, Catherine showers Pope Pius VI with blows from her scepter. The *sans-culottes*, who have added to the misery of their victims by starving them, deliver with much ceremony a barrel of biscuits. Depicted as the dogs they really are, the kings fight for the bread. Catherine demands the biggest share. During the altercation the volcano erupts. All the monarchs are killed.

The insanity evident from the foregoing analysis defies the expression of any critical opinion. To protest the existence of monarchs is one thing, but to sanction their starvation and virtual condemnation to hell is inhuman. The *Journal des Spectacles* (October, 1793), however, called *Le jugement dernier des rois* «...sujet à l'unisson des désirs des spectateurs, glorieux pour les Français et d'un intérêt général...» [76] The critic writing in *Le Moniteur* (December 22, 1793) was less effusive. He wrote: «Dans cette irruption barbare d'ouvrages pitoyables dont nos théâtres sont inondés depuis quelques mois... *Le jugement dernier des rois* fait beaucoup pour faire tomber dans l'avilissement le théâtre français». [77]

During 1794 more than two hundred new plays were presented. [78] Until the reaction that followed Robespierre's downfall, most of the dramatic offerings were of a political nature. In that period when madness was the order of the day, actors joined the army or else performed important public offices.

Having been occupied during the imprisonment of its troupe by a group specializing in opéra-comique, the Comédie-Française was ordered reopened by a decree, dated March 10, 1794, issued from the Committee of Public Safety. [79] Instead of bearing the name of Théâtre de la Nation, it was to be known as the Théâtre de l'Egalité. [80]

After the dissolution of the Montausier-Neuville troupe in April, 1794, Molé and Mlle. Devienne, who had been active members, brought together as many of their former associates as possible; and, thus

---

[76] Cited by Frères Goncourt, *L'histoire de la société française pendant le Directoire*, p. 29.

[77] Cited by Frères Goncourt, *Histoire de la société française pendant la Révolution*, p. 299.

[78] Lumière, *op. cit.*, p. 115.

[79] Welschinger, *op. cit.*, pp. 62-63.

[80] *Ibid.*, p. 62.

reunited, the old Théâtre de la Nation opened on June 27, 1794.[81]

The *Gazette Nationale* (June 30, 1794) included a long article on the theater's furbishings:

> ...les distributions de ces décorations intérieures ne sont plus les mêmes. Il paraît qu'on a eu en vue, cette fois-ci, de faire un théâtre plus populaire, dans lequel les citoyens ne seront plus séparés, les uns des autres dans les loges, mais où ils se réuniront et se confondront sur des amphithéâtres circulaires. Cet arrangement rappelle l'égalité, la fraternité républicaines, et justifie le nom donné à ce théâtre.[82]

The *Petites affiches* also reported on the new republican air that was apparent from the decorations:

> Plus d'aristocratie de loges ni de balcons! Le rang des premières ne porte plus qu'une vaste galerie tournante. Plus de loges d'avant-scène: à leur place, des niches où s'élèvent les statues, de la Liberté et de l'Egalité, une coupole tricolore, et aux colonnes des troisièmes, les bustes des amis ou martyrs de la Liberté.[83]

The group that had used the Comédie-Française during the imprisonment of its actors was scarcely happy to see the old troupe return home again. Difficulties naturally arose.[84] Disheartened at having to share their theater with a strange brood, the parent group of actors adandoned their old home and were welcomed with open arms by Sagaret, director of the Théâtre de la rue Feydeau, who had already engaged Molé and Devienne. The agreement reached between Sagaret and the newcomers stipulated they were to present their repertory every other day. They opened in the new theater on January 27, 1795, with a presentation of *La mort de César* and *La surprise de l'amour*.[85]

---

[81] Lumière, *op. cit.*, p. 238. After Robespierre's downfall, the name was changed from Théâtre de l'Egalité to Théâtre de l'Odéon. For a history of the Odéon see Paul Porel et Georges Monval, *L'Odéon* (Paris: Alphonse Lemerre, 1876).

[82] Cited by Lumière, *op. cit.*, p. 238.

[83] Cited by Frères Goncourt, *Histoire de la société française pendant le Directoire* (Paris: Flammarion, 1864), p. 23.

[84] Dussane, *op. cit.*, p. 107.

[85] *Ibid.*, p. 107.

In the meanwhile, Mlle. Raucourt had prevailed upon some of her former associates to join her troupe at the Théâtre de Louvois. She opened there on December 25, 1796 (5 Nivôse An V). With an impressive array of actors, among whom were Larive, Saint-Prix, Saint-Phal, Naudet, Dupont, Joly, Fleury, Thénard, Mézeray and Simon, she offered *Phèdre*, presented traditionally by the Comédie-Française as the first tragedy of the season.[86] However, Contat, Lange, Fleury, Molé, and Dazincourt refused to leave the Feydeau.[87]

At first highly successful, Raucourt and her colleagues were under close surveillance by the government. The tag of subversion that plagued the Comédie-Française from the opening years of the Revolution to its closure in 1793 prompted the government's suspicions. Consequently, the Louvois was ordered closed on the slightest pretext. In an inferior comedy by Dorvigny, *Trois frères rivaux*, presented on August 4, 1797 (17 Thermidor An V), an allusion to the honesty of Merlin, one of the characters, was thought to be an intentional criticism of the present minister of Justice, M. Merlin de Douai.[88] The play was immediately withdrawn, but Merlin had his vengeance. The theater was ordered closed on September 10, 1797 (24 Fructidor An V).

The official opinion toward the Louvois was expressed in an item appearing in the *Journal des hommes libres*:

> On sait que la police a fait fermer le tripot royal de la rue de Louvois, pompeusement nommé le seul Théâtre-Français par messieurs les nobles champions du trône et de l'autel...[89]

With the closing of the Louvois, the next recourse for Raucourt was to join either the troupes of the Odéon, Feydeau or that of the Théâtre de la République. She made a judicious decision in selecting the Odéon, and had her debut there on January 18, 1798 (29 Nivôse An VI).[90]

---

[86] Lucien Dubech, *La Comédie-Française d'aujourd'hui* (Paris: Le Divan, 1926), p. 16.

[87] Etienne et Martainville, *op. cit.*, IV, 16-19.

[88] The controversial line was: «Vous êtes un coquin. M. Merlin, vous finirez par être pendu».

[89] Cited by Frères Goncourt, *Histoire de la société française pendant le Directoire*, p. 314.

[90] Dussane, *op. cit.*, p. 109.

The arbitrary closing of the Théâtre du Louvois gave a momentary rise of popularity to the Théâtre de la rue Richelieu, but the latter soon fell into almost total abandon, and crowds rushed to the Feydeau or Odéon.[91]

The Odéon, Feydeau, and Théâtre de la rue Richelieu, came under the supervision of an energetic but not very astute director, Sagaret. A former banker, Sagaret hoped to found a theater where all the dramatic arts could be united.[92] With this in mind, actors were engaged to play comedy and tragedy at the Odéon and at the République. The opera was installed at the salle Feydeau.[93]

Because of lavish expenditures in furbishings for his theaters and extremely high salaries for the actors, Sagaret could not meet the demands of his creditors and was soon brought to declare a state of bankruptcy. He resigned his position, and shortly thereafter, during the night of March 18, 1799 (28 Ventôse An VII), the Odéon burned.[94] Although reasons for the blaze were never discovered, Sagaret was accused of arson and thrown into prison.[95]

With the Odéon destroyed, the way was cleared for the establishment of a single Comédie-Française as had existed before the Revolution. After long negotiations, members of the old troupe were reunited at the Théâtre de la rue Richelieu, today the salle Richelieu of the Comédie-Française. The first plays presented were *Le Cid* and *L'Ecole des maris* performed on May 30, 1799 (12 Prairial An VII).[96]

Following the execution of Robespierre, an entirely new reaction swept France. Relieved that the horror of daily executions was passed, Parisians moved again freely through their city ruined by civil war. The population wallowed in every excess. Never before had the

---

[91] Etienne et Martainville, *op. cit.*, IV, 86.
[92] Frères Goncourt, *Histoire de la société française pendant le Directoire*, p. 309.
[93] Etienne et Martainville, *op. cit.*, IV, 137.
[94] *Ibid.*, IV, 182.
[95] Frères Goncourt, *Histoire de la société française pendant le Directoire*, p. 311.
[96] Lumière, *op. cit.*, p. 356. The personnel of the Comédie-Française on May 30, 1799, was composed of the following: Molé, Monvel, Dugazon, Dazincourt, Fleury, Vanhove, Florence, Saint-Prix, Saint-Phal, Naudet, La-Rochelle, Talma, Grandménil—all *ex-sociétaires de l'ancien Théâtre-Français*. Alexandre Duval, Michot, Baptiste (cadet), Baptiste (aîné), Dumas—formerly of the Théâtre de la République.

theater been so popular.⁹⁷ Capacity crowds, displeased with comedy and tragedy, clamored for the presentation of lachrymose dramas. Thus the melodrama received the emphasis needed to catapult it into predominance. Audiences were not very discriminating to say the least. Soldiers, workers, clerks, lackeys, and just plain riffraff came because it was the fashion.⁹⁸

Curtain time for most theaters was 5:30 p.m. They were required to be emptied by 10:00 p.m. If the plays ran a little over the alotted time, directors were promptly warned by the government. Such was the case with the Théâtre Favart:

> On se plaint de voir les théâtres finir trop tard; celui de la rue Favart finit toujours à dix heures passées. Il serait essentiel pour le bon ordre d'ordonner aux artistes de ce théâtre de ne pas s'écarter de la règle ordinaire, et de finir au moins à neuf heures et demie.⁹⁹

From 1793-1800 few plays that could be classified as bona fide *tragédies nationales* were written. The great majority of more than two thousand dramatic offerings during this period should properly be categorized as phrenetic harangues destined to formulate or encourage certain attitudes toward Revolution popular at the time. Those works classified under tragedy were taken from contemporary events and mirrored sentiments appropriate to the moment. Charlotte Corday murdered Marat on July 13, 1793. Ten days later a five act tragedy appeared depicting the event. Historical happenings are properly understood and appreciated only after the passage of time; it is therefore unlikely that works written almost at the moment of their occurrence can be termed anything more than journalistic dialoguizing. Since the period, particularly the years from 1793-1800, was a time when heads fell most often whitout convincing evidence, it is understandable why writers indulged in the ignominious task of sparring to save their very lives.

---

⁹⁷ Frères Goncourt, *Histoire de la société française pendant le Directoire*, p. 324.
⁹⁸ *Ibid.*, p. 325.
⁹⁹ Cited by Lumière, *op. cit.*, p. 318. This was a notice posted on May 9, 1796 (10 Floréal An IV).

Chapter V

FACTORS INVOLVED IN THE PRESENTATION OF DRAMA

To bring the evolution of the *tragédie nationale* into clearer focus, a survey of factors involved in the presentation of drama is necessary. This concluding chapter will deal with such aspects as the growth of the theater in France, the number of people who attented theatrical performances, the prices that were paid for admission, the composition of audiences, the inauguration of benches on the stage and their influence in creating a minimum of action and spectacle, the *décor* used to stage plays, lighting in the theater, and costumes worn by actors and actresses.

The Edict issued by the Parlement de Paris in 1548 prohibiting the presentation of mystery plays in generally indicated as the official proclamation marking the end of the theater of the Middle Ages. The prohibition of the *mystères* encouraged the creation of new genres, and thus the modern theater was born. Emphasis on *décor* and action, characteristic of drama in the Middle Ages, shifted in the Renaissance to an exposition of psychological theories which became more perfected and sophisticated in the seventeenth and eighteenth centuries.

During the sixteenth and well into the seventeenth century the one public theater in Paris was the Hôtel de Bourgogne. Built in 1548, and owned by the Confrérie de la Passion, the Hôtel de Bourgogne was about thirty-five meters long and much less wide. Although the seating arrangement at first was rather primitive, that which eventually evolved was simple. The arrangement used in the Hôtel de Bourgogne was the model for other theaters. Divided into two levels, the ground floor contained: (1) *parterre*—the area immediately in front of the stage and containing no seats; (2) *théâtre*—seats on the stage (installed perhaps in 1630); and (3) the *amphithéâtre*—raised platform provided with benches back of the *parterre*. On the upper level were three sets of loges or balconies consisting of *loges du premier rang, loges hautes (2ᵉ rang),* and *loges du troisième rang.* The loge was a row of boxes, hired as units or in single seats. [1]

During the course of the latter half of the sixteenth century the Hôtel de Bourgogne had fallen into disrepair and disrepute. [2] Although it remained the one public theater in Paris at the beginning of the seventeenth century, those of the Foires Saint-Germain and Saint-Laurent should be included, but they were not permanent. Having collapsible sets, the actors carried them from town to town and installed them on the fairgrounds where they presented their plays during the season of the fair, which was once a year. [3]

The many *Jeux de Paume* in Paris were acceptable places for dramatic performances. Molière left a description of the *Jeu de Paume de la Croix-Noire,* in the section of the Arsenal, where he played for two years at the beginning of his career. The walls were about five meters high. At a certain distance above, the roof was supported by a complicated framework of timbers and wooden pillars. In order that players could have light, and the balls prevented from bounding out of the building, the space between the walls and the roof was filled with either nets or straw mats. The entire building was about thirty meters long and much less wide. [4]

---

[1] The Salle du Petit-Bourdon, belonging to the court and occupied by the Italians (Gelosi) from 1571, had a much larger auditorium. It measured seventy meters in length and was twelve meters wide. Two staircases led to an equal number of balconies. The stage was as deep as it did not occupy the traditional *trou* midway at the front of the stage but took their places on one of the sides next to the wings. See Germain Bapst, *Essai sur l'histoire du théâtre* (Paris: Librairie Hachette, 1893), p. 150.

In the Palais-Royal, the theater of Molière, the *salle* had three *étages* or *galeries.* The first two had loges, but not the third in which the people could sit where they pleased. The *orchestre,* composed of *douze violons,* was seated in front of the *parterre. Ibid.,* pp. 364-365.

For most theaters, including the old *Jeux de Paume,* Petit-Bourbon, and the Hôtel de Bourgogne, spectators entered through a single door at the back of the building. *Ibid.,* p. 370.

[2] *Ibid.,* p. 152.
[3] *Ibid.,* p. 157.
[4] *Ibid.,* p. 168.

In 1634 Mondory rented the *Jeu de Paume* on the street of Vieille-du-Temple.[5] For loges, he built two galleries on each side divided transversally by wide boards. The less fortunate element of the public stood in the *parterre*.

At the end of the seventeenth century and until 1791, there were only two theaters subsidized by the State: (1) La Comédie-Française, and (2) L'Opéra. The eighteenth century was an era of private theaters; almost every important nobleman and rich bourgeois had his own. The most famous of these was perhaps that at Ferney belonging to Voltaire.[6]

From August 25, 1680, the most important troupe of actors in Paris was at the Comédie-Française, formed from the combined membership of Molière's company, which had played at the Théâtre Guénégaud, the Théâtre du Marais and that of the Hôtel de Bourgogne. The personnel of the company from 1680 numbered twenty-seven persons.[7] Following Molière's death on February 6, 1673, his troupe was expelled from the Palais-Royal, which was relinquished to Lully, and given the Théâtre de la rue Guénégaud, opposite the rue Mazarine. This theater had been built in the *Jeu de Paume de la Bouteille* in 1670 by the Marquise de Sourdéac and the Sieur de Champeron.[8] From 1682 the troupe of the Comédie-Française continued to enjoy the title of *Comédiens Ordinaires du Roi* and had the exclusive right of playing tragedy and comedy.

The troupe remained in the Théâtre Guénégaud until 1687. Being almost directly behind the collège Mazarin worked against the Théâtre Guénégaud. Hostility was quickly manifested by the Sorbonne. This unfriendly attitude brought pressure to bear upon Louis XIV. A letter signed by Louvois, who had become Superintendent of Buildings at the death of Colbert in 1683, and dated June 17, 1687, or-

---

[5] *Ibid.*, p. 171.

[6] M. De Chevrier, in his *Observations sur le théâtre* (Paris: Debure le jeune, 1755), p. 58, comments on the many spectacles in Paris at that time. He maintained there were at least twenty spectacles in Paris in 1755 «livrés à la curiosité publique».

[7] Lough, *op. cit.*, p. 9.

[8] Nicole Bourdel, «L'établissement et la construction de l'Hôtel des Comédiens Français rue des Fossés-Saint-Germain-des-Prés (ancienne comédie) 1687-1690», *Revue d'histoire du théâtre*, VII (1955), 146.

dered the *Comédiens* to vacate their present quarters before the following October.⁹

Faced with imminent expulsion, the *Comédiens* sought a new theater. After inquiring into a dozen different possibilities, the *Jeu de Paume de l'Etoile*, in the faubourg Saint-Germain, was the final selection.¹⁰ It was decided to demolish the *Jeu de Paume* and erect a new theater in the form of an ellipse with a stage which was 31½ feet at its widest point. The construction of the new theater was universally admired. In drawing up the plans the architect, François d'Orbay, had leaned heavily on his knowledge of Italian theater buildings.¹¹

In spite of protests from the priests of Saint-Sulpice, the *Comédiens* persisted in their intent to remain put and gave *Phèdre* and *Le médecin malgré lui* for their first performance in the new theater on April 18, 1689.¹² This theater served as the headquarters of the Comédie-Française until March 31, 1770. The troupe also played at court, mainly at Fontainebleau and at Versailles, and in the homes of nobles. When the building occupied in 1689 became too dilapidated for further use, the actors moved to the Tuileries until a new theater was ready. The new theater, known today as the Odéon or Salle Luxembourg of the Comédie-Française, was erected on the spot where the Hôtel de Condé had stood.

The Chevalier de Mouhy has left a vivid description of that theater:

> ...il est isolé dans les quatre faces, et offre, sur sa face principale, trois entrées, et autant sur chacun des côtés qui bordent les rues de Corneille et de Molière. Le peristile d'ordre dorique, communique à une galerie couverte régnant au pourtour. A droite et à gauche l'édifice, sont deux pavillons, qui y tenant par des arcades, laissent, dans les mauvais tems, la facilité de descendre de voiture sans en être incommodés, et forment des terrasses où, pendant l'été, on peut prendre l'air, et jouir d'une vue agréable. On arrive par deux grands escaliers, à des galeries qui menent à un beau foyer, décoré des

---

⁹ *Loc. cit.*
¹⁰ *Ibid.*, p. 163.
¹¹ *Ibid.*, p. 170. The theater had 1704 seats.
¹² *Loc. cit.*

bustes des grandes hommes de la scène; et du palier haut des mêmes escaliers on va aux premières loges.

L'intérieur de la salle présente un cercle allongé. Cette forme donne aux spectateurs l'agrément de jouir de tout le spectacle. Il y a quatre rangs de loges... [13]

From its inception, the Comédie-Française was promised an annual subsidy of 12,000 *livres* by the King. Although this aid was welcomed, the greatest source of revenue was admissions.[14] The standard charges for entrance from 1680 to 1699 were fifteen *sous* to the *parterre*, one *livre* to the third tier of boxes (*loges du 3ᵉ rang*), one and a half *livres* to the second tier (*loges hautes*), three *livres* to the first tier (*loges*) and to the stage (*théâtre*). Admission to the *amphithéâtre* was usually three *livres*, but sometimes one and a half were charged.[15]

Due to heavy taxes, prices were raised after 1699.[16] Admission to the *parterre* was for eighteen *sous*, one *livre* four *sous* to the third tier of boxes, one *livre* sixteen *sous* to the second tier, three *livres* twelve *sous* to the first tier and the stage, and three *livres* to the *amphithéâtre*.[17] Boxes sold as units varied from twelve to forty-four

---

[13] The Chevalier de Mouhy, *Abrégé de l'histoire du Théâtre-Français, depuis son origine jusqu'au premier juin 1780* (Paris: De Mouhy, L. Jorry and J.-G. Mérigot), IV, 193-194. The fourth volume was not published until 1783. In the new theater described by Mouhy, there were nineteen loges to each balcony. Each loge contained eight seats.

[14] An interesting sidelight on the price of theater tickets concerns the earnings of playwrights down to the Revolution. In seventeenth century France no dramatist could expect to reap a great fortune from his work. There were two or three sources of payment: (1) royalties from actors and publishers, and (2) gifts or a pension from a patron. Plays did not have a ready market. Actually the playwright was neglected. The profits derived by him from the performances of his work were limited to those which he drew from its first run, receiving one-ninth of the money collected. A play scarcely had more than ten performances during its first run, thus the author's share was indeed small. After the first run, the play could be performed by anyone anywhere without any consideration of an author's rights. See Lough, *op. cit.*, pp. 321-323, and Henry O. Lancaster, «The Comédie-Française 1701-1774—plays, actors, spectators, finances», *The American Philosophical Society Publications*, XLI (1951), 596.

[15] Eugène Despois, *Le théâtre français sous Louis XIV* (Paris: Hachette, 1894), p. 107. The *livre* in 1672 was the equivalent of 15 francs in 1939. A franc was equal, at that time, to $ .70 United States money.

[16] One-sixth of the total receipts was a tax levied for the benefit of the poor.

[17] Despois, *op. cit.*, p. 107.

livres. Balconies are mentioned as selling for twenty-five *livres*. There were even balconies behind the curtain. Individual seats in them probably were at the same price as those on the stage.[18] Prices were *au double* when there was a machine or new play. Admission to the *parterre* and third tier of boxes was one and a half *livres*, three *livres* to the sencond tier, five and a half *livres* to the first tier, *amphithéâtre* or stage. After September 20, 1753, no distinction was made as to whether a play was new or old.[19]

The population of Paris in 1700 was about 500,000. From 1680-1780 around 150,000 people went to the Comédie-Française yearly.[20] The theatrical season ran from Easter to Easter. During that period the actors played some 335 days in the year.[21] The audiences were small; yet they were composed of people from all levels of society. In the theater occupied by the Comédie-Française between 1689 and 1770 in the rue des-Fossés-Saint-Germain the largest number of paid admissions on any one day was 1,586 in March, 1704.[22]

The composition of theatrical audiences in Paris before 1760 is reflected in the places where notices were posted advertising plays. Before the seventeenth century a play was announced by a crier, who was the *orateur de troupe,* or by a harlequin. The use of printed announcements was supposedly an innovation of Cosme d'Oviedo, a sixteenth century Spanish dramatist.[23] The printed announcement was instituted in France around 1635 and indicated the name of the play, the place of performance, the hour, and the price and the day of a given presentation. The names of actors were not included until 1789. The notices of the Théâtre de Monsieur were the first in Paris to adopt this practice. In verse, the advertisement spoke occasionally of the many spectators who had seen the play during its previous performances, extolled its merits and threw in a little gossip. Announcements were differentiated for the various theaters by color. Those of

---

[18] Henry C. Lancaster, *The Comédie-Française 1680-1701—Plays, Actors, Spectators, Finances* (Baltimore: The Johns Hopkins Press, 1941), p. 16.
[19] Henry C. Lancaster, «*The Comédie-Française 1701-1774—Plays, Actors, Spectators, Finances*», p. 595.
[20] Based on a yearly count made by Lough, *op. cit.*, p. 50.
[21] Henry C. Lancaster, «The Comédie-Française 1680-1701», p. 20.
[22] Lough, *op. cit.*, p. 101.
[23] François de Dainville, «Les lieux d'affichage des comédiens à Paris en 1753», *Revue d'histoire du théâtre*, III (1951), 248-252.

the Comédie-Française were red, green for the Comédie-Italienne, and yellow for the Opera. A person was hired by the theater to post the announcements. In 1753 no announcements were posted in the proletarian areas of the faubourg Saint-Marcel or Saint-Antoine. There were very few around Notre-Dame or at the Sorbonne. The great majority were in more prosperous areas such as the Marais, the Louvre, the Palais-Royal, the faubourgs Saint-Germain and Saint-Honoré. Out of 175 announcements posted, 50 were reserved for the front doors of private residences. In spite of the foregoing evidence, the greatest number of admissions was sold for the *parterre*, composed primarily of solid bourgeois citizens, soldiers, students, intellectuals, and a sprinkling of noblemen. Few women went into the *parterre* until toward the end of the eighteenth century.[24] The numerical importance of the *parterre* can be illustrated by comparing the total number of spectators at a given performance. For example, a crowd of 1,600 people saw a performance in 1692 of Boursault's *Esope*, a new comedy, and of this number 777 stood in the *parterre*.[25] Although the people who stood in the *parterre* actually contributed a very small amount to the total receipts and were often unruly, they usually determined the success or failure of a play.

In spite of its numerical preponderance, the *parterre* was not the most influential element of the theater audience, at least this is the case for the latter half of the seventeenth century and until 1789. The aristocratic spectators exercised an amazing influence over the content and form of French drama. A graphic illustration of the power of the aristocracy in drama is reflected in the *drame sérieux* ostensibly destined to «moraliser les bourgeois» but whose main characters were of the highest social levels.[26] Indeed, it was the aristocratic element of theatrical audiences upon whom the actors depended largely to swell the receipts with the purchase of highpriced seats.

---

[24] The *parterre* was not seated at the Comédie-Française until its installation at the Odéon in 1782. Despois, *op. cit.*, p. 115.

[25] Lough, *op. cit.*, p. 101. Hubert's register of the last year (1672-1673) of Molière's theater has revealing facts along the line of spectators. At the opening night, *Les femmes savantes* was performed. This was the twelfth performance of the play. Only 374 admissions were sold; of these 316 were for the *parterre*. See William L. Schwartz, «Molière's theater in 1672-1673», *Publications of the Modern Language Association of America*, LVI (1941), 399.

[26] Lough, *op. cit.*, p. 236.

One of the greatest hindrances to action and spectacle and instrumental in imposing the inflexible rule of unity of place on the stage was the presence of *banquettes* or tiered benches. The practice of having spectators on the stage was generally widespread in Europe and is known to have existed in Germany from the sixteenth century, and in England from the time of Shakespeare. In England the spectators could sit on the stage only on days when the house was full. When the practice of *banquettes* was first inaugurated in France is not known. Some historians, however, maintain that they were first introduced in the Hôtel de Bourgogne at the presentation of *Le Cid* (1636). [27]

In the new theater of the Fossés-Saint-Germain the stage was reduced to fifteen feet across the front and eleven across the back because of the *banquettes* (four rows) which filled one-half of each side of the stage. [28] This represented about one-third of the space on the stage. [29] These seats were regularly purchased by noblemen, fops, financiers, rich bourgeois and in general anyone who, with money enough to pay the price of admission, wanted to make his presence known. The vanity of those who sought seats there encouraged them to be noisy and inconsiderate even during the action of the play being given.

It would seem that the presentation of a machine play would have necessitated the removal of benches from the stage. Hubert's attendance records of the Palais-Royal throw light on that problem. Evidence demonstrates spectators on the stage were always welcomed by Molière. For example, during the revival of *Psyché* in 1672-73, four to thirty-two tickets for seats on the stage were sold for all performances. [30]

Sometimes the occupants of the *banquettes* would relinquish their seats and stand at the back of the theater thus barring the actors' en-

---

[27] Bapst, *op. cit.*, p. 372.
[28] Jean Lucien Adolphe Jullien, *Les spectateurs sur le théâtre* (Paris: A. Detaille, 1875), p. 6.
[29] Ibid., p. 5.
[30] Schwartz, *op. cit.*, p. 419. The program of a *tragédie arlésienne* of 1729 admonishes patrons on the stage: «On prie tout le monde de ne point se trouver sur le théâtre, dans le tems de la représentation. Ceux qui n'y sont pas nécessaires ne feroient qu' embarrasser les machinistes exposeroient les enfans au risque d'être blessés». Cited by De Dainville, *op. cit.*, p. 372 (from Bibliothèque d'Arles, MS 425, p. 5).

trance. Many anecdotes have been preserved relating disturbances arising due to spectators on the stage. At the première of *Childéric* by Louis de Cahusac on December 19, 1736, the play almost was stopped because of interference from spectators on the stage. The incident as recounted by the Chevalier de Mouhy is highly amusing:

> Dans une des meilleures scènes de la pièce un des acteurs portant une lettre eut bien de la peine à passer pour la remettre selon son rôle, à celui auquel il devoit la rendre, à cause de la foule des spectateurs qui barroit son passage; un moine travesti, qui étoit au Parterre s'écria hautement, «Place au Facteur». Cette fade plaisanterie fit un si grand effet qu'à peine la Tragédie put-elle être achevée, tant les huées succédèrent. Celui qui avoit occasionné la rumeur, fut conduit en prison. A la représentation suivante, l'auteur supprima la lettre. [31]

In order to quell disturbances similar to that mentioned by De Mouhy, many ordonnances were issued, but they had little effect. [32]

Naturally there was much opposition to the presence of spectators on the stage. The leaders among those who opposed the *banquettes* were primarily dramatists who disliked the intrusion of an element that prevented action and spectacle. The most outspoken enemy of the *banquettes* was Voltaire. Writing in the *Discours sur la Tragédie*, addressed to Mylord Bolingbooke, and destined as a preface to *Brutus* (1731), he said:

> Les bancs qui sont sur le théâtre, destinés aux spectateurs rétrécissent la scène et rendent toute action impracticable. Ce défaut est cause que les décorations tant recommandées par les anciens, sont rarement convenables à la pièce. Il empêche surtout que les acteurs ne passent d'un appartement dans un autre aux yeux des spectateurs, comme les Grecs et les Romains le pratiquent sagement, pour conserver à la fois l'unité de lieu et la vraisemblance. [33]

Through his constant criticism and the efforts of actors under the leadership of Le Kain to disband the *banquettes*, the issue was brought

---

[31] De Mouhy, *op. cit.*, III, 37-38.
[32] Jullien, *op. cit.*, p. 13.
[33] Voltaire, *op. cit.*, II, 315.

to its conclusion in 1759.[34] The suppression of such expensive and sought after seats would naturally result in smaller receipts. To offset this, Louis de Brancas, Comte de Lauraguais, (1733-1824), himself a devotee of the theater, was persuaded to underwrite the expenses incurred in the removal of the *banquettes*. He earmarked 12,000 *livres* for the *comédiens* to defray expenses of removing the benches.[35] Although recognized almost universally as an odious practice, the removal was opposed even in the ranks of the Comédie-Française. Each time that the problem was mentioned, the majority of the troupe, aware of the funds received from the *banquettes,* objected to their removal. The Count's offer gave the needed impetus, and on March 31, 1759, in his speech before the Easter closing the actor Brizard announced the removal of the benches among the changes to be wrought during the recess.[36] The theater re-opened on April 23, 1759. In order to accentuate the differences that the removal had made, it was decided to present a play which required a large number of actors on stage and stipulated much action. The play chosen was *Les Troyennes* of Châteaubrun.[37]

In referring to the reaction of the public upon seeing the stage emptied of the cumbersome *banquettes,* De Mouhy wrote:

> Un applaudissement général réitéré avec transport partit au lever de la toile, à l'aspect de la Scène, devenue libre par le retranchement des balustrades.[38]

Voltaire was inordinately happy. He expressed his appreciation, and that of all lovers of the theater, to the Comte de Lauraguais in the *épître dédicatoire* of *L'Ecossaise* (July 26, 1760):

---

[34] Frères Goncourt, *L'histoire de la société française pendant la Révolution*, p. 20.

[35] The actual cost was much more than this. Some say 60,000 *livres*, others 34,000. See Frères Goncourt, *L'histoire de la société française pendant la Révolution*, p. 22.

[36] To make up for the loss of seats on the stage additional boxes and balconies were installed. See Lancaster, «The Comédie-Française 1701-1774», p. 594.

[37] Thirty assistants (figurants), soldiers, and guards. About 1200 people saw this performance. Frères Concourt, *L'histoire de la société française pendant la Révolution*, p. 25.

[38] De Mouhy, *op. cit.*, III, 66.

Vous avez rendu un service éternel aux beaux arts et au bon goût en contribuant, par votre générosité, à donner à la ville de Paris un théâtre moins indigne d'elle. Si on ne voit plus sur la scène César et Ptolémée, Athalie et Joad, Mérope et son fils, entourés et pressés d'une foule de jeunes gens, si les spectacles ont plus de décence, c'est à vous seul qu'on en est redevable. [39]

With the suppression of the benches, the way was clearly paved for the introduction of tragedies characterized by action and spectacle. The national history would have afforded excellent materials; but the writers were so thoroughly accustomed to following the tradition of concentrating on love intrigues, long conversations, and psychological analysis, no immediate appreciable change was noticed in the themes treated. However, the *décor* and costuming underwent drastic change.

From the sumptuous *décor* of a *mystère* as depicted in the manuscript of *La Passion de Valenciennes* (1547) in which the various mansions could be closed by a curtain, indicating that the scene was over and warning the public to look elsewhere or else shutting from the spectator's view an episode that was too scabrous, we note vast differences were inaugurated with the birth of tragedy and comedy.

The only scenery in the sixteenth century was a flat rising from the floor of the stage and representing some object in nature such as a clump of bushes, cliff or bank. [40] The stage was hung with tapestries on three sides. The area between the back of the tapestry and the wall was called the wings. [41]

In the seventeenth century and until late in the last half of the eighteenth century stage scenery as such was of little or no consideration. As a result of the imposition of the unities in tragedy, the famous *palais-à-volonté* served as the setting. Usually portraying the vestibule of a palace of classical architecture ornamented with columns and statues from four to six flats were placed obliquely, thus prevent-

---

[39] Voltaire, *op. cit.*, IV, 405. Spectators were still on the stage at the Comédie-Italienne in 1784. See Jullien, *op. cit.*, p. 30.

[40] Bapst, *op. cit.*, p. 147.

[41] The stage sets at the *collèges* were no better than at public theaters. For the presentation of *La Cléopâtre captive* at the collège de Boncour in 1552, the stage was set up in a courtyard. Windows in the neighboring buildings served as loges. The *parterre* was the ground. It was there that Henri II and the court sat. Jodelle played Cléopâtre himself. (Bapst, *op. cit.*, p. 146.)

ing the spectator from seeing into the wings. The flats were of unequal size with the largest near the front of the stage and diminishing in size toward the back. The last was so small that a man of ordinary stature was taller.[42] The flats on either side were joined at the back by a rod thereby leaving an opening for a passageway beyond which was another flat.[43]

Lighting is, of course, an important consideration in any discussion of *décor*. An order issued in November, 1609, testifies that the performance of plays began at 2 p.m. and were over around 4:30 p.m. During the reign of Louis XIII, the performances began around 3:00

---

[42] In the eighteenth century the *palais-à-volonté* became a *cour d'honneur* simulating those of private Parisian mansions. Bapst, *op. cit.*, p. 384 and Nicole Décugis et Suzanne Reymond, *Le décor de théâtre en France du Moyen Age à 1925* (Paris: Compagnie Française des arts graphiques, 1953), p. 121.

[43] Stage furniture was reduced to a bare minimum. In the presentation of *Adélaïde du Guesclin* (January 8, 1734), the directions indicated the scene was to represent a palace. There were to be two armchairs and a table placed on the left. The play lasted one hour fifty minutes. See J. B. Colson, *Répertoire du Théâtre Français ou détails essentiels sur trois cent soixante tragédies et comedies* (Bordeaux: Colson et J. Foulquier, 1817), III, 5.

For *Childéric* (December 19, 1736) the action was to take place in a room of the king's palace at Tournay. *Ibid.*, III, 48.

For *Le siège de Calais* (February 13, 1765), lasting two hours, taking place in an audience room of the Governor and in the prison at Calais, some armchairs and chairs were the only furniture. *Ibid.*, III, 176.

The furniture for *Gaston et Bayard* (April 24, 1771) was much more elaborate. The stage, representing a gallery of the arsenal at Brescia, bore flags, guns, pieces of cannon, piles of bullets and other instruments of warfare. In the fourth act, the scene changes to a room just off the gallery. Bayard is seen lying on a cot, a chair and his sword are nearby. The play lasted two hours twelve minutes. *Ibid.*, III, 68.

It is not known when the front curtain made its first appearance in France. It was first inaugurated at the Hôtel de Bourgogne in 1630. (See Bapst, *op. cit.*, p. 173). After the front curtain was installed, it was customary to close it only at the end of a play.

Even as late as 1662 the front curtain was not used in theatrical presentations in some *collèges*. See DeDainville, *op. cit.*, p. 358.

Père Abram, the historian of the University of Pont-à-Mousson, mentioned the presence of a front curtain there as early as 1622. At a theatrical celebratrion noted:

> Le théâtre fut remarquable par les scènes qui étoient peintes pour le sujet de la pièce et surtout par le grand rideau qui se levoit et s'abbaissoit tout d'un coup. (Cited by Delainville, *op. cit.*, p. 372 from Manuscript 930 of the Bibliothèque de Nancy, p. 136).

p.m. Under Louis XIV curtain time was delayed still longer for two reasons. The priests of Saint-Eustache succeeded in seeing a proclamation issued to the Hôtel de Bourgogne prohibiting the opening of the theater until after vespers. Secondly, the habit of eating a large meal at noon, as was the practice during Boileau's youth, was altered to postpone dinner until much later. Louis XIV continued, however, to eat a large meal at noon. The courtisans who were present to witness this ritual were forced to delay their noon meal at least an hour. This, of course, was imitated in the bourgeoisie. Theaters were forced to delay their performances until at least 2 p.m. or later; finally, 5 p.m. seems to have become the usual hour. [44] The final curtain rang down around 8 p.m. or 8:30 p.m. [45]

The nature of the program followed a set pattern. Tragedies were presented three times a week and long comedies on other days. [46] The long play was presented first and then during an interlude there was ballet; this was followed by a play of one act. In the eighteenth century the theater was generally opened every day in the week during the winter months, but was often closed in summer on Tuesdays and Fridays because of the opera, the heat or some other cause. [47] Tragedies were reserved for winter months and comedy for the summer. This tradition had definitely been discarded by 1732; for *Zaïre* was presented in August.

In 1635 theaters in Paris had very little lighting. About 1640 at the Bourgogne and Marais theaters lighting was installed; however, it was not until the middle of the reign of Louis XIV that serious attention was paid to it. [48] At first a few candles were placed backstage behind the actors. With light behind them, the actors' faces were only silhouetted. In order to correct this situation torches were placed along the front of the stage instituting the principle of footlights. Toward 1650 overhead lights made from crystal hung in front of the stage. They were lowered and raised at will. Six such lights were hung from the stage ceiling at the Hôtel de Bourgogne, and the

---

[44] In provincial theaters the hours were the same with curtain time at 5 p.m. and the performance over by 8:30 p.m.
[45] Despois, *op. cit.*, pp. 144-145.
[46] De Mouhy, *op. cit.*, III, 389.
[47] Lancaster, «The Comédie-Française... 1701-1774», p. 595.
[48] Bapst, *op. cit.*, p. 173.

footlights were made from small lamps placed behind latticework and at spaced intervals.[49]

In 1781 the famous chemist Lavoisier presented a plan to the Academy of Science which would revolutionize the outmoded system of lighting in theaters.[50] The speaker launched into his discussion with a précis of the historical background. He was particularly critical of the present system and referred to the overhanging lights just above the heads of the patrons in the loges thus obfuscating the view of some in seeing the stage. This system was eventually corrected and only one light for the entire theater overhung the center of the stage[51] The result was completely undesirable and prevented the spectators from reading their programs and seeing any distance around them. Lavoisier also complained of the front of the stage being too brightly lighted while the *décor* backstage was almost shut out by darkness.[52] He maintained that part of the stage directly in line with the spectators' view should be the brightest because «...cette partie du théâtre qui est toujours vue de face, et qui représente des perspectives et des lointains, est une des plus imposantes, relativement à l'illusion qu'elle doit produire sur les spectateurs...»[53]

Lavoisier's solution to the entire problem was a series of *réverbères* to reflect light and placed at strategic points throughout the theater and out of sight of the spectator. The *réverbère*, as Lavoisier explained it to his colleagues, was a light backed by a cylindrical piece of metal and resting on a reservoir of fuel. With the installation of *réverbères* the number of lights required at the present time could be reduced considerably; less smoke would be created thereby rendering the theater more pleasant.[54] The number of *réverbères* to be used would depend entirely on experiment. He was given permission to test his experiment in the Salon des Tableaux at the Louvre. Two weeks later Lavoisier reported to the Academy that he had carried out the experiment most successfully.[55]

---

[49] *Ibid.*, p. 375.
[50] Antoine de Lavoisier, *Oeuvres* (Paris: Imprimerie imperiale, 1865), III, 91.
[51] *Ibid.*, p. 92.
[52] *Ibid.*, p. 93.
[53] *Ibid.*, p. 94.
[54] *Ibid.*, p. 96.
[55] *Ibid.*, p. 100.

The deplorable lighting system was an open invitation to the spread of fire. In France, during the sixteenth and seventeenth centuries there was no officially organized firefighting groups. The little service offered was performed by monks of mendicant orders, usually the Capucins.[56] The firefighting equipment furnished by theaters was indeed primitive and consisted of buckets of water placed at determined points, usually behind the scenery on the stage. Sponges attached to long sticks or else syringes hung on a nail above the buckets.

In studying the growth of the *tragédie nationale* in France a very pertinent question is posed by the costuming used in staging these tragedies of which the success was enhanced by attempts at historical exactitude in the dress of actors. Until the time of Voltaire, little effort, as in *décor*, was made to achieve historical exactitude in dress on the stage. There was an extreme change in the manner of costuming on the stage from the fifteenth to the sixteenth centuries. Whereas stage costumes were very sumptuous in the fifteenth, the opposite was true in the sixteenth. No attempt was made at wearing costumes appropriate to the period concerned in the play; actors were contemporary dress.[57] When, under Louis XIII, the Hôtel de Bourgogne began devoting itself to serious plays, the same costume was used indiscriminately for historical rôles. David and Charles V had their hair loose and flowing, covered by a toque amply supplied with panaches, bore a wide cuirass, wore knee-breeches and brodequins, and their shirt sleeves—only elbow length—ended in big puffs. Sometimes if the character in tragedy belonged to a period more modern than that of antiquity, he wore the costume of his own time.

It was not until the time of Voltaire that any significant progress was made in adapting costumes that were historically exact. Until 1755 actresses usually played their rôles dressed as they were in daily life. They wore long dresses with hooped skirts and their coiffure was usually topped by tall panaches.[58]

Although some costumes belonged to the theater, it was possible to rent or buy them. The latter possibility was very rare since pay was low for actors. One of the most frequent practices was to seek

---

[56] Bapst, *op. cit.*, p. 379.
[57] *Ibid.*, p. 148.
[58] *Ibid.*, p. 396.

the favor of a rich nobleman who would donate costumes from his wardrobe or have them made.[59]

The first important step in revolutionizing stage costumes was due to the efforts of Mlle. Clairon and LeKain, who had perhaps received encouragement from Voltaire. It was with his *Orphelin de la Chine* (August 20, 1755) that actors and actresses tried to effect any striking degree of historical exactitude in costuming.[60] To show full approval, Voltaire gave his earnings from the performances to help in defraying the cost of scenery and costumes.[61] Grim saluted the ingenuity of Mlle. Clairon (1723-1803) and Le Kain (1728-1778).

> Il faut espérer que la raison et le bon sens triompheront avec le temps de tous ces ridicules usages qui s'opposent à l'illusion et aux prestiges d'un spectacle tel qu'il doit être chez un peuple éclairé.[62]

The triumph of *L'orphelin de la Chine* signaled a new era for the stage.[63] With some attempt at historical exactitude, the way was cleared for a great spectacle such as *Tancrède* (1759) which brought to the scene for the first time French chivalry in all its glory with armor, banners and imposing parades. The success enjoyed by *Tancrède* assured the triumph of historical costuming which was not truly realized, however, until Talma insisted on historical exactitude in the costume of Charles IX whom he played for the first time on November 4, 1789, in Marie-Joseph Chénier's first important work, *Charles IX*.

Nevertheless, it was not until the beginning of the nineteenth century that all actors donned costumes in accord with the period depicted

---

[59] Wilma Deierkauf-Holsboer, *L'histoire de la mise en scène dans le théâtre française de 1600 à 1657* (Paris, E. Droz, 1933), pp. 59-60. The habit of giving costumes to actors and actresses continued until the Revolution when it was completely disbanded. See Bapst, *op. cit.*, p. 465.

[60] A. DuCasse, *Histoire anecdotique de l'ancien théâtre en France* (Paris, E. Dentu, 1864), I, 83.

[61] *Zaïre* had been presented in 1732 with actors wearing Polish costumes. See Bapst, *op. cit.*, p. 466.

[62] Grimm, *op. cit.*, III, 89.

[63] The most revolutionary step taken by Mlle. Clairon was the replacement of the hoop skirt with an oriental costume. The play lasted one hour fifty-five minutes. See Colson, *op. cit.*, III, 142.

in the plays being presented. While Talma insisted on the exactness of every detail in his costume, those of secondary actors were sorely neglected. During the Revolution, costuming was of no consideration in staging a play, but as a sign of the times the tricolor was unmistakably worn on every costume.

CHAPTER VI

CONCLUSION

Tragedy emerged as a genre in French literature during the sixteenth century. Concerned primarily with creating a great national tragedy, the first dramatic theorists writing on tragedy took their models in form and content from the Greeks and Romans. The history and mythology of these countries served as the main sources of French tragedy until after the middle of the eighteenth century. By 1730 public demand for variety encouraged exploitation of modern history as a source for tragedy, but the use of French national history received unqualified acclaim only toward the end of the eighteenth century. Although national history had been used before, the first so-called *tragédie nationale*, *Le siège de Calais*, had its initial performance on the stage of the Comédie-Française on February 13, 1765. The work was written by Buirette de Belloy, and, although it was immediately famous, another tragedy, *Charles IX*, by Marie-Joseph Chénier, presented at the Comédie-Française on November 4, 1789, received much more attention.

From the presentation of *Cléopâtre captive* in December, 1552, marking the emergence of French tragedy as a genre, to January 1, 1800, the date chosen as the limit of this study, there were about six hundred new tragedies on the stages of Parisian theaters. Of this number less than seventy-five were based on events drawn from French history. Therefore, the *tragédie nationale* was a rather insignificant branch of tragedy. There were many reasons why the *tragédie nationale* in France never gained much impetus. The limited interpretations of Aristotle and Horace, advanced by early dramatic theorists dealt a crushing blow to the use of French history as a source for tragedy.

The use of French national history as a source for tragedy was rarely mentioned in critical treatises. Among critics considering this field, Voltaire was the first outstanding advocate of its use. Although frequent reference to French history was made in his many discourses on drama, the most concise statement along those lines appeared in a letter to Madame de Pompadour dated September 3, 1760, which is included as a preface to *Tancrède*. The manner in which Voltaire addressed the favorite of Louis XV is worthy of note:

> Je ne saurios trop recommander qu'on cherche à mettre sur notre scène quelques parties de notre histoire de France. On m'a dit que les noms des anciennes maisons qu'on retrouve dans *Zaïre*, dans *Le Duc de Foix*, dans *Tancrède*, ont fait plaisir à la nation. C'est peut-être un nouvel aiguillon de gloire pour ceux qui descendent de ces races illustres. Il me semble qu'après avoir fait paraître tant de héros étrangers sur la scène, il nous manque d'y montrer les nôtres. [1]

With such an outspoken endorsement by the most famous dramatist of the century, many less noted writers quickly turned to the exploitation of the national history for their themes. From the production that resulted, most successful was *Le siège de Calais* (1765) by Buirette de Belloy. Although purported to be a tragedy, *Le siège de Calais* was a highly melodramatic bourgeois drama. Its success was due to a mixture of chauvinism and sentimentalism.

Following Voltaire, the most enthusiastic exponent of the *tragédie nationale* was Marie-Joseph Chénier. He placed emphasis, like his predecessor Louis-Sebastien Mercier, on the political and propagandistic import of this branch of tragedy. His work, *Charles IX*, ushered in the Revolution on the stage. This tragedy, which was a condemnation of the monarchy, served, for a decade, as the model of serious drama.

The first tragedy in French literature that could be called a *tragédie nationale* dates from 1575. It was *La tragédie de feu Gaspard de Colligny* and served as an outstanding example of that myriad body of literature that evolved from the Protestant-Catholic controversy in

---

[1] Voltaire, *op. cit.*, V, 497-498.

the sixteenth century. From its very inception, the *tragédie nationale* in France seemed inexorably destined to serve primarily as a propaganda weapon used all too frequently by the French against their fellow countrymen. Indeed, less than ten of the tragedies treated in this study were devoted to a glorification of the French nation. The primary aim, however, of the national tragedy of other nations had been their exaltation.

The formation of the *tragédie nationale* followed the same lines as regular classical tragedy, and thus was constrained because it was totally devoid of spectacle and action, two of the most salient characteristics of national historical tragedy in other nations, and two elements which usually warranted great success for such plays. Dependent almost entirely on French classical tragedy for its form, the *tragédie nationale* never was blessed with a bold and capable writer to demonstrate its latent possibilities. The *tragédie nationale* tended to be in alexandrine verse, have five acts, obeyed the unities of time, place and action, depicted persons of a noble station, required that no violent action be enacted on the stage, permitted no mixing of the comic and tragic, and had its main interest in the analysis of passion, usually of an amorous nature. The latter quality pointed to the ruin of the *tragédie nationale* even before the first strides were made in its development. As a consequence of the all-absorbing concern with love, an historical personage was drawn at will and caused to be violently in love. The main interest of the author was then devoted to the successful solution of problems posed by the intrusion of the love element. Little attention was given to a truthful representation of historical events. In fact, with the eclipse wrought by love, history was distorted even beyond recognition.

To what extent historical fact could be changed and yet be acceptable in drama had been of great concern to the early theorists of French tragedy whose principles were instrumental in the final evolution of that genre. Dramatists who delved into the realm of the *tragédie nationale* seemed unaware of their responsability to represent French history with some evidence of verisimilitude. With the sole exceptions of *La Pucelle d'Orléans* (1581), *François II* (1747), *Louis XI* (1783) and *Charles IX* (1789), French history was subjected to caricature represented most poignantly perhaps in *La Pucelle* (1641) of the Abbé d'Aubignac who, in order to introduce the love element, caused Joan of Arc to be in love with the Count of Warwick. The love element, so devastating to the development of the *tragédie nationale*, contributed in a large measure to the eventual propagation of the *drame sérieux* whose prime tenet was the portrayal of conditions and not character.

Although it has been stated that the *tragédie nationale* patterned itself along lines taken by French classical tragedy, consideration should be given to an analogy between the style of the two. Whereas, at the zenith of its development, the classical tragedy could claim beauty and simplicity of language as its most appealing characteristics, the *tragédie nationale* was typified in 1800, as in 1575, by periphrasis, neologism, bombast and other such elements that obfuscated clarity of expression. The end result of such practice was, of course, unnaturalness.

In the staging of the *tragédie nationale* little attention was given to historical exactitude in costume until the interest generated in it by the tragedian Talma. Had it been possible to effect costumes suitable to a given period, the efforts would have hardly been rewarded. The existence of the *banquettes* on the stage until 1759 was a source of ready income for theaters but impeded movement and elaborate scenery on the stage to such an extent that action in tragedy was reduced to conversation. Because of the evident lack of space, the *décor* usually remained the same for the entire play.

Many of the outstanding tragedies in other European nations were drawn from their national history. At best those inspired by events in French history were, until the Romantic period, propagandistic harangues surfeited with highly unrealistic intrigues. These tragedies bore little historical verisimilitude. Many were taken from romances and not from historical accounts. Moreover, histories available were, until the middle of the eighteenth century, themselves romanticized. [2] During periods of national crisis tragedies drawn from the national history were not staged in France, as they were elsewhere, to increase the patriotic fervor of its citizenry. Instead, classical plays based on Greek or Roman history, yet distinctly French in spirit, were presented. The perennially famous *Horace* (1640) of Pierre Corneille was

---

[2] A list of the histories available to writers of the *tragédie nationale* can be found in the *Catalogue de l'histoire de France* of the Bibliothèque Nationale, Département des Imprimés (Paris: Firmin Didot, 1855-1895).

and still is such a tragedy. Failure of the *tragédie nationale* as an important branch of tragedy in France was also demonstrated by a lack of interest among outstanding writers. In fact, no very important writer of national historical drama appeared until the Romantic period.

APPENDIX

A LIST OF *TRAGÉDIES NATIONALES* FROM 1800 TO 1830

All tragedies listed here are in five acts and in verse and were presented at the Comédie-Française (Salles Richelieu or Luxembourg).

TITLE	AUTHOR	DATE OF PRESENTATION
Montmorenci	André Carrion-Nisas	12 prairial An 8 (1803)
Guillaume Le Conquérant	A. Duval	February 4, 1804
Les Templiers	F. Raynouard	May 14, 1805
La mort de Henri IV	G. M. J. B. Legouvé	June 25, 1806
Brunehaut, ou les successeurs de Clovis	Etienne Aignan	February 24, 1810
Les états de Blois	F. J. M. Raynouard	May 31, 1814
Charlemagne	N. Lemercier	June 27, 1816
Jeanne d'Arc à Rouen	Loevillard d'Avrigni	April 4, 1819
Louis IX	Jacques Ancelot	May 11, 1819
Charles de Navarre	Charles Brifaut	March 1, 1820
Clovis	Jean Viennet	October 18, 1820
Jean de Bourgogne	Guilleau de Formont	December 4, 1820
Jean-Sans-Peur	P. C. Liadieres	September 1, 1821
Frédégonde et Brunehaut	N. Lemercier	March 27, 1821
Louis IX en Egypte	N. Lemercier	August 5, 1821
Mathilde	Du Parc Locmaria	January 1, 1821
Le maréchal de Biron	Du Parc Locmaria	September 27, 1824
Alain Blanchard, citoyen de Rouen	A. Dupias	September 27, 1825
Jeanne d'Arc	A. Soumet	March 14, 1825
Sigismond de Bourgogne	J. Viennet	September 10, 1825
Charles VI	La Ville de Mirmont	March 6, 1826
Le siège de Paris	Charles-Victor D'Arlincourt	April 8, 1826
Blanche d'Aquitaine, ou le dernier des carlovingiens	Hippolyte Bis	October 29, 1827

TITLE	AUTHOR	DATE OF PRESENTATION
Elisabeth de France	A. Soumet	April 28, 1828
Isabelle de Bavière	E. L. de la Mothe Langon	October 10, 1828
Le roi fainéant, ou Childébert III	J. Ancelot	October 7, 1830
Clovis	N. Lemercier	January 7, 1830

BIBLIOGRAPHY

ARNAUD, CHARLES. *Les théories dramatiques au XVIIe siècle; étude sur les oeuvres de l'abbé d'Aubignac*. Paris: Alphonse Picard, 1888.
AUBERTIN, CHARLES. *L'esprit public au XVIIIe siècle*. Paris: Perrin, 1889.
AUBIGNAC, FRANÇOIS HÉDELIN (abbé d'). *La pratique du théâtre*. Edited by Pierre Martino. Alger: Carbonel, 1927.
BACULARD D'ARNAUD, THOMAS. *Le Coligni*. Lausanne: Bousquet, 1789.
BAPST, GERMAIN. *Essai sur l'histoire du théâtre*. Paris: Hachette, 1893.
BEAUPRÉ, JEAN NICOLAS. *Nouvelles recherches de bibliographie Lorraine, 1500-1700*. Nancy: Grimblot, 1856.
BESANT, WALTER. *Gaspard de Coligny*. New York: G. P. Putnam's sons, 1881.
BILLARD, CLAUDE. *Tragédies*. Paris: Denys Langlos, 1610.
―――. *Gaston de Foix*. Edited by Eliot H. Poligner. New York: Publications of the Institute of the French Studies Incorporation, 1931.
BILLARDON DE SAUVIGNY, Edme. *Gabrielle d'Estrées*. Paris: Robustel, 1778.
BONNASSIES, JULES. *Le théâtre et le peuple, esquisse d'une organisation théâtrale*. Paris: Armand le Chevalier, 1872.
BOTO, CLAUDE. *Calendrier de la Révolution*. Paris: Imprimerie Nouvelle, 1928.
BRAY, RENÉ. *La formation de la doctrine classique en France*. Paris: Hachette, 1927.
BOURDEL, NICOLE. «L'établissement et la construction de l'Hôtel de Comédiens Français rue des Fossés-Saint-Germain-des-Prés (ancienne comédie) 1687-1690», *Revue d'histoire du théâtre*, VII (1955), 145-172.
BREITHOLTZ, LENNART. *Le théâtre historique en France jusqu'à la Révolution*. Uppsala: A. B. Lundequistska, 1952.
BRENNER, CLARENCE D. «L'histoire nationale dans la tragédie française du XVIIIe siècle», *University of California Publications in Modern Philology*, XIV (1929-30), 195-329.
BRODY, CLARA C. *The Works of Claude Boyer*. New York: King's Crown Press, 1947.
CAHUSAC, LOUIS DE. *Pharamond*. Paris: Prault, 1741.
CELLER, LUDOVIC. *Les décors, les costumes et la mise en scène au XVIIe siècle*. Paris: Dufour, 1869.
CHAMPION, PIERRE. *Louis XI*. 2 vols. Paris: Champion, 1927.
CHARLTON, H. B. *The Senecan Tradition in Renaissance Tragedy*. Manchester: University Press, 1946.
Chefs d'oeuvre tragiques. 2 vols. Paris: Firmin-Didot, 1877.

CHÉNIER, MARIE-JOSEPH. *Théâtre*. 3 vols. Paris: Foulon et Cie., Baudouin Fréres, 1818.

COHEN, GUSTAVE. *Etudes d'histoire du théâtre en France au Moyen-Age et à la Renaissance*. Paris: Gallimard, 1956.

COLSON, J. B. *Répertoire du Théâtre Français ou détails essentiels sur trois cent soixante tragedies et comédies*. 3 vols. Bordeaux: Colson et J. Foulquier, 1817.

COPIN, ALFRED. *Talma et la Révolution*. Paris: Bibliothèque des Deux Mondes, Frinzine, 1887.

CORNEILLE, PIERRE. *Théâtre de Pierre Corneille*. 5 vols. Paris: Librairie des bibliophiles, 1877.

DABNEY, LANCASTER E. «Claude Billard, minor French Dramatist of the Early Seventeenth Century», *The Johns Hopkins Studies in Romance Literatures and Languages*, XIX (1931), 1-125.

———. *French Dramatic Literature in the Reign of Henri IV*. Austin: The University Cooperative Society, 1952.

DE BELLOY, BUIRETTE. *Gaston et Bayard*. Paris: Veuve Duchesne, 1770.

DE CHEVRIER, M. *Observations sur le théâtre*. Paris: Debure le jeune, 1755.

———. *Causes de la décadence du goût sur le théâtre*. Paris: Dufour, 1758.

DECUGIS, NICOLE ET REYMOND, SUZANNE. *Le décor de théâtre en France du Moyen-Age à 1925*. Paris: Compagnie française des arts graphiques, 1953.

DE DAINVILLE, FRANCOIS. «Les lieux d'affichage des comédiens à Paris en 1753». *Revue d'histoire du théâtre*, III (1951), 248-255.

———. «Décoration théâtrale dans les collèges de Jésuites au XVIIe siècle», *Revue d'histoire du théâtre*, IV (1951), 355-374.

DEIERKAUF-HOLSBOER, SOPHIE W. *L'histoire de la mise en scène dans le théâtre français de 1600 à 1657*. Paris: E. Droz, 1933.

DE L'ESTOILE, PIERRE DE. *Journal de Henri III ou mémoires pour servir à l'histoire de France*. 5 vols. La Haye: Pierre Gosse, 1744.

D'ESTRÉE, PAUL. «Un auteur imcompris, Pierre de Morand l'homme et l'oeuvre (1701-1757)», *Revue d'histoire littéraire de la France*, XVI (1909), 302-328.

———. *Le théâtre sous la terreur*. Paris: Emile-Paul Frères, 1913.

———. «Farmin de Rozoi», *Revue d'histoire littéraire de la France*, XXV (1918), 211-242; 408-422.

———. «Farmin de Rozoi: Journaliste contre-révolutionnaire», *Revue d'histoire littéraire de la France*, XXIX (1922), 409-432.

DE GONCOURT, EDMOND ET JULES. *Histoire de la société française pendant le Directoire*. Paris: Flammarion, 1864.

———. *Histoire de la société française pendant la Révolution*. Paris: Bibliothèque Charpentier, 1914.

DE LA TAILLE, JEAN. *De l'art de la tragédie*. Edited by Frederick West. Manchester: University Press, 1939.

DE MOUHY, LE CHEVALIER. *Abrégé de l'histoire du théâtre français depuis son origine jusqu'au premier juin 1780*. 4 vols. Paris: De Mouhy et al., 1780.

DESPOIS, EUGENE. *Le Théâtre Français sous Louis XIV*. Paris: Hachette, 1894.

DUBECH, LUCIEN. *La Comédie-Française d'aujourd'hui*. Paris: Le Divan, 1926.

Du Bellay, Joachim. *La deffence et illustration de la langue française.* Edited by Henri Chamard. Paris: Didier, 1948.
Dubeux, Albert. *Les traductions françaises de Shakespeare.* Paris: Les Belles Lettres, 1928.
Du Casse, A. *Histoire anecdotique de l'ancien théâtre en France.* Paris: E. Dentu, 1864.
Dussane, Beatriz. *La Comédie-Française.* Paris: La Renaissance du Livre, 1921.
Edelman, Nathan. *Attitudes of Seventeenth Century France toward the Middle Ages.* New York: King's Crown Press, 1946.
Etienne, Charles G. et Martainville, A. *Histoire du théâtre français depuis le commencement de la Révolution jusqu'a la réunion générale.* 4 vols. Paris: Barba, 1802.
Faguet, Emile. *La tragédie française au XVIe siècle.* Paris: H. Welter, 1897.
Fournier, Edouard. *Le théâtre française au XVIe et au XVIIe siècle.* Paris: LaPlace, 1871.
Fuchs, M. *La vie théâtrale en province au XVIIIe siècle.* Paris: E. Droz, 1933.
Funck-Brentano, Frantz. *La Bastille des Comédiens, Le Fôr l'Evêque.* Paris: Albert Fontemoing, 1903.
Gaiffe, Félix. *Le drame en France au XVIIIe siècle.* Paris: Armand Colin, 1910.
Gofflot, L.-V. *Le théâtre au collège du moyen âge à nos jours.* Paris: Honoré Champion, 1907.
Green, F. C. *Minuet, a Critical Survey of French and English Literary Ideas in the Eighteenth Century.* London: M. Dents and Sons, 1935.
Grimm, Frederick M. et Denis Diderot. *Correspondance littéraire philosophique et critique, 1770-1782.* 5 vols. Paris: F. Buisson, 1812.
Guillaumont, A. (fils). *Costumes de la Comédie-Française XVIIe-XVIIIe siècles.* Paris: Jules Lemonnyer, 1885.
Guilland, L. *Oeuvres complettes de M. de Belloy.* 6 vols. Paris: Moutard, 1778.
Hallays-Dabot, Victor. *Histoire de la censure théàtrale en France.* Paris: E. Dentu, 1862.
Hénault, Charles-Jean-François. *Nouveau théâtre françois.* No name of place or publisher given, 1747.
Hill, L. Alfreda. «The Tudors in French Drama,» *The Johns Hopkins Studies in Romance Literatures and Languages,* XX (1932), 1-171.
Jauffret, Eugene. *Le théâtre révolutionaire, 1788-1799.* Paris: Furne, Jouvet, 1869.
Joannides, A. *La Comédie-Française de 1680 à 1900.* Paris: Plon, 1901.
Jones, Alice C. *Frederick Melchior Grimm as a Critic of Eighteenth Century French Drama.* Bryn Mawr, 1926.
Jourdain, Eleanor F. *Dramatic theory and Practice in France, 1680-1808.* London: Longmans, Green, 1921.
Jullien, Adolphe. *Les spectateurs sur le théâtre.* Paris: A. Detaille, 1875.
———. *Histoire du costume au théâtre.* Paris: Charpentier, 1880.
Lacan, Adolphe et Paulmier, Charles. *Traité de la legislation et de la jurisprudence des théâtres.* 2 vols. Paris: A. Durand, 1853.
Lacroix, Paul. *Bibliothèque dramatique de Monsieur de Soleinne.* 5 vols. Paris: Hennuyer et Turpin, 1844.

LANCASTER, HENRY C. *A History of French Dramatic Literature in the Seventeenth Century*. 5 pts. 9 vols. Baltimore: The Johns Hopkins Press, 1929.

———. *Sunset, a History of Parisian Drama in the Last Years of Louis XIV, 1701-1715*. Baltimore: The Johns Hopkins Press, 1945.

———. *French Tragedy in the Time of Louis XV and Voltaire, 1715-1774*. 2 vols. Baltimore: The Johns Hopkins Press, 1950.

———. *French Tragedy in the Reign of Louis XVI and the Early Years of the French Revolution, 1744-1792*. Baltimore: The Johns Hopkins Press, 1953.

———. *The Comédie-Française, 1680-1701; Plays, Actors, Spectators, Finances*. Baltimore: The Johns Hopkins Press, 1941.

———. «*The Comédie-Française, 1701-1774; Plays, Actors, Spectators, Finances.*» Philadelphia: The American Philosophical Society Publications, XLI (1951), 593-849.

———. *Le Mémoire de Mahelot, Laurent et d'autres décorateurs de l'Hôtel de Bourgogne et de la Comédie-Française au XVIIe siècle*. Paris: Champion, 1920.

LANSON, GUSTAVE. «Etudes sur les origines de la tragédie classique en France,» *Revue d'histoire littéraire de la France*, X (1902), 177-231; 413-436.

———. *Esquisse d'une histoire de la tragédie française*. New York: Columbia University Press, 1920.

L'attentat de Versailles ou la Clémence de Louis XVI. Genève: n. p., 1790.

LAVOISIER, ANTOINE. *Oeuvres*. Vol. 3. Paris: Imprimerie impériale, 1865.

LAWTON, H. W. *Handbook of French Renaissance Dramatic Theory*. Manchester: University Press, 1939.

LEBÈGUE, RAYMOND. *Tableau de la tragédie française de 1573 à 1610*. Paris: Société d'édition d'enseignement supérieur, 1951.

LEJEAUX, JEANNE. «Les décors de théâtre dans les collèges de Jésuites,» *Revue d'histoire du théâtre*, VII (1955), 305-315.

LIÉBY, A. *Etude sur le théâtre de Marie-Joseph Chénier*. Paris: Société Française d'imprimerie et de librairie, 1901.

LION, HENRI. *Les tragédies et les théories dramatiques de Voltaire*. Paris: Librairie Hachette et Cie., 1895.

———. *Le Président Hénault 1685-1770; sa vie, ses oeuvres*. Paris: Librairie Plon, 1903.

LISLE, J.-A. *Essais sur les théories dramatiques de Corneille, d'après ses discours et ses examens*. Paris: Durand, 1852.

LOUGH, JOHN. «The Earnings of Playwrights in 17th Century France,» *Modern Language Review*, XLII (1947), 321-336.

———. *Paris Theatre Audiences in the 17th and 18th Centuries*. London: Oxford University Press, 1957.

LUMIÈRE, HENRI. *Le Théâtre-Française pendant la Révolution*. Paris: E. Dentu, 1894.

MARÉCHAL, SYLVAIN. *Jugement dernier des rois*. Paris: C. Patris, 1794.

MÉLÈSE, PIERRE. *Le théâtre et le public à Paris sous Louis XIV 1659-1715*. Paris: E. Droz, 1934.

MERCIER, LOUIS-SÉBASTIEN. *Théâtre complet*. 3 vols. Amsterdam: B. Vlam, 1778.

———. *La destruction de la Ligue*. Amsterdam: n.p., 1782.

———. *La mort de Louis XI, roi de France*. Neûchatel: La Société typographique, 1783.

MOFFAT, MARGUERITE. «Le siège de Calais et l'opinion publique en 1765,» Revue d'histoire littéraire de la France, XXXIX (1932), 339-354.
MOLAND, LOUIS. Théâtre de la Révolution. Paris: Garnier Frères, 1877.
MONVEL, C. Les victimes cloîtrées. Paris: Chambon, 1796.
MORNET, DANIEL. «Les enseignements des bibliothèques privées, 1750-1800» Revue d'histoire littéraire de la France, XVII (1910), 449-496.
——. «La question des règles au 18e siècle,» Revue d'histoire littéraire de la France, XXI (1914), 241-268; 592-617.
MURET, THÉODORE. L'histoire de France par le théâtre, 1789-1851. 3 vols. Paris: Amyot, 1865.
MYERS, ROBERT L. «Fréron's Theories on Tragedy,» The French Review, XXI (1958), 503-508.
NODIER, CHARLES ET LACROIX, PAUL. Bibliothèque de M. G. de Pixérécourt. Paris: Mme. de Lacombe, 1838.
PARFAICT, LES FRÈRES. Histoire du théâtre françois. 15 vols. Paris: LeMercier et Saillant, 1735-1749.
PASQUIER, ETIENNE. Oeuvres. 2 vols. Amsterdam: La compagnie des libraires associés, 1723.
PAUPHILET, ALBERT. Le legs du Moyen-Age. Melun: Libraire d'Argences, 1950.
PÉRICAUD, LOUIS. Histoire des grands et petits théâtres de Paris pendant la Révolution, Le Consulat et l'Empire. Paris: E. Jorel, 1908.
——. Théâtre des Petits Comédiens de S.A.A. Monseigneur le Comte de Beaujolais. E. Jorel, 1909.
PETIT DE BACHAUMONT, LOUIS. Les mémoires secrets pour servir à l'histoire de la république des lettres en France depuis 1762 jusqu'à 1787. 36 vols. London: John Adamson, 1780-1789.
Pièces de théâtre (tragédies). 3 vols. Paris: Didot l'aîné, 1790.
PITOU, ALEXIS. «Les origines du mélodrame français à la fin du 18e siècle,» Revue d'histoire littéraire de la France, XVIII (1911), 256-296.
POREL, PAUL ET MONVAL, GEORGES. L'Odéon. Paris: Alphonse Lemerre, 1876.
PUSEY, W. W. Louis-Sébastien Mercier in Germany, his Vogue and Influence in the 18th Century. New York: Columbia University Press, 1939.
PUYMAIGRE, THÉODORE JOSEPH DE BOUDET DE. Jeanne d'Arc au théâtre, 1439-1875. Paris: Albert Savine, 1890.
RACINE, JEAN. Bajazet. Edited by Cuthbert Girdlestone. Oxford: Basil Blackwell, 1955.
ROCHEDIEU, CHARLES. Bibliography of French Translations of English Works 1700-1800 Chicago: The University Press, 1948.
SCHWARTZ, WILLIAM LEONARD. «Molière's Theater in 1672-1673,» Publications of the Modern Language Association, LVI (1941), 395-427.
SEDAINE, MICHEL J. Maillard ou Paris Sauvé. Paris: n.p., 1788.
SPINGARN, J. E. A History of Literary Criticism in the Renaissance. New York: Columbia University Press, 1920.
STREETER, HAROLD WADE. The 18th Century English Novel in French Translation, a Biographical Study. New York: Publications of the Institute of French Studies, 1936.
STUREL, RENÉ. «Essais sur les traductions du théâtre grec en français avant 1550,» Revue d'histoire littéraire de la France, XX (1913), 269-296; 637-643.
TALMA, FRANÇOIS-JOSEPH. Mémoires. Edited by Alexandre Dumas. 4 vols. Paris: Hippolyte Souverain, 1849.

TEXTE, J. J.-J. *Rousseau et les origines du cosmopolitisme littéraire.* Paris: Hachette, 1895.

THOMPSON, J. M. *The French Revolution.* New York: Oxford University Press, 1945.

VIAL, FRANCISQUE ET LOUIS, DENISE. *Idées et doctrines littéraires du XVIIIe siècle.* Paris: Delagrave, 1920.

VILLEHERVÉ, BERTRAN DE LA. *François-Thomas de Baculard d'Arnaud, son théâtre et ses théories dramatiques.* Paris: Edouard Champion, 1920.

VIVENT, JACQUES. *La tragédie de Blois, le roi de France et le Duc de Guise, 1585-1588.* Paris: Hachette, 1946.

VOLTAIRE, F. *Oeuvres complètes.* Edited by Louis Moland. Théâtre, 6 vols. Paris: Garner Frères, 1877.

WELSCHINGER, HENRI. *Le théâtre de la Révolution, 1789-1799.* Paris: Charavay Frères, 1880.

WHITE, HENRI. *The Massacre of St. Bartholomew.* New York: Harper and Brothers, 1868.

WICKS, BEAUMONT. *The Parisian Stage; Alphabetical Indexes of Plays and Authors.* Part I: 1800-1815; Part II: 1816-1830. University, Alabama: University of Alabama Press, 1950.

The Department of Romance Studies Digital Arts and Collaboration Lab at the University of North Carolina at Chapel Hill is proud to support the digitization of the North Carolina Studies in the Romance Languages and Literatures series.

www.ingramcontent.com/pod-product-compliance
Lightning Source LLC
Chambersburg PA
CBHW022020220426
43663CB00007B/1150